Civic Center

THE MYSTERY OF THE
HANGING GARDEN OF BABYLON

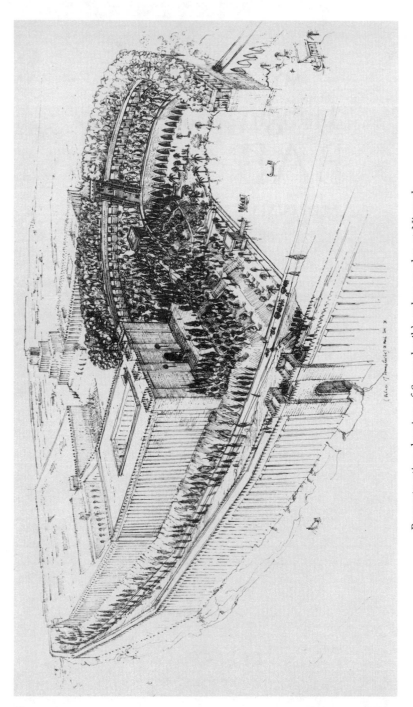

Reconstruction drawing of Sennacherib's palace garden at Nineveh

THE
MYSTERY OF THE
Hanging Garden of
BABYLON

AN ELUSIVE WORLD WONDER
TRACED

STEPHANIE DALLEY

OXFORD
UNIVERSITY PRESS

OXFORD

UNIVERSITY PRESS

Great Clarendon Street, Oxford, OX2 6DP,
United Kingdom

Oxford University Press is a department of the University of Oxford.
It furthers the University's objective of excellence in research, scholarship,
and education by publishing worldwide. Oxford is a registered trade mark of
Oxford University Press in the UK and in certain other countries

First Edition published in 2013

Impression: 3

British Library Cataloguing in Publication Data

Data available

ISBN 978-0-19-966226-5

Printed in Great Britain by
Clays Ltd, St Ives plc

This book is dedicated to the memory of my parents
Denys and Katie Page
who packed me off to Nimrud in northern Iraq in 1962
for the first of many adventures in archaeology and epigraphy

Acknowledgements

So many people have contributed to the development of this work that it is impossible to name them all, for the research began more than eighteen years ago. Since it overturns a long-established understanding, I would like to thank particularly warmly those who were early supporters of the work when doubts were still strong. They include Christopher Dalley especially for discussion of engineering aspects and great help in reading and criticizing successive drafts; Kai Brodersen; Margaret Drower, David Oates and Geza Vermes after hearing lectures; David Stronach; Simon Raikes and his team for making the BBC programme *Secrets of the Ancients* in 1999, especially Andrew Lacey for discussion of bronze-casting and for drafting reconstruction drawings; Eleanor Robson who pointed to a useful clue in a cuneiform mathematical text; John Dransfield of the Royal Botanical Gardens at Kew for help with details of date palms; and David Ussishkin for urging me to look for imitators.

For discussion of particular issues I thank Mark Brown of Spaans Babcock, George Cawkwell, Robin Lane Fox, Norma Franklin, Liz Frood, Joyce Reynolds, John Russell, Sue Sherratt, Grahame Soffe, Arie van der Kooij, Stephanie West and Martin Worthington. For general encouragement I thank John Boardman, Iain Cheyne, Mario Geymonat, Kathryn Gleason, Audrey Gordon-Walker, Sarah Gurr, Elizabeth Macaulay, Arthur MacGregor, David Ottewill and Chris Scarre. The staff and the facilities of the Sackler Library in Oxford were invaluable. Christopher Dalley, Rebecca Dalley and Sarah Shaw read a late draft of the book, and their very different critical insights led to improvements, not least when they tripped up on the jargon of Assyriology, the infelicities compounded by computer-writing, and inadequate explanations for non-specialist readers. I also thank particularly warmly one of the anonymous readers for the Oxford University Press. None of them is to blame for remaining errors of judgement, fact or style.

In a different way I would like to thank those who opposed the work, initially at least, for they galvanized me to greater efforts. A few of them have already acknowledged conversion.

I thank the following for inviting and arranging lectures: The British School of Archaeology in Iraq in 1993; the late Rosemary Nicholson for the Museum of Garden History in Lambeth; Elizabeth Foy, Sarah Carthew and Henrietta McCall for the British Museum Society in 1995; Liz Potterton for the Oxford Archaeological Society in 1995; Lutfi Al-Soumi for the Aleppo Historical Society in 1996; Lamia Al-Gailani for the Kufa Gallery in Westbourne Grove, London, in 1998 (in aid of Help the Children of Iraq); Christopher Coleman for the Bloomsbury School, London, in 1999; Lucinda Lewis-Crosby for the Oxford Garden Society in the Sunningwell Art School in 2001; Philippe Talon and the late André Finet for the Institut des Hautes Études de Belgique in 2003; Virginia Hastings for the University of the Third Age, Headington, Oxford, in 2004; the Department for Continuing Education at Rewley House, Oxford, in 2005; Irene Winter of Harvard University in 2005; Kai Brodersen who arranged for me to lecture in Mannheim, Heidelberg, Freiburg and Innsbrück in 2005; the Royal Literary and Scientific Institution in Bath in 2005; the Pitt Rivers Museum in Oxford in 2007; Lucio Milano at the Advanced Seminar for the Humanities in Venice, 2008; and Diederik Meijer for Ex Oriente Lux in the Netherlands in 2011. On all of those occasions the ongoing research benefited from comments and from questions asked by members of the audience.

I am deeply indebted to the late Terry Ball for the fine drawing he made after careful discussion on how to reconstruct the garden at Nineveh, and to Andrew Lacey for a draft drawing; also to Marion Cox for drawing the brazier with the dog.

Most of all I warmly acknowledge the tremendous work on many facets of the history and archaeology of Nineveh done by other scholars, especially Julian Reade. It will be clear not least from the bibliography that much of this book could not have been written without his detailed studies which span the years from 1967 until recently.

Stephanie Dalley

The Oriental Institute
University of Oxford
March 2012

Contents

List of Colour Plates

1. View from Nebuchadnezzar's Summer Palace at Babylon. (Author's colour slide, 1967)

2. The Negoub tunnel, made in the 9th century BC. (Author's colour slide, 1962)

3. The Chicago prism of Sennacherib Museum no. A11255. (© Oriental Institute Museum, University of Chicago)

4. *Chamaerops humilis*, a type of palm tree. (Author's colour slide)

5. Andrew Lacey's casting of a mini-screw in bronze, for the BBC programme *Secrets of the Ancients*. (Author's colour slide)

6. Wooden full size screw under construction. (Reproduced by kind permission of John Oleson)

7. The wooden screws set up over cisterns. (Reproduced by kind permission of John Oleson)

8. Pebble mosaic floor at Tushhan, modern Ziyaret Tepe. (Reproduced by kind permission of T. Matney and J. Macginnis)

9. The river at Khinnis. Looking upstream.

10. Looking downstream. (Author's colour slides, 1967)

11. Large panel of sculpture on a rock face at Khinnis. (Author's colour slide, 1967)

12. Ruins of the stone aqueduct at Jerwan. (Author's colour slide, 1967)

13. The sculptured block of rock at the weir. (Author's colour slide, 1967)

14. Shalmaneser III clasps hands with the king of Babylon on the throne-base at Nimrud. (Author's colour slide, 1962)

15. Cast bronze panel showing Sennacherib's widow Naqia, from Hilleh near Babylon. (Louvre, AO 20185, reproduced by kind permission, © RMN (Musée du Louvre)/Franck Raux)

16. *Gossypium arboreum*, and *Gossypium herbaceum*. (J. F. Royle, *Illustrations of the Botany and Other Branches of the Natural*

List of Figures

Time-line

Almost all dates are approximate.

	BC
Sammu-ramat, the first Semiramis	floruit 805
Sennacherib built SW Palace and garden at Nineveh	c.700
Ashurbanipal showed garden on palace sculpture	c.660
Fall of Nineveh to Babylonians and allies	612
Nebuchadnezzar II built palace in Babylon	before 562
Fall of Babylon to Cyrus the Great	539
Nakht-hor's journey through Assyria	c.410
March of Xenophon's Ten Thousand	401
Xenophon's *Anabasis* written	c.370–367
Alexander at battle of Gaugamela	331
Berossus	floruit c.290
Stratonice became queen of Seleucus I	c.290
Archimedes	floruit c.287–212
Latest known copy of *Gilgamesh Epic*	c.127
Philo of Byzantium the Engineer	floruit c.200
Apollonios altar inscription at Nineveh	c.100–200?
Tigranes of Armenia conquered Nineveh	90
Diodorus Siculus	floruit c.56–30
Rome defeated at battle of Carrhae (Harran)	53
Apollophanes *strategos* at Nineveh	c.31
Herod built palaces in Palestine	ruled 73–04
Antipater, poet, writing	c.4
Strabo	64 BC–after AD 24

	AD
Quintus Curtius Rufus	floruit c.43
Mithridates captured Nineveh	c.50
Nero built Domus Aurea	c.64–68
Josephus wrote	c.93
Deiogenes sculptor of Heracles' statue at Nineveh	c.100 (?)
Deiogenes graffito on bas-relief in N. Palace at Nineveh	c.100 (?)
Plutarch	floruit 100
Trajan made Mesopotamia a province	115–17
Statue of Hermes from Nineveh	c.200
Bahram II (rock carvings)	ruled 276–93
Philo of Byzantium the Paradoxographer	c.350?
Ammianus Marcellinus	c.330–395

Not all our power is gone—not all our Fame—
Not all the magic of our high renown—
Not all the wonder that encircles us—
Not all the mysteries that in us lie—
Not all the memories that hang upon
And cling around about us as a garment
Clothing us in a robe of more than glory.

Edgar Allen Poe, 'The Coliseum' (1833)

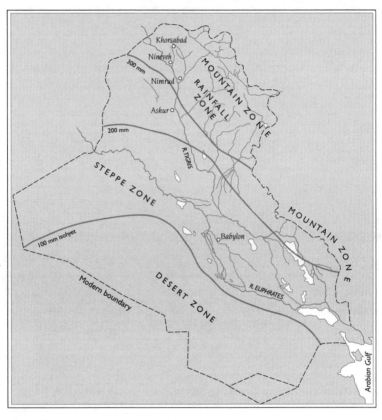

Fig. 1 Sketch map showing rainfall zones and rivers around Mesopotamia

Introduction

From the water and alluvial mud of the mighty rivers Tigris and Euphrates arose two of the earliest great powers in the world, Babylonia in the south and Assyria in the north. Both lay in ancient Mesopotamia within the borders of modern Iraq. Babylonia included territory along both rivers and had access to the sea at the head of the Arabian Gulf, whereas Assyria began as a small, landlocked state based on the upper Tigris. One of the few things known to the general reader is that Babylon was the city where the famous Hanging Garden was located, one of the seven wonders of the ancient world, built by Nebuchadnezzar the Great (see Plate 1).

As an Assyriologist I work on clay tablets written in cuneiform script by Babylonians and Assyrians, whether they have been freshly excavated by archaeologists working in Iraq and Syria, or languish in the great museums and collections of the world. Most of them were only sun-dried, not baked, and they are usually damaged, often badly broken. It is a slow job, with frustrations as well as excitements, to piece together the material remains and their written contents. Some ancient sites have yielded thousands of tablets within a few seasons, so there is always new work to be done, and old interpretations have to be revised in the light of new discoveries. A recent word-count estimates that the body of known writings in Babylonian and Assyrian already matches that of the entire body of Latin texts, and there is more to come from future excavations.[1] My work deals primarily with such cuneiform texts, although other kinds of information, especially Greek and Hebrew literature, and scenes on panels of bas-relief sculpture, help with interpretation in this piece of research.

When I was an undergraduate studying Assyriology at Cambridge in 1962–6 the Hanging Garden was not mentioned in my studies. Many years later, as part of a weekend course on ancient gardens, I gave a lecture to the Department of Continuing Education in Oxford. In preparing for the talk, I was surprised to find nothing intelligent to say about the Hanging Garden of Babylon; but plenty of other interesting material about the gardens of Assyria allowed me to concentrate on what was positive, and I omitted mention of the famous World Wonder. At the end of the lecture, a lady in the audience said, with reproachful indignation, that she had come expecting to hear about the World Wonder-garden, so I sheepishly exculpated myself by saying that there was nothing much to be said from the viewpoint of Babylonian texts or archaeology. I don't think she believed me. She was disappointed, I was embarrassed. That unsettling experience led me to try at least to analyse the problem, without at that time trying to solve it. Chapter 1 describes how archaeologists and Assyriologists made strenuous attempts to find the garden in Babylon, sometimes distorting or ignoring genuine information. Several Greek and Latin sources described the garden—they are the subject of Chapter 2—but they were written many centuries after the time when the garden was supposedly built. Most attempts to locate the garden in Babylon, using the results of excavation there, were forced to brush aside those Classical texts, because no information of any kind allowed a connection. The excavations too were disappointing. I could see no way through the difficulties. For several years the problem remained at the back of my mind while other work took precedence.

Meanwhile, working on a lecture about forms of currency before the invention of coinage for an undergraduate course at Oxford, I found much confusion in translations of a text written for an Assyrian king. Some lines were taken to mean that he had cast coins early in the 7th century BC, several centuries earlier than the earliest known coinage in that area. The anomaly was striking, and impelled me to look again at the text. There I found that a different interpretation, avoiding the anachronistic introduction of coinage, was more likely. The king was describing how his workmen cast gigantic animal figures in solid bronze by a new method which was so successful that the production was as easy as if the figures had weighed a mere half-shekel each rather than 43 tons.[2] The old translation was 'as easily as if they were half-shekel coins'. The text was also striking because royal inscriptions hardly ever show an interest in a technological innovation or mention the skill of craftsmen. Not until I could talk with Andrew Lacey, an experimental bronze-caster, in the course of making a programme for the BBC many years later, did I find out how to understand some of the detail given in that inscription, related to the king's new method of casting bronze. From that experience I became interested in problems of recognizing technical details in cuneiform texts, and in the use of similes and metaphors to describe innovations. The results of the new understanding were included in a paper written for a conference on ancient bronze-working,[3] and the implications for this book are discussed in Chapter 4.

As a royal city the prominence of Babylon can be highlighted by contrast with the royal cities of Assyria. During the first four centuries of the first millennium BC the Assyrians moved northwards from the western bank of the middle Tigris, where their old capital city Ashur bore the same name as the national god, still preserved in our word Assyria. They transferred their royal residence to the eastern bank of the Tigris, first to Nimrud, ancient Calah, then to Khorsabad, ancient Dur-Sharrukin, and lastly to the largest and oldest city of them all: Nineveh, which bears its ancient name to this day. Those three cities all lay within a short distance of each other. The Babylonians, by contrast, remained faithful throughout to their traditional capital city Babylon. At times Assyrian kings brought Babylonia under their control, but Babylon never conquered Assyria.

The two powers had much in common, not least language and a cuneiform system of writing, much of their literature and most of their gods and goddesses. Building with mud bricks, and writing on damp clay, they recorded literature, history and administrative details. But they differed greatly in their surroundings: Assyria was a land with several tributaries flowing through hill country into the Tigris from the mountains of Persia, past fertile valleys and plains benefiting from reliable rainfall. Babylon, on the other hand, lay in flat territory, criss-crossed by canals, fed by the abundant lower Euphrates and Tigris, lacking reliable rainfall. In Assyria the use of cuneiform (wedge-shaped) script died out in the 6th century BC, much earlier than in Babylonia where it continued in use for many centuries.[4]

The cuneiform script and the languages of Mesopotamia began to be deciphered a little more than 150 years ago. The work of understanding, editing, and making reliable translations of their texts continues to this day. So much information is now at our disposal that the failure to find the Hanging Garden of Babylon has been extremely frustrating.

The idea of seven wonderful places in the known world, exceptional sights to visit, is known from Greek and Roman texts from the 2nd century BC onwards. That is several centuries after the famous garden was created. The earliest text is a fragment of papyrus found when a mummy from an Egyptian tomb was unwrapped, for it was common to use old, discarded rolls of text to enshroud corpses. Its text preserves, with gaps, the words: 'the seven sights, the temple of Artemis in Ephesus, (... gap ...) the Pyramids ... (gap) ... the funerary monument of Mausolus in Halicarnassus ... (gap) ... '[5] Around the same time a scholar known as Callimachus of Cyrene (305–240 BC) wrote *A Collection of Sights in Lands throughout the World* from his seat in the great library of Alexandria in Egypt. Whether he had a list of seven is uncertain because his work is known only from its title and some fragments, but Diodorus Siculus, writing in the following century, mentioned an obelisk installed in Babylonia by Semiramis 'beside the most famous street' which, he said, people included 'among the seven sights of the world',[6] and Marcus Terentius Varro (116–27 BC) wrote a work on 'Seven works to be marvelled at in the world'. This shows that the number seven was by then a well-known attachment to the idea of marvellous sights to see. No later writers who listed seven sights included Semiramis' obelisk, an omission which indicates that the listing was a flexible one, presumably prone to the vagaries of fashion and availability.[7] As time went on, the original wonders were updated; new wonders were added to the list, enlarging the total number of famous places 'to see before you die', but with the number seven still attached. Various different lists are known: Romans and Byzantines added their own marvels, such as the Colosseum in Rome, and the Church of Santa Sophia in Constantinople.[8]

As for the main Greek and Roman writers who mentioned or described the Hanging Garden, most of them, Diodorus Siculus, Strabo, Antipater, Josephus and Quintus Curtius Rufus, were contemporary with Roman rulers from Julius Caesar to Nero, and all except the last wrote in Greek. During that time Roman armies and administrators were moving around western parts of the Near East, stimulating a popular interest in the marvels of the Orient. Many centuries later, writing in Greek during the Byzantine period, was

Philo of Byzantium 'the Paradoxographer'. All of those writers had access to earlier texts and legends that are now lost, so there is no definitive account—the origin of the concept of listing seven World Wonders is lost in the mists of early antiquity. Some of those earlier writers whose books are lost actually served under Alexander the Great, suggesting that the tradition may first have arisen when there were many Macedonian and other Greek soldiers and administrators in Mesopotamia. In any case, the earliest listings date from many centuries after the time of Nebuchadnezzar the Great (604–562 BC).

The Hanging Garden of Babylon, the walls of Babylon, and the Obelisk of Semiramis are by far the easternmost of the early candidates to be included in lists of seven World Wonders. All the others are easily accessible from the east Mediterranean. Egypt claimed the great pyramid and the lighthouse known as the Pharos in the harbour at Alexandria; the Aegean island of Rhodes had its Colossus, a gigantic bronze-cast man whose huge legs spanned the harbour entrance; western Anatolia boasted of the huge Mausoleum with its fabulous sculptures made for the satrap of Caria at Halicarnassus (modern Bodrum), and the Artemisium of Ephesus with its extraordinary statue of Diana—Artemis (her many 'breasts' are now thought by some to be pollen sacks representing her role as patron of apiculture in an area where honey is still famous); Olympia on mainland Greece claimed the statue of Zeus crafted by the great Athenian sculptor Phidias. All of those lie between longitude 21 and 31, and could be visited with relative ease by travellers from the Greek and Roman world whose writers publicized the tradition of seven, and added others to it; whereas Babylon lies between longitude 44 and 45, far beyond easy reach of the Mediterranean. It is remarkable that Babylon is the location of three early World Wonders. All the other wonders lie in lands more likely to be on a tourist route for Greeks and Romans; one might suppose that remoteness and great antiquity gave Babylon a specially romantic allure, allowing the imagination to roam, free from the smells, dust and epidemics of reality.

Several centuries earlier, Herodotus had written with admiration of the pyramids in Egypt and of the walls of Babylon without mentioning or implying a group of seven. Those two phenomenal constructions had stood the test of time, and reminded the Greeks that they were relative newcomers on the scene of great civilizations. In Herodotus' day some of the works that would eventually join lists of wonders such as the Lighthouse of Alexandria and the Colossus of

Rhodes were not yet created, and King Mausolus was not yet born. In the various lists known from later times, very ancient constructions sit alongside recent ones, the juxtaposition implying that men could still rival the wonders of the remote past, in lists advertising with the rhetoric of the travel agent 'modern' marvels as worth a visit for enterprising travellers. Some of the later lists have fewer or more than seven, yet the idea of seven persisted.

What was so important about the number seven, and where did the idea of seven for this context of World Wonders come from? In quite different spheres of Greek culture, such as the *Seven Against Thebes*—a legend used for a famous play of that name written by Aeschylus—or the Seven Sages, the choice of that number is thought to come from ancient Mesopotamia.[9] In the literatures of Mesopotamia, seven was the number of heavens and of earths; seven the gates to the Under-world, seven the Sages who brought the arts of civilization to man-kind, and above all, seven the celestial bodies—sun, moon and five great planets—whose movements and conjunctions affected the fate of men, cities and nations.[10] The war-mongering group of gods Sibitti whose very name means 'Seven' was identified with the constellation of the Pleiades, and was also known as 'Stars'. In myths and legends there was a tendency for demons to appear in groups of seven, and winds, quite improbably, could rise up seven at a time. Many actions in rituals and magic had to be performed seven times. Seven con-tained the concept of totality, Akkadian *kiššatu*, the number serving as a logogram for that word. In later times and in some spheres such as the number of heavens and the recitation of spells, three super-seded seven, but did not always replace it because seven carried the authority of earliest antiquity.

The walls of Babylon, with their great gates and cunning access through them from the citadel to the river, were described by Herod-otus in detail. Although they are included in several of the Greek lists—those given by Antipater, Strabo, Philo of Byzantium, and a few Roman and Christian writers subsequently—they are often omitted in modern listings. We know that some walls for the city must have been constructed before the time of king Hammurabi who ruled Babylon early in the second millennium BC, and no doubt there were many occasions during the following centuries when they were remodelled, restored and repaired.[11] This was done, to our certain knowledge, by Assyrian kings as well as Babylonian ones. Four generations of great Assyrian kings carried out building work on the walls of Babylon before the dynasty of Nebuchadnezzar. The mixture of Babylonian and Assyrian kings responsible for restorations added to confusion when later conflation simplified a long and varied history.

The citadel was encircled by two concentric walls which were given names as if they were people: the inner one was Imgur-Enlil 'the god Enlil approved', and Nemetti-Enlil 'Enlil's Bulwark' was the outer one. These names for the two walls are known at least 500 years before Nebuchadnezzar II. The inner one was by far higher and thicker than the outer one, which was built at a lower level.

In the late 8th and 7th century when Assyria ruled Babylon directly, repair and partial rebuilding were carried out frequently. Sargon II (721–705 BC) repaired and strengthened both walls, piously claiming to have moulded bricks for baking. His son Sennacherib at first did building work there, but later besieged and sacked the city, and when eventually peace was restored, Esarhaddon (680–669 BC), followed by his son Ashurbanipal,[12] made a major effort of atonement by repairing the walls, recording his work on formal inscriptions:

With the large cubit I measured the dimensions of Imgur-Enlil, its great wall—each length and width was 30 cubits. I had it built just as formerly, and raised its top like a mountain. I built it perfectly, and filled it with splendour, for the wonder of all people.[13]

The word used to express 'all' is *kiššatu*. Here we encounter the remarkable fact that an Assyrian king of the 7th century BC describes as a wonder a wall listed half a millennium later likewise as a wonder, and incorporates the concept of seven into the expression. But the usage is different, and one might think of a link through creative misunderstanding or a deliberately clever shift of interpretation rather than coincidence. About fifty years after Esarhaddon, when power had passed from Assyria to Babylon, Nabopolassar, who founded the new dynasty in Babylon, wrote a much more fulsome account, linking his victory over Assyria to the rebuilding of that wall. It has been found on seven barrel cylinders.

I chased the Assyrians out of Akkad and so the Babylonians threw off their yoke. At that time I, Nabopolassar . . . —Imgur-Enlil the great wall of Babylon, the primeval boundary that has been famous since the distant past, the firm frontier as old as time, the lofty eyrie as high as the heavens, the strong shield that bars access from enemy lands, the spacious enclosure of the Igigi-gods . . . [14]

After the fall of Nineveh Nabopolassar also repaired the outer wall of Babylon, helped by his son, the king-to-be, Nebuchadnezzar,[15] depositing a building inscription in it. Although Nabopolassar did not use the expression 'wonder of all peoples', his poetic language shows the supreme status attributed to the city wall in his time. When Nabonidus, who ruled Babylon half a century later, repaired the same wall, he imitated the wording of his predecessor, added to it the phrase 'for a wonder', and not only inserted one of Nabopolassar's cylinders alongside his own into a brick box within the wall,[16] but also found and reinstated an inscription of Ashurbanipal.[17] Even Cyrus the Great, a foreigner who conquered Babylon, issued an edict written in deliberate imitation of the style of Ashurbanipal,[18] while at the same time quoting the previous work on the inner wall done by Nebuchadnezzar.[19] Such inscriptions could still be found and read when the successors of Alexander ruled Babylon.

This extended and self-conscious tradition—a long line of powerful kings aware of their predecessors' fame in building the walls, and a virtual chain of inscriptions deposited in the walls to perpetuate their memory—is exceptional.

The importance and emphasis placed on building the city wall reflects the Mesopotamian ideal of kingship in the character and achievements of the legendary Gilgamesh whose epic deed as a builder is recorded in this way:

> He had the wall of Uruk built, the Sheepfold
> Of holiest Eanna, the pure treasury.
> See its wall, which is like a copper band,
> Survey its battlements, which nobody else can match, ...
> Inspect the foundation platform and scrutinize the brickwork!
> Testify that its bricks are baked bricks,
> And that the Seven Sages must have laid its foundations!

So to Babylonians wall-building was a supreme act of kingship. This passage from the *Epic of Gilgamesh* shows it was worthy of a great hero, linked to the Seven Sages.[20]

Tracing back to look at the use of the expression 'wonder' in inscriptions of an earlier period, we find that its earliest known use was when the Assyrian king Tiglath-Pileser III (744–727 BC) described his new palace at Nimrud on the Tigris, with special emphasis placed on 'the colossal lions and bulls with very skilfully wrought forms, clothed with allure, I placed at the entrance and set up as a wonder'.[21] A couple of decades later Sargon II, describing his new capital at Khorsabad, used the same term for the doors and the pictures on their bronze bands in his palace. His son Sennacherib, after describing the decorative features of his 'palaces' at Nineveh, wrote, 'I made them "wonders".' Then, after the lines describing a new water-raising device, he wrote, 'I made those palaces beautifully. I raised the area surrounding the palace to be "a wonder for all peoples", I named it Unrivalled Palace.'[22] Esarhaddon in the 7th century, expanding the use of the term, used it on at least six occasions: for his restoration of a temple to Ashur, for the temple of Marduk in Babylon, for his restoration of the walls of Babylon, for his restoration of the Military Review Palace at Nimrud and his new Review Palace built in Nineveh, and for the palace he built for the crown prince in the town Tarbiṣu close to Nineveh. This was part of a competitive spirit that drove each new king to claim that he was even better than his predecessors, in phrases such as 'more than previously', and 'more than the kings my predecessors'.

The expression was taken up by later kings of Babylon. Nebuchadnezzar used the phrase for at least four public spectacles: a cultic boat used for processions of Marduk's statue; one of his palaces in Babylon (using the term at the beginning and end of an inscription, but with no mention of a garden); the city gates of Babylon; and the main temple in Borsippa. Finally, Nabonidus used it at least twice: for the walls of Babylon, and for the great temple of the sun-god in Sippar.

All of these were spectacles. The Babylonian term corresponds closely to the Greek word *theamata* 'sights' first used for World Wonders, later changed to *thaumata* 'wonders'. In the expression used, 'wonder for all people' *tabrâti kal niši*, the word *tabrâti* means literally something to gaze upon with admiration, and corresponds to the earlier Greek *theamata*. This correspondence between Babylonian and Greek may be coincidence, but it raises the possibility that the Greek expression was modelled upon the Babylonian phrase. Both the concept and the expression could thus have been taken over by Greeks from a tradition that had begun in 8th-century Assyria, continued in Babylonia, and would have been known to the Seleucid kings from their study of neo-Babylonian inscriptions.

Cuneiform records often seem to offer a scatter of unrelated minutiae, bits of information that refuse to yield a coherent story, scraps of detail transmitted by ancient writers in several languages—

Fig. 2 East India House inscription of Nebuchadnezzar II, a complete text written in an archaic script in stone, recording the king's building work, but no garden, in Babylon where it was found. 56.51 × 50.16 cm.

Assyrian, Babylonian, Greek and Latin, and in different scripts—cuneiform and alphabetic—covering a span of many centuries. In addition to the crucial role played by the study of cuneiform texts, excavation, field survey and art history play their part in finding the solution to this puzzle through persistent research. Inscriptions show that many exceptional constructions had been proclaimed as wonders in Assyria as well as in Babylonia, with a concentration on the city of Babylon. The inner wall of Babylon was explicitly a wonder under an

Assyrian king, a Babylonian king, and in lists of wonders compiled by Greek authors from at least the time of Alexander onwards.

This book is the result of a long process of investigation which has uncovered at last the reality behind the legend of the Hanging Garden of Babylon.

1

Drawing a Blank in Babylon

> Beware lest you lose the substance by grasping at a shadow
>
> Aesop, *Fable of the Dog and his Shadow*

When a German team led by Robert Koldewey excavated in Babylon from 1898 to 1917, it made a thorough excavation of the citadel on which the royal palaces stood, along with the splendid processional way, the great temples, and the Ishtar Gate. Of course those archaeologists were keen to discover at least the site of the Hanging Garden, both out of interest and because further funding would follow from the resulting publicity. They treated Josephus' information as correct, and expected to find inscriptions of Nebuchadnezzar confirming that he built the garden. To their dismay they could not find any possible location with enough space in the vicinity of the palaces, nor did they dig out any written confirmation from the many texts they unearthed.

To uncover the site of the World Wonder would have given a great impetus to their work. Every visitor to the site, every journalist, every colleague, must have asked the same questions: where is the Hanging Garden, and why haven't you found it? Every audience at Koldewey's public lectures in Germany would have expected an answer. Eventually the excavators made an unsatisfactory case for interpreting a complex of rooms within the Southern Palace, where the walls were especially thick, and where baked brick rather than sun-dried brick was used, along with much bitumen to make the building waterproof. A roof-top garden might explain the use of those materials. But there was no sign of how it might have been watered, no sign of tree roots, and the building was much too far from the river for water to be raised up to supply the supposed trees (see Figure 3).

As Koldewey well knew, the suggestion of a roof-top garden did not agree with the descriptions of the Classical authors. Wells inside the building would have been the only feasible source of water, and they would have been unsatisfactory for the purpose of keeping trees alive, besides the objection that the Classical texts certainly do not name wells as providing irrigation for the garden. In that part of the building suggested for the roof garden were stored administrative records of unbaked clay.[1] Such a function would be impractical beneath a roof garden, from which leakages of water might from time to time reduce clay tablets to puddles of mud. Nevertheless, the idea of a roof garden that would give a bird's eye view of the city caught the imagination of the public, and gave rise to a number of florid reconstructions, regardless of the fact that plants would have shrivelled in the fierce heat of a Babylonian summer when shade is utterly desirable during those long, hot days and months.

Much later, in 1979, Wolfram Nagel, soon followed by Donald Wiseman, Professor of Assyriology at SOAS in London, made an alternative suggestion, going to the opposite extreme.[2] Realizing that the garden must have been located beside a river, as Strabo described, they proposed the area to the west of the main palace, where the massive structure known now as the Western Outwork lay, a narrow near-rectangular building which the excavators had assumed simply protected the palace against erosion when the river level rose with the spring floods. The disadvantages of Nagel's idea, however, outweighed its advantages, for there were several thick walls barring the king's way from the palace to the garden, and the walls would have denied the plants any sunshine for most of the daylight hours.

A further objection to both those locations is that there had been a change in the course of the Euphrates. The phenomenon is thought by some to have been the result of a deliberate act, whether on the part of Cyrus the Great when he advanced to capture the city in 539 BC, or on the part of Darius I when he quelled the rebellion of 522–521 BC in Babylon, or much later in the Seleucid period.[3] But this is only guesswork based on historical probability, for although the altered river bed is clear from aerial photographs and surface surveys, surface observation does not allow precise dating.[4] The river was diverted just upstream from the Western Outwork, and then flowed to the east of the Southern Palace, leaving the Western Outwork high

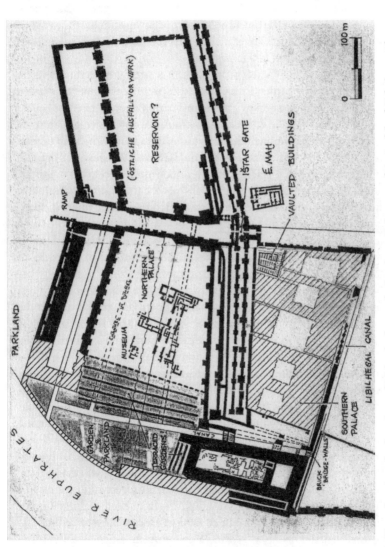

Fig. 3 Plan showing the location of Nebuchadnezzar's Southern Palace on the citadel of Babylon with suggested locations of the garden: in the palace and in the Western Outwork.

and dry. Any mechanisms set up to water the garden from the river would have been useless, and the plants would quickly have dried out. A garden marked only with dead trees, abandoned whether before Greeks came to work and travel in Mesopotamia under the benevolent protection of the Seleucid kings, or during Roman times, would not have been worth a visit when the World Wonders were such a popular theme for Classical writers.

Ignoring these difficulties, several artists attempted to draw a reconstruction of the garden in Babylon, showing the walls of the Western Outwork or the Southern Palace enclosing the garden at too great a height to have made a pleasant environment for growing plants, and they were obliged to include very steep steps to allow the king to reach the top of the garden before he could enjoy the view (see Figure 4). Others showed a terraced garden sunk within a courtyard inside a palace, enclosed again by high walls on each side, and accessible by walking up and down a steep stairway: claustrophobic, tiring, lacking a view or a breeze, it would have been a gloomy place, producing etiolated plants. Other reconstructions ignored the walls, and set the garden on a series of terraces out in the open. One of them depicts enormous water wheels on each terrace, but as we shall see, water wheels are not an option for Babylonia in the 6th century BC, nor is there any reference to their use in Babylonian or Greek texts. Another reconstruction drawing showed the garden on that site as an internal courtyard surrounded by high walls decorated in an Assyrian, not a Babylonian, style of palace decoration.[5] It has none of the characteristics described by any of the sources; laid out as an essentially flat, formal garden with a Persian-style pool at its centre, it does not resemble the forested mountains for which the queen had supposedly pined according to some of the later accounts, and lacks many other features described in ancient testimonies. Another idea, placing the World Wonder at Nineveh rather than Babylon, was for a 'carpet garden', sunken and flat, a style for which there was no evidence of any kind.[6]

As one casts a critical eye over these many attempts at reconstruction, aware that the ancient descriptions have been wilfully ignored, one asks oneself why a roof or courtyard garden, or a sunken flat one, should qualify to be a World Wonder, since all the other World Wonders are marvels of engineering, construction, technical ingenuity, size and artistic accomplishment. Those who have asked themselves such a question, finding no answer, have fallen back on a denial that the gardens ever existed, preferring to relegate them to the realms

"*Don't forget to compliment him on his green thumb.*"

Fig. 4 Cartoon of Robert J. Day from the *New Yorker*, 1960. Several reconstructions show long, steep staircases and jungle-like plants.

of romantic imagination and the fantastic fabulations of late antiquity. This offers an unsatisfactory solution to the problem, partly because the various Classical descriptions were quite coherent while arousing no suspicion of a common source such as a folktale or novel, and partly because all the other six World Wonders certainly existed. A non-existent wonder did not fit the category.

A different suggestion that ignored the Classical sources gained credence by disregarding descriptions of the garden as an adjunct to the royal palace, and placing it on the stages of the ziggurat at Babylon, the temple tower of the great god Bel–Marduk, famously described by Herodotus. The idea obviated the need to find a site on the ground with space for a garden. It germinated from a discovery made by Leonard Woolley, excavating the great ziggurat at Ur in southern Iraq, when he found holes at regular intervals in the solid mass of brickwork. Ziggurats are solid mud-brick structures with a skin of baked brick. If anyone had planted trees upon the terraced stages of the ziggurat and then watered them (hauling water unceremoniously from a well up the long flights of stairs in buckets) the brickwork would soon have disintegrated. The purpose of the so-called 'weeper holes' was to help the mass of solid brickwork to dry out evenly, so that a differential in moisture content between the core and the surface brick would not cause splitting and cracking; this was Woolley's original interpretation.

But then Woolley changed his mind, and associated the holes with drainage for plants, a suggestion that appealed to the public, inspiring many reconstruction drawings of the Hanging Garden to show plants dangling from the terraces of a ziggurat, like a fancifully decorated wedding cake made of superimposed squares that decrease in size the higher they go, so that the foliage hung over from each terrace on the side of the building, rather like gigantic hanging baskets. His second interpretation is wrong for several reasons, including those just described, and has been discounted by later archaeologists.[7] Unfortunately it was so picturesque, and seemed, on the face of it, so suitable for applying to Babylon, and the book in which Woolley published it so popular, that many of his readers looked no further, remembering what they had read; and Moorey retained the second interpretation in his otherwise fine revision of Woolley's book.[8] This is the image that has endured in many artistic reconstructions of the Hanging Garden.

Another reason to discard the idea comes from several depictions of ziggurats engraved on cylinder seals. Plants are never shown

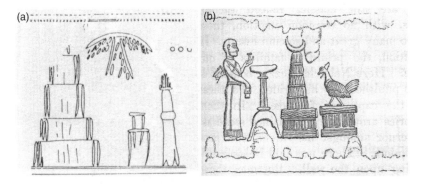

Fig. 5 Cylinder seal impressions showing ziggurats without any plants on their terraces. (a) From Tell Muhammed Arab, Late Bronze Age. (b) Provenance unknown, Babylonian Iron Age. Ht. 3.85 cm.

rising from the terraces of those temple towers, which are bare of ornamentation (see Figure 5).[9] A few Assyrian sculptures showing tall buildings were occasionally thought by early interpreters to show plants growing from the walls, but further careful study showed either that flames of destruction were intended, or the horns of wild deer and gazelles, such as one still sees decorating the walls of houses in the Arabian peninsula (as well as German hunting lodges and Scottish baronial castles).[10] The misconception gives an insight into the difficulties of interpreting an ancient form of art, especially when the carved surface is damaged and no colour survives. Flames and leaves are both grey on bare limestone sculptures.

Above all, the idea of a ziggurat-garden bears no relationship at all to the rather detailed descriptions of the Hanging Garden given by the Classical authors, from whose accounts the main evidence is drawn. We cannot simply dismiss our chief sources of information, which were ostensibly written while the garden still existed.

Some confusion arose from misunderstanding of the English word 'hanging'. In modern times we may think of hanging baskets, in which drooping plants have their roots at a higher level than much of their pendant foliage (see Figure 6). Or, in a less urban environment, we may think of 'hangers', steeply sloping hillsides covered in forest trees such as Gilbert White described in his village of Selbourne in Hampshire.[11] Sir Thomas Browne's 'pensile paradise' was preferred for its poetic alliteration derived from a Latin description.[12] For people who only knew of the World Wonder as Hanging Gardens

THE HANGING BASKET OF BABYLON

Fig. 6 Cartoon by 'Knife'. The word 'hanging' has caused much confusion.

(in German, *hängende Gärten*),[13] the semantic range of the English word could be exploited regardless of the Classical texts, encouraging the idea of plants on the stages of a temple tower. 'Hanging' is the English word that translates the ancient Greek word *kremastos*, applied to the Hanging Garden, and its meaning may be discerned from other contexts: it does not have the same range of meaning in Greek as in English. I have not identified an Akkadian equivalent. In Greek it was used by Sophocles to describe Antigone, found hanging by the neck, suspended by a noose of fine linen, and Oedipus' mother hanging by a plaited rope. Less dramatically the word is used of a hammock, of the rigging of a ship, and of dried grapes.[14] Some of the Greek descriptions of the Hanging Garden make it clear that the upper part was built upon artificial terraces of stone, like a Greek theatre, so that the trees planted there could not reach the water table with their roots, and had to be kept moist artificially, as Strabo, Diodorus Siculus, Q. Curtius Rufus and Philo of Byzantium describe them. Thus the terraces which were actually elevated on vaults above the ground appeared as if suspended from the sky. This is not a feature of the ancient Mesopotamian ziggurat, which is made of solid brick.

Nebuchadnezzar II, who ruled Babylon for forty-three years, is named by Josephus as the creator of the Hanging Garden, and it is his name that has generally been accepted in that context, helping to qualify him for the modern epithet 'the Great'. Contemporary records show that he had at least seven sons and three daughters whose names are known;[15] that he benefited from a long reign to complete the enormous building works that his father had begun, in and around Babylon, and he took the credit for them by recording his works in quite lengthy inscriptions, and by inscribing hundreds of bricks that were inserted into the constructions (see Figures 2 and 7). We have more than 200 of his official building inscriptions, many of them complete, which he wrote at various times after he became king. Even as crown prince he had taken an active part in building work. In the words of his proud father Nabopolassar, 'I had builders' baskets made of gold and silver, and I made Nebuchadnezzar, my eldest son, beloved of my heart, carry soil mixed with wine, oil and aromatic shavings, alongside the workmen.'[16]

Nebuchadnezzar had campaigned as crown prince with great success, driving the Egyptians out of Syria and back into the Nile valley. After inheriting the kingship from his father he established control over Syria and Palestine in the course of many campaigns, but never controlled Egypt, Anatolia or Iran.[17] This limitation sometimes causes surprise because the modern epithet 'the Great' invites comparison

Fig. 7 Barrel cylinder of Nebuchadnezzar II. His long and complete inscriptions do not mention any garden. Length 20 cm.

with Alexander, whose conquests included those lands. After his death legends inflated Nebuchadnezzar's achievements, giving him an undeserved reputation as a world conqueror; but his triumphs in the Levant, and the riches heaped up earlier from the conquest of Assyria, must have given him enough wealth for his ambition to make his city the greatest in the known world. He celebrated his prowess by inscribing on two rock faces in the Wadi Brisa, a ravine in the cedar mountains of Lebanon (see Figure 8 a, b).[18] This was the region where the legendary Gilgamesh and Enkidu had fought and killed the monster Humbaba. Nebuchadnezzar referred to it as a place where he had cut down gigantic cedar trees for his temple doors—implying that he was like Gilgamesh. On the surface of the rock he also had scenes carved that showed himself grasping a tree, presumably intending to cut it down, and fighting a lion,[19] as Gilgamesh had done with Enkidu:

> Gilgamesh was cutting down the trees;
> Enkidu kept tugging at the stumps . . .
> We who met and scaled the mountain, . . .
> Killed lions in the passes of the mountains.

The Roman emperor Hadrian was to imitate him by carving his own rock inscriptions in the same area, many centuries later.[20]

Nowadays Nebuchadnezzar is most famous for taking direct control of Jerusalem, plundering and destroying its temple, and taking its rebellious kings into exile in Babylon. Other kings suffered a similar fate—at Arvad, Sidon, Tyre, Ashdod and Gaza—in episodes that had no biblical texts to prolong their notoriety; we know about them mainly from very brief chronicle texts. Compared with Assyrian kings, whose annalistic royal inscriptions relating military events are known in abundance, Babylonian kings were much more reticent about the details of their conquests, and put their main emphasis on pious works, building temples, making objects for use in the cult, and listing the exact offerings they instituted for the deities. The different nature of their texts, and the lack of narrative sculpture, makes it impossible to trace the kinds of details that might reveal a particular king's character and his intellectual interests. We do not know if he liked hunting, or collecting plants,[21] or whether his official piety was linked to personal religious fervour, or whether he loved his wife. Our knowledge of the king is far more restricted than of late Assyrian kings.

After his death Nebuchadnezzar's reputation polarized sharply. For the Babylonians he was, like Gilgamesh, a model king, to such an extent that two rebels who briefly snatched the kingship from

Achaemenid Persian control both called themselves 'Nebuchadnezzar'. When eventually Seleucid kings ingratiated themselves with the Babylonians, nearly 250 years later, they imitated the famous king's inscriptions for at least one of their building works, and one of their number wore his ancient robe for celebrating the festival of the New Year in Babylon. But for Jews and Christians he was the wicked, cruel emperor who had destroyed the temple in Jerusalem, caused the Babylonian Captivity, and sent Daniel into the lion's den. Some of the later traditions confused him either with the Assyrian king Sennacherib because both had attacked Jerusalem, or with Nabonidus the last king of Babylon, distorting the facts to allow the inference that God had punished the great leader for his sacrilege in Jerusalem, by causing the fall of Babylon to the foreigner Cyrus.

To Nebuchadnezzar the Hanging Garden is nowadays attributed, so it comes as a surprise to find that most of the Greek and Latin texts mentioning the garden do not name him as the builder. Diodorus Siculus said it was built 'not by Semiramis but by a later Syrian king' ('Syrian' meant 'Assyrian' from at least the 7th century BC onwards); and Quintus Curtius Rufus wrote, 'Tradition affirms that a king of Assyria reigning in Babylon executed this work'. Strabo specified Babylon and the river Euphrates, but did not name the builder. The only ancient author to name Nebuchadnezzar was Josephus. He ostensibly quoted from the writings of Berossus, a Babylonian scholar-priest who wrote an account of Babylonian traditions in Greek for his patron the Seleucid emperor.

These attestations, and the single attribution to Nebuchadnezzar, give rise to doubts, whether about the veracity of Berossus himself, or about the use of his work by Josephus. But it is not just a question of denying Nebuchadnezzar his rightful place as builder of the World Wonder on the suspect testimony of much later sources. As luck would have it, among the many building records of Nebuchadnezzar that have come to light from Babylon and other Babylonian cities, not least is the great *East India House Inscription* on stone which describes the building of his palace. (See Figure 2) The king was far from reticent about his achievements in building: the marvellous walls of the city as well as wonderful temples and palaces; but he never mentions a garden.

Later, Greek writers describe Babylon without referring to the garden. Chief among them is Herodotus, writing in the time of Artaxerxes I (464–424 BC) who would surely have mentioned that the city contained a World Wonder, whether he had seen it himself,

Fig. 8a Two rock sculptures at Wadi Brisa, Lebanon showing Nebuchadnezzar II killing a lion, and cutting down trees, reflecting the deeds of the legendary hero Gilgamesh: (a) 200 × 550 cm.

Fig. 8b (b) 280 × 350 cm.

or had relied on hearsay for his information.[22] Much later the Roman writer Pliny the Elder described the city, again without referring to the garden. Equally surprising, the patchwork of texts in several different languages and widely divergent versions now known as the *Alexander Romance* does not mention it even though the final days and premature death of Alexander the Great in Babylon gave every opportunity to incorporate a reference at the very least to one of the world's marvels. There is no mention in the writings of Plutarch, or of Quintus Curtius Rufus, when they refer to Babylon. Nor does the Book of Daniel mention it; Nebuchadnezzar went up on to the roof of the royal palace to admire his city, but the tale does not mention the supposed garden. It is as though the World Wonder never existed.

The problems seemed insuperable to many scholars. When Irving Finkel wrote his chapter for Peter Clayton's book *The Seven Wonders of the Ancient World* in 1988, he began his contribution with these words: 'It must be admitted at the outset that the Hanging Gardens of Babylon, although famed far and wide as one of the celebrated Seven Wonders of the World, have never been conclusively identified, nor, indeed, has their existence been proved.' John and Elizabeth Romer came to an even more negative conclusion, writing in 1988 that 'of all the Seven Wonders, they are the one that everyone first names, but they are also the one that is most insubstantial and elusive . . . for there never was such a thing in Babylon'.[23]

Since all the World Wonders in early lists were in some way astonishing not just for aesthetic reasons, but also from a technical point of view, in looking for the original Hanging Garden we have to find rather more than just an attractive garden such as many kings would have enjoyed in their capital cities, whether within their palaces as a courtyard garden, or on a more malleable plot of land adjacent to a palace. This excludes all of the reconstructions described earlier.

For those who suggested that the garden never existed, but was a purely fictional tradition invented to satisfy a Greek appetite for oriental marvels, it was not just a matter of invoking the infamous name of Nebuchadnezzar, sacker of Jerusalem, or the feminist allure of Semiramis the warrior queen. They thought that Babylon during the Achaemenid Persian period went into a severe decline which was subsequently exacerbated by the foundation of a new capital, Seleucia, when Hellenistic rule eventually settled down after the death of Alexander the Great and the ensuing power struggles.[24] But new evidence has overturned that view. Babylon lay on the Euphrates, whereas Seleucia lay on the Tigris, so the new capital had little effect on trade or population around the old city. When the strife that followed the death of Alexander the Great subsided, Antiochus I (281–261) and his successors engaged in the traditional rituals of Babylon, and worked to restore the temple of Marduk there, as well as the temple of the god Nabu in the neighbouring city of Borsippa, encouraging a renaissance of indigenous traditions.[25] More than that, recent excavations have discovered that renovations previously attributed to Nebuchadnezzar may be dated to the Seleucid period, a revision which calls into question the whole understanding of Babylon's history at that time.[26] Presumably those Seleucid rulers found the inscriptions of Nebuchadnezzar within the brickwork, and piously replaced them when the work of renovation was completed—many examples of such a practice are known from the reigns of indigenous kings in much earlier times. We can no longer claim, therefore, that Babylon was too ruined to support a famous garden as World Wonder at a time when the Hanging Garden was famous for Greek and Roman writers, and when it had not been displaced from the listing by a more recently built marvel. Nor can it be supposed that the people of Babylonia were no longer interested in their glorious past.[27]

As for records written on clay tablets, it was thought until recently that by the end of the Seleucid period a very few esoteric scholars still wrote and studied literature written in cuneiform. We now know that not only was there a cuneiform library with an archive at Babylon, but also no less than three cuneiform libraries with archives in the southern city of Uruk.[28] Among the tablets from those late libraries comes the latest piece of the *Gilgamesh Epic* in cuneiform, dated to the Parthian period perhaps a few years before 127 BC, written by the son of a top astrologer-scholar.[29] Those libraries with their literary tablets and archives have helped to amplify our view of the city of Babylon and its more or less uninterrupted tradition of education and scholarship beyond the end of the Seleucid period.[30] In the time of Parthian rule, when many of the Greek and Roman books describing the Hanging Garden were written, there is not a trace of indigenous evidence for its existence, past or present, in Babylon.

We have reached the point when there is so much negative evidence that the absence is significant. If only there were the slightest evidence from cuneiform inscriptions or archaeology that the Hanging Garden was built in Babylon by Nebuchadnezzar, there would be no need to search for a solution, for there would be no mystery.

2

Classical Writers and their Testimony

> What more agreeable entertainment to the mind, than to be
> transported into the remotest ages of the world, and to observe
> human society, in its infancy, making the first faint essays
> towards the arts and sciences?
>
> David Hume (1711–76), *Of the Study of History*

Past attempts to identify and reconstruct the famous Hanging Garden
dismissed wholesale the explicit evidence given in Greek and Latin
texts. Proponents of the ziggurat theory disregarded the clear connection
with the royal palace and a total lack of any mention of a temple
or temple tower. The proponent of a reconstruction with water
wheels cast aside references to water-raising screws. Almost all have
turned a blind eye to the persistent theme that the garden was built
to resemble a hilly or semi-mountainous landscape, shaped like a
theatre: it was a landscape garden.

How should each of the Classical sources be evaluated? Do they
give literal descriptions of a real garden, or imaginative fiction? Are
they based on serious historical records, on eye-witness accounts, or
on rhetorical stereotypes and the tall tales of travellers? A thorough
training in rhetoric allowed Hellenistic authors, like barristers making
a case against the odds, to embellish or alter facts to support their
argument when they wrote of great men from the past, for their
primary interest lay in the character of leaders whether arrogant
and dissolute or admirable and effective. Within that essential framework
they would insert, for variety, passages on geography, zoology,
foreign customs: marvels of various kinds. One type of insertion was
the ecphrasis, a painting in words often depicting a particular

building or monument, allowing the audience to respond according to each individual's imagination. According to ancient handbooks on rhetoric, there were four elements in the ecphrasis: a focus on event and characters, physical appearance of the object, the method of construction, and the reaction of the viewer.[1] World Wonders were ideal subjects for that purpose. Owing to the suspected but imponderable influence of rhetoric and satire, the reliability of any of the Hellenistic sources is seldom agreed by scholars, but one can detect a trend in recent times towards a more critical, even sceptical understanding of supposedly historical detail as relayed by some of the authors.

Without a clear idea of what is being described, translators have done their best with some of the more difficult passages, but in some cases translations differ in important respects. In the hope of representing fairly the problems involved, and to highlight different interpretations, I have given more than one translation for certain passages.

Two of the earliest Roman authors to describe the garden of 'Babylon' as a World Wonder, in texts that have survived through time to our own generation, are Diodorus Siculus and Strabo. They lived when the Seleucid empire in Mesopotamia had given way to Parthian domination, around the time when Babylonian texts written in cuneiform were in the final years of use, when Rome's Parthian wars would have stimulated popular interest as soldiers returned from the field with tales to tell. They took much of their material from earlier Greek writers such as Callisthenes, who accompanied Alexander the Great in the 4th century BC but died before him, leaving an account no longer extant but presumably free of hindsight. Strabo extracted material from one Onesicritus who had also campaigned with Alexander. Diodorus Siculus described the walls of Babylon quoting from a lost account written by the Greek Ctesias who had supposedly served as a doctor at the Persian court, long before the conquests of Alexander. But for his account of the Hanging Garden Diodorus is now generally reckoned to have relied mainly on the writings of Cleitarchus who wrote a history, no longer extant, of Alexander the Great.[2] Another possible influence on Diodorus' writing was that of his contemporary Pompeius Trogus, whose universal history is known, from a surviving prologue, to have begun with Ninos and Semiramis, legendary characters whose part in this story is described in later chapters.[3]

Diodorus Siculus, a contemporary of Julius Caesar, wrote his description of the garden in the second book of his great *Library of History* between about 60 and 30 BC, five centuries after the time of Nebuchadnezzar II. He depended uncritically, many scholars suppose, on earlier sources available in Rome.

There was also, beside the acropolis, the Hanging Garden, as it is called, which was built, not by Semiramis, but by a later Syrian king to please one of his concubines; for she, they say, being a Persian by race and longing for the meadows of her mountains, asked the king to imitate, through the artifice of a planted garden, the distinctive landscape of Persia. The park extended 4 *plethra* on each side, and since the approach to the garden sloped like a hillside and the several parts of the structure rose from one another tier on tier, the appearance of the whole resembled that of a theatre. When the ascending terraces had been built, there had been constructed beneath them galleries[4] which carried the entire weight of the planted garden and rose little by little one above the other along the approach; and the uppermost gallery, which was 50 cubits high, bore the highest surface of the park, which was made level with the circuit wall of the battlements of the city. Furthermore, the walls, which had been constructed at great expense, were 22 feet thick, while the passage-way between each two walls was 10 feet wide. The roofs of the galleries were covered over with beams of stone 16 feet long, inclusive of the overlap, and 4 feet wide. The roof above these beams had first a layer of reeds laid in great quantities of bitumen, over this two courses of baked brick bonded by cement, and as a third layer a covering of lead, to the end that the moisture from the soil might not penetrate beneath. On all this again earth had been piled to a depth sufficient for the roots of the largest trees; and the ground, when levelled off, was thickly planted with trees of every kind that, by their great size or any other charm, could give pleasure to the beholder. And since the galleries, each projecting beyond another, all received the light, they contained many royal lodgings of every description; and there was one gallery which contained openings leading from the topmost surface and machines for supplying the garden with water, the machines raising the water in great abundance from the river, although no-one outside could see it being done.[5]

From the beginning of Diodorus' account it is clear that a version of legend existed in which the Hanging Garden was built by Semiramis, a variant which he felt obliged to deny, putting forward his own version of how the Wonder originated. Some reasons for attributing the garden to her, not as a wilting, homesick queen but as a robust builder, are described in Chapter 8, among the historical and legendary sources for Semiramis.

Diodorus' description is especially significant for stating that the water-raising mechanism was not visible. This eliminates the possibility of a water wheel or any type of shaduf, both of which are highly visible (see Figure 9).[6] An Assyrian sculpture shows shadufs, but no water wheel is ever depicted or mentioned in Assyrian texts, and there is no reason to think that the situation was different in the time of Nebuchadnezzar. Diodorus' description of the topmost gallery, roofed, with trees planted on top, matches well the depiction in a palace sculpture from Nineveh (discussed in detail in the next chapter) although he does not mention pillars. Some of the details are different from those of Philo who does not mention lead, bitumen, or reed mats, but rather tells of the trunks of palm trees. Reed mats were often used between layers of mud brick to help bond a structure. Diodorus' comparison of the whole garden with a theatre supplies the overall visual effect that we have used for the reconstruction drawing (Frontispiece).

As for deciding whether the term 'Syrian' meant the same as 'Assyrian', this has long been a cause for doubt among scholars, but

Fig. 9 Drawing showing a man raising water by shaduf, from a bas-relief found in Sennacherib's South-West Palace.

it has been resolved recently by the discovery of a bilingual inscription which came to light in Cilicia. One version has 'Syrian' and the other 'Assyrian', proving that the two terms were variants of a single word in the 8th century BC, a time when the Assyrian empire was expanding into that area.[7] Therefore the earlier supposition, that Syria and Assyria meant two different regions in Greek texts at that time, must be abandoned, and the 'Syrian king' of Diodorus Siculus can safely be understood as 'Assyrian king'.[8]

Strabo was an Anatolian from Pontus, a region bordering on the Black Sea, close to Armenia, although he spent much of his adult life in Rome. His great seventeen-volume *Geography* was completed by 7 BC, so during his lifetime he would have been stimulated by the Armenian withdrawal from Syria in 69 BC, the shocking defeat of Crassus at Carrhae in 53 BC, and Parthian invasions of Roman Syria in 51 and 41 BC. Great voyager though he was, he may have exaggerated the extent of his travels, and he used some earlier work by the great writer Eratosthenes, who had become head of the Library at Alexandria. Although Strabo referred specifically to seven Wonders, he described only five of them. According to his account Babylon boasted two World Wonders: its walls, and its palace garden.

The circuit of the walls (of Babylon) is 385 stadia.[9] The width of its wall is 32 feet. The height of it between the towers is 50 cubits, that of the towers is 60 cubits. And the path on top of the wall is so wide that 4-horse chariots can easily pass each other. And for that reason this as well as the Hanging Garden are called one of the Seven Wonders of the World. It (the garden) is quadrangular in shape, and each side is 4 plethra in length. It consists of arched vaults which are set, one over the next, on a chequer-board of cube-like foundations. The hollow chequerboard foundations are covered with earth so deep that they sustain the largest of trees, for they were constructed of baked brick and bitumen—they (the foundations) and the vaults and the arches. The ascent to the uppermost terrace is made by a stairway, and alongside these stairs there were screws, through which the water was continually drawn up into the garden from the Euphrates by those appointed for the purpose.[10] For the river, a stadium in width, flows through the middle of the city, and the garden is on the bank of the river.[11]

Strabo is not the only author to refer directly to screws for watering, for Philo, much later, says the same, and gives an account that does not resemble that of Strabo, so was presumably independent of it. As for Archimedes (*c.*287–212 BC), who is often credited with inventing the water-raising screw, Strabo would certainly have known that he

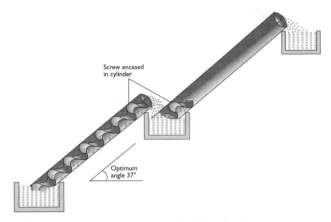

Screw encased
in cylinder

Optimum
angle 37°

Fig. 10 Sketch to show a water-raising (Archimedean) screw.

had lived long after the time when the Hanging Garden was built, because the two men were only a couple of centuries apart (see Figure 10).

An epigram written in Greek by Antipater of Thessalonica, probably soon after 11 BC, is of particular interest.[12]

I have seen the walls of rock-like Babylon that chariots can run upon, and the Zeus on the Alpheus; and the Hanging Gardens, and the great statue (Colossus) of the Sun, and the huge labour of the steep pyramids, and the mighty tomb of Mausolus.

He goes on to praise the statue of Artemis at Ephesus. If the right man is identified,[13] he would indeed have had occasion to visit Rhodes, Ephesus, and Mausolus' monument at Halicarnassus, so taking in three World Wonders on his way to visit his patron, L. Calpurnius Piso, whose successful campaign of 13–11 BC he was authorized to commemorate in verse. That man, whether before or after his triumph, served as Roman governor of Galatia–Pamphylia.[14] Antipater wrote another epigram beseeching Phoebus Apollo to grant him a safe journey to 'Asian land',[15] so he is possibly the first writer to list wonders as a traveller who had first-hand knowledge of at least some of the places in his list. Although he might have gone on to visit Mesopotamia, describing its impressively high citadels by comparison with the rocky prominence of Greek citadels, more likely he claimed to have seen Babylon by poetic licence. The Colossus at Rhodes which he also says he saw, existed for only sixty-six years, until 225 BC, so he could only have seen the base for it, and any shattered pieces that were still visible.

Josephus, who was born in AD 37/8, exactly contemporary with the Roman emperor Nero, wrote a brief passage about the Hanging Garden of Babylon, and inserted the same text into two different compositions: *Jewish Antiquities* X.11 and *Contra Apionem* I.19—a good example of how a section could be pasted into more than one narrative.[16] He is the only author, whether Greek, Hebrew or Mesopotamian, who specifically connected the garden with Nebuchadnezzar, and he claimed to be quoting Berossus, the priest of Marduk who lived in Babylon under the early Seleucid kings. Berossus was contemporary with Callimachus of Cyrene, who, as we saw in the Introduction, is the earliest writer known to have listed seven World Wonders.

Josephus lived in Jerusalem, so his main readership was Jews or those who were interested in the history of the Jews. For them Nebuchadnezzar's name and fame mainly derived from two biblical texts: as the conqueror who sacked the temple in Jerusalem (2 Kings 24 and 2 Chron. 36), and as the cruel tyrant who subjected the pious Daniel to the terrors of a lion's den (Book of Daniel). His account has been given priority by several scholars.[17] Two different translations are given for the same passage, to show how two different translators have interpreted the description:

At his (Nebuchadnezzar's) palace (in Babylon) he had mounds made of stone which he made to look like hills, and planted with all kinds of trees, and he built the 'Hanging Gardens'; because his wife, who came from Media, longed for her mountain homeland.[18]

In this (Nebuchadnezzar's) palace he built and arranged the so-called Hanging Garden by setting up high stone terraces which he made appear very similar to mountains planted with all kinds of trees. He did this because his wife, who had been raised in Media, longed for mountainous surroundings.[19]

What Josephus wrote needs to be evaluated in the light of recent research on the writings attributed to Berossus. Berossus himself may not have mentioned Nebuchadnezzar in connection with the garden, but rather that passage was probably added to his original text by one of the authors who quoted from him in the two centuries that separate Berossus from Josephus; and it is that secondary author from whom Josephus quotes.[20] The possibility arises because Greek texts have no way of showing when a quotation begins and ends, so authors insert extracts from other writers seamlessly into their own prose.

Had Josephus himself inserted Nebuchadnezzar's name, his motive would be hard to fathom, since Nebuchadnezzar was a notorious king whose name, among Josephus' readers in Jerusalem, stood as the wicked destroyer of the First Temple. The evil reputation that Josephus wished to attribute to Babylon can be seen in a passage in which he re-interpreted the biblical story of the Tower of Babel. Whereas in the biblical text[21] God introduced confusion of speech to hinder the power of mankind because the building of the tower by men who spoke a single language showed excessive achievement, Josephus changed the motive, to show that God punished Babylon for its arrogance.[22] Since the passage in Josephus concerning the Hanging Garden does nothing to tarnish the reputation of Nebuchadnezzar, but rather enhances it as an example of his brilliance as an imaginative builder, it is possible that an earlier transmitter of Berossus' text inserted that passage. But Josephus' audience in Jerusalem would have been interested to read of the famous garden because Herod's Winter Palace and garden in Judaea, and Nero's Domus Aurea in Rome, were probably both inspired by the Hanging Garden, as discussed in Chapter 8.

The theme of homesickness to which Josephus' text refers is emphatically not one that is known, nor likely, from Babylonian and Assyrian literature, nor is it compatible with what we know of Berossus' style. However, it is typical of some heroines of Greek novels, and notably occurs in *Chaereas and Callirhoe*, a tale of true love triumphing over a series of frightful adversities, written by Chariton who came from Aphrodisias, a fine city on the Meander river in south-western Turkey. Since Chariton's lifetime is now dated between the 1st century BC and AD 50,[23] his novel would have been available to Josephus, and it contains the theme of a woman abroad, crossing the Euphrates from the West, homesick for her native land.

As far as Syria and Cilicia, Callirhoe readily put up with the journey, for she still heard Greek spoken and could look upon the sea ... But when she arrived at the River Euphrates, ... beyond which lies the vast continent, then she was filled with longing for her home and family.[24]

Thus that novel, or a similar one, is a possible source of inspiration for the passage included by Josephus.

Berossus was a temple official of the highest rank who wrote in Greek for the newly established dynasty of Seleucid kings, successors of Alexander the Great in the Near East. The importance of Babylon to the Seleucids is apparent not least from their keeping the name of the city, and their honouring the fame of Nebuchadnezzar. We now recognize that Berossus faithfully used cuneiform texts in composing the historical parts of his text; parts of his account correspond directly to a series of Babylonian chronicles which dealt with the main events, including problems of succession, during the reigns of the great Neo-Babylonian kings.[25] Where Berossus described the building works of Nebuchadnezzar, he paraphrased that king's great and complete *East India House Inscription* (see Figure 2). It was not a rare text: several versions, written on clay, are extant. The Babylonian original and Berossus' Greek text can be matched, side by side, for episodes and their sequence, but the Greek passage about the Hanging Garden has nothing to match it.[26] This makes it virtually certain that a later writer added it, providing readers with a bit of extra marvel at a time when marvels were especially popular with Greek readers.

As a result of now understanding Berossus' account so much better than before, his supposed reference to the Hanging Garden can be eliminated. We can also set aside the mistaken view of the Seleucid kings' attitude to the ancient civilization they had inherited: that Seleucus I carried out 'a deliberate policy of degrading Babylon and its shrines'.[27] In fact, those kings continued to take an interest in Babylonian traditions, its shrines and its scholarship, as contemporary cuneiform records show.[28]

Although it was a Greek custom to refound an old city and to establish a Greek identity by naming a mythological founder, such as Heracles or Aeneas, or an eponymous one such as Ninus or Alexander, in Babylon Seleucus I and his son Antiochus with queen Stratonice, keen to integrate themselves into the prestigious antiquity of Babylonia, conducted a policy rather different from the one that might have been expected. Babylon was not renamed Seleucia—that name was given to a new city founded on the Tigris. Nor was it renamed Alexandria, as one might have expected from it being the place where Alexander died. Babylon remained Babylon. Its most famous indigenous king, whose brilliant reign and magnificent building works were now two centuries old, was Nebuchadnezzar II.

Nebuchadnezzar's possessions had been safeguarded throughout more than two centuries of Persian domination and the long civil war that followed Alexander's death. His royal robe was available to be used for the coronation of a later Seleucid king, Antiochus III, who desired to be associated very closely with the legendary Babylonian emperor. By wearing Nebuchadnezzar's robe for such an important occasion, the Seleucid king was performing a deeply symbolic act. In stripping off his normal garments, a king prepared for death; in putting on other robes, he transformed himself for a new life.[29] The symbolism is explicit in the Babylonian myth *Descent of Ishtar to the Underworld*, one of the best-known and longest-lasting texts of Babylonian literature: the great goddess is stripped of her various garments and jewellery as she passes through the seven gates into the Underworld, where she then lies naked and dead until she is revived and returns to the world of the living, donning her garments and jewellery at each gate on her way out.

Those acts of association—the restoration of an ancient temple, and the donning of the most prestigious royal robe for an ancient ceremony—belong within a wider policy to ease the new dynasty into Babylonian traditions and win popular support.[30] One of Berossus' aims in writing his *Babyloniaca* was therefore to integrate the new regime into past history, showing the new kings as rightful heirs to the throne of Babylon.[31] It is thus significant that he did not, we now think, mention the Hanging Garden as one of the glories of Babylon. The analysis of the passage in Josephus allows the possibility that Nebuchadnezzar was not responsible for creating the Hanging Garden, and that Diodorus and Q. Curtius Rufus were correct when they stated that the Hanging Garden was built by an Assyrian king.

Quintus Curtius Rufus wrote in Latin around the mid to late 1st century AD, in a highly rhetorical style, with a main interest in the character and motives of Alexander the Great. He was certainly careless with some details in the interests of journalistic entertainment, and inserted his description of the garden into a passage about Alexander's arrival in Babylon.[32] The details of construction that he gives appear non-poetic, as if based on a pragmatic account. After describing the Euphrates at Babylon, the embankments built to prevent flood damage, and a stone bridge, he continued:

On the top of the citadel are the Hanging Gardens,[33] a wonder (*miraculum*) celebrated in the tales of the Greeks, equalling the extreme height of the walls, and made charming by the shade of many lofty trees. Columns of stone were set up to sustain the whole work, and on these was laid a floor of squared blocks, strong enough to hold the earth which is thrown upon it to a great depth, as well as the water with which they irrigate the soil; and the structure supports trees of such great size that the thickness of their trunks equals a measure of eight cubits. They tower to a height of fifty feet, and they yield as much fruit as if they were growing in their native soil. And although lapse of time gradually undermines and destroys, not only works made by the hand of man, but also those of Nature herself, this huge structure, although worked upon by the roots of so many trees and loaded with the weight of so great a forest, endures unchanged; for it is upheld by cross walls twenty feet wide at intervals of eleven feet, so that to those who look upon them from a distance real woods seem to be overhanging their native mountains. There is a tradition that a king of Syria, who ruled in Babylon, undertook this mighty task, induced by love for his wife, who from longing for the woods and groves prevailed upon her husband to imitate in the level country the charm of Nature by a work of this kind.[34]

This description confirms that the height of the garden, at the top of the citadel, was equal to that of the city walls. It emphasizes the spectacular growth of the trees, and seems to describe the ones planted above the pillared walkway. Curtius barely mentions the means of irrigation, but relays the romantic story that the garden was built to please the queen. His claim that the gardens were still flourishing centuries after they were constructed could be explained as relating to the time of Alexander rather than Curtius' own lifetime, or may simply be a rhetorical flourish to make the passage vivid.[35] Alternatively, his description could have been based upon a still-visible bas-relief, and the partly ruined palaces that could still be visited.

A Handbook to the Seven Wonders of the World, written by Philo of Byzantium, is by far the latest in date of all the Classical sources. There are two possible writers named Philo, which has caused confusion in the past.[36] Both men acquired the epithet 'of Byzantium', which caused further confusion.[37] Our man is not the engineer of the 3rd century BC, but a much later Philo, the so-called Paradoxographer of the 4th–5th century AD. A paradoxographer can be defined as writer of a 'semi-scientific study of the origins and causes of contemporary wonderful happenings'.[38] Rather than being an engineer, the latter Philo of Byzantium was a writer who described marvels throughout the known world, but did so with a considerable understanding of construction and materials. This contributed to the confusion with the earlier writer who bore the same name. On the other hand, his use of language was quite flowery, a characteristic that allowed some scholars to dismiss him as an unreliable source. His account, written in Greek but also known in an early Latin translation, appears to be independent of earlier Greek texts, although it repeats the statement of Curtius that the gardens still flourished. As we have seen, this claim need not mean literally what it says, but could be a rhetorical device, or a quotation from a much earlier writer, or could imply ecphrasis based on a surviving panel of sculpture. Survival of the actual garden into the 4th century AD seems unlikely, as it would imply an unbroken existence with many intermittent restorations. In particular the trees planted on top of the pillared walkway would have had to be replaced on a regular basis.

Philo also provided a technical, if rather poetic, description of how the Colossus of Rhodes, another World Wonder, was made. Although scholars in the past were sceptical of his account, doubting that he had real knowledge of the casting processes involved in such a gigantic work, his account has been carefully analysed to show that it is indeed of practical value, and records accurately an unusual technical process.[39]

Philo's text had not been edited since 1858, when fewer manuscripts were known than is now the case.[40] The challenge of incorporating new texts was taken up by Kai Brodersen, who published an edition with a German translation in 1992.[41] Even then he did not have available the understanding of the cuneiform inscription that is analysed in the next chapter. With the benefit of Brodersen's edition, an English translation of the Greek text is given here.[42]

The so-called Hanging Gardens have plants above ground, and are cultivated in the air, with the roots of trees above the (normal) tilled earth, forming a roof.[43] Four stone columns are set beneath, so that the entire space through the carved pillars is beneath the (artificial) ground. Palm trees lie in place on top of the pillars, alongside each other as (cross-) beams, leaving very little space in between. This timber does not rot, unlike others; when it is soaked and put under pressure it swells up and nourishes the growth from roots, since it incorporates into its own interstices what is planted with it from outside. Much deep soil is piled on, and then broad-leaved and especially garden trees of many varieties are planted, and all kinds of flowering plants, everything, in short, that is most joyous and pleasurable to the onlooker. The place is cultivated as if it were (normal) tilled earth, and the growth of new shoots has to be pruned almost as much as on normal land.[44] This (artificial) arable land is above the heads of those who stroll along through the pillars.

When the uppermost surface is walked on, the earth on the roofing stays firm and undisturbed just like a (normal) place with deep soil. Aqueducts[45] contain water running from higher places; partly they allow the flow to run straight downhill, and partly they force it up, running backwards, by means of a screw;[46] through mechanical pressure they force it round and round the spiral of the machines.[47] Being discharged into close-packed, large cisterns, altogether they irrigate the whole garden, inebriating the roots of the plants to their depths, and maintaining the wet arable land, so that it is just like an ever-green meadow, and the leaves of the trees, on the tender new growth, feed upon dew and have a wind-swept appearance. For the roots, suffering no thirst, sprout anew, benefiting from the moisture of the water that runs past, flowing at random, interweaving along the lower ground to the collecting point, and reliably protects the growing of trees that have become established. Exuberant and fit for a king is the ingenuity, and most of all, forced, because the cultivator's hard work is hanging over the heads of the spectators.

By the time that account was penned, Mesopotamia had been penetrated and lost many times by Parthians, Romans and Lakhmids, when military and mercantile travels would have given further opportunities for eye-witness reports. Philo's description of how water is raised matches the screw explicitly claimed by Strabo (but very differently expressed), and would not match any other way of raising water. His extraordinary detail of stone columns roofed with trees on top matches details preserved in a drawing made of a lost group of panels found in the mid 19th century at Nineveh, discussed in the next chapter.

What we have learned from the Classical texts alone is quite a useful description of the garden as a World Wonder. Set beside the king's palace high up on the citadel, it imitated natural hillside by means of artificial terraces and was planted with forest trees; water flowed on to the upper terraces, raised by machinery involving screws. It was shaped like a Greek theatre, about 120 m on each side—roughly the size of two football pitches set side by side—and the top terrace supported a pillared walkway which had trees planted on its roof. A homesick queen inspired the design.

3

Three Pictures, and Archimedes

When the facts change, I change my mind. What do you do, sir?

Maynard Keynes

In 1854 a now famous panel of sculpture showing a garden was found at Nineveh in the North Palace of Ashurbanipal, grandson of Sennacherib, king of Assyria. Sir Henry Creswicke Rawlinson saw it there, and exclaimed that it must show the fabled Hanging Garden at Babylon, because it had several features in common with the descriptions of Classical authors (see Figure 14).[1] His immediate reaction gave way to the idea that the garden depicted there was a prototype for a later one.

Rawlinson's exclamation resulted from his knowledge of the Classical authors who had described the Hanging Garden of Babylon. Several of them, notably Josephus and Diodorus Siculus, described the garden as imitating mountain and forest scenery, a description ignored in most reconstructions and at variance with the type of garden found in Babylonia. It does, however, match the type known in Assyria including the one at Khorsabad made by Sargon II, father of Sennacherib (see Figure 11).

A high garden imitating the Amanus mountains in which are planted all the aromatic trees of northern Syria, all the mountain's fruits, I created alongside (Khorsabad).[2]

Sennacherib used an identical simile for his own palace garden at Nineveh. This comparison with the tree-clad mountains of north-west Syria and southern Turkey was common in Assyrian inscriptions at that time because Assyrian armies were crossing through that

Fig. 11 Drawing of a stone panel carved in bas-relief, found in the palace of Sargon at Khorsabad, showing his garden. Ht. 98 cm.

terrain as they extended the empire into Cilicia. The Amanus range lies from north to south, forming a natural barrier between modern Syria and Turkey; catching rainfall between the Mediterranean and Asia, its slopes are covered in fine trees, many aromatic pines, cedars and junipers, streams of water, lovely glades for picnics. Tired and overheated soldiers must have been glad to rest there. Sargon's garden at Khorsabad is illustrated on a sculpture found in his palace, and shows some of those features. Prototypes for the later Hanging Garden in the city of Babylon were thus thought by some scholars to have been designed in Assyria, both at Khorsabad and Nineveh.

The various writers who described the garden in Greek and Latin gave descriptions that are consistent in some important respects, but do not have close matches with each other in vocabulary and phrases that might arouse a suspicion of a common source. We are hampered by being uncertain whether the gardens were still visible when they wrote, and whether they relied on written sources of information that had begun in the time of Alexander or at an earlier date. But we can say that they were describing a type of garden known from northern Mesopotamia, which was very different from the type characteristic of southern Mesopotamia, where Babylon lay.

Josephus among others described the garden as an imitation of a natural landscape. This is an important point because Babylonian gardens were designed in a style quite different from those of Assyria. Two distinct garden traditions can be discerned from cuneiform inscriptions written on behalf of Babylonian and Assyrian kings and from differences in landscape: a southern one and a northern one. Owing to the type of terrain in southern Iraq, Babylonian gardens were set in a flat alluvium, where networks of little irrigation ditches favour rectangular parcels of land. Often they featured parallel rows of date palms which are not only beautiful and productive in themselves, but also afford shade to the smaller plants. They are watered from the river by means of shadufs. The land is unremittingly flat, desperately featureless to the eyes of a traveller coming from the east Mediterranean. Therefore the river Euphrates, which ran through the middle of Babylon, has no tributaries but splits into various branches that change their course from time to time, and there were no nearby hills or mountains such as might allow an aqueduct of some kind to bring water into the city by gravity from higher up. (See Figure 1) The natural river banks generally lie low, and are easily breached when the warmth of spring brings melt-water down from its source in the mountains of eastern Turkey—hence the need for the Western Outwork, to protect the Southern Palace from erosion. (See Figure 3) The city was almost entirely built with mud brick, since that was the traditional building material, copiously available; but bricks are easily damaged and often need replacing. In the course of time, repeated demolition and rebuilding caused the whole area to rise high above the plain upon which the first buildings were presumably located.

By the time Nebuchadnezzar built his palaces in Babylon, the Processional Way on the citadel stood 13 m above the level of the plain through which the river runs. Such an elevation made it difficult to bring enough water from the river to the citadel, to augment the supply hauled up from deep wells. Therefore provision of water to the height of the citadel was done partly through the arduous use of rows of shadufs drawing water from the river, nodding and creaking on the bank of the river; and partly by means of wells with pulleys within buildings and their courtyards. An enormous elevated reservoir was discovered to the north of the palaces, presumably supplied partly through the careful collection of winter rain-water, and partly from shaduf-raised water. An elaborate system of conduits, sturdily built in terracotta and bitumen, helped to distribute the water.[3] The terrain in

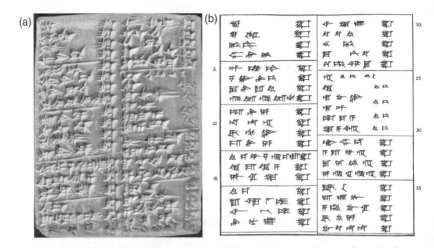

Fig. 12 (a) Obverse of the cuneiform tablet with the text listing plants in the garden of Merodach Baladan, king of Babylon in the time of Sennacherib. The ruled lines separating sections of text may correspond to the layout of the plants in their beds. (b) Hand-copy of the obverse. 6.5×4.0 cm.

and around Babylon, therefore, was not suitable for the kind of landscape garden described by the Classical writers.

A type of design for southern gardens may be deduced from the cuneiform text in which groups of similar plants are named in sections divided by ruled lines (see Figure 12). That clay tablet is a copy made in antiquity, not long after the original composition which names the king whose ownership is recorded: he was Marduk-apla-iddina II, also known as Merodach Baladan early in the 7th century BC. His was probably a formal kitchen garden, in which the beds were criss-crossed by irrigation channels to form a kind of parterre. The text suggests a type of physic garden, in which one bed contains varieties of mint, another has types of onion, garlic and leek, another has different kinds of thyme and origanum, and so on. Such an arrangement requires a piece of flat land with a network of small water channels for irrigation on the same level as the plants by opening and closing gaps in the channels.

Assyrian gardens in the north, on the other hand, were created in or near cities with far more energetic design, expressly to imitate a natural mountain landscape, by heaping up artificial hills, by planting fragrant mountain trees on their slopes, and by engineering running water to cool the air, keep the herbage green and provide the soothing sound of rippling streams. Where the royal palaces of Nineveh, Nimrud and Khorsabad were built for the great Assyrian emperors, the river Tigris runs through undulating landscape. To the east a spectacular range of mountains limits the horizon. Therefore tributaries come down to the Tigris, bringing clear mountain water which can be diverted through channels and aqueducts to serve the high citadels with their palaces, even though the bed of the Tigris itself lies far below the citadel. The Khosr was a tributary that brought mountain water swiftly down to Nineveh, and the Upper Zab flowed down likewise to Nimrud (see Figures 1 and 66).

So prolific are the waters from the tributary river Khosr and the streams that feed into it that they caused damage to buildings on the citadel at Nineveh when the spate of spring was excessive, as several Assyrian building inscriptions record.

The flood-prone river, a raging, destructive stream, which in its commotion had destroyed the *gegunnu*-shrines in the middle of the city and had exposed to sunlight their heaped up burials, and from long ago had flowed past close to the palace, and in its powerful spate had washed out its foundations . . . [4]

By controlling the flow of several mountain streams, by judicious use of canals, sluice-gates, dams and aqueducts, the Ninevites could obviate the damage and reap the benefits of a water supply that reached the citadel at the appropriate height, providing fresh mountain water for palaces and temples, and irrigation for surrounding fields and gardens alike. Thus the natural environment made it possible to plant a landscape garden within a citadel—even though, as at Babylon, the latter rose high above the level of the plain—and to plan it with slopes so that streams of running water continually refreshed the plants and the senses of pleasure-seekers. In Assyria the aim was to recreate beauty-spots, natural groves and tree-clad hills, with running water and serendipitous pleasures, conveniently located beside the king's palace. This is the type of garden described by the Greek authors. The type of royal garden known for Nimrud, Khorsabad and Nineveh in Assyria could not simply be the prototype for one that was eventually created in Babylon, because conditions in the south were too different.

Sargon and Sennacherib, both of whom created extraordinary palace gardens, stood in a long line of Assyrian tradition. In the 9th century BC Ashurnasirpal II (883–859 BC) had constructed this type of garden with its associated engineering at Nimrud. He diverted water from the river Zab before it debouched into the Tigris through the famous Negoub tunnel in which the flow could be regulated by sluice-gates (see Plate 2). Maintenance was facilitated by shafts with steps leading down from the ground surface. His description of the garden is inserted into a long text recording the king's conquests, the building of his new palace, his renovation of temples in Nimrud, his hunting exploits, and the huge quantities of food supplied for the party held at the inauguration of his palace. He mentions with delight the streams of water that chuckle through the plantings of fruit and nut trees.

I dug out a canal from the Upper Zab, cutting through a mountain peak, and called it Abundance Canal. I watered the meadows of the Tigris and planted orchards with all kinds of fruit trees in the vicinity. I planted seeds and plants that I had found in the countries through which I had marched and in the highlands which I had crossed: pines of different kinds, cypresses and junipers of different kinds, almonds, dates, ebony, rosewood, olive, oak, tamarisk, walnut, terebinth and ash, fir, pomegranate, pear, quince, fig, grapevine . . . The canal-water gushes from above into the garden; fragrance pervades the walkways, streams of water as numerous as the stars of heaven flow in the pleasure garden . . . Like a squirrel I pick fruit in the garden of delights . . .

This clear description shows the type of garden favoured in Assyria where each king tried to create his own horticultural haven even more ingeniously than his predecessors.

The 'joyful palace, the palace full of wisdom' that Ashurnasirpal built at that time was the marvellous North-West Palace at Nimrud which has been excavated with many of its interior sculptured panels intact. The king called it 'a royal residence for eternity' and enjoined future kings to maintain and protect it. Like Sargon and Sennacherib more than a century later, his monumental achievements combined a major project of water management with a garden and an exceptional palace.

The great Assyrian palaces of the 9th to 7th centuries BC all had state rooms decorated with a dado of stone panelling. The types of stone were carefully chosen, mainly different kinds of limestone, and were carved in low relief with scenes that displayed the king's power in conquest, receiving tribute, and building works. Many of them were excavated in the 19th century and brought back to western museums, but no doubt others had been eroded beyond recognition, or had long been removed as useful building materials for buildings in the vicinity. Some panels were packed and sent off but never reached the west.[5] No panel surviving from Ashurnasirpal's palace at Nimrud shows his garden, and it is possible that the subject was considered unsuitable for display in palace sculpture at that time. Later, however, it became fashionable to include a garden scene. In the palace of Sargon II at Khorsabad a rather eroded garden scene was drawn at the time of discovery, and the drawing is easier to look at than the original stone, which is now in the museum of the Oriental Institute in Chicago. (See Figure 11) It shows a lake with a boat, a boat-house or pavilion, and an artificial-looking hill with an altar on top; the ground is planted with trees. The sculpture was found in excavations of the early 20th century, long after the discovery that excited Rawlinson at Nineveh, and shows many similarities of design. The latter panel was in a better state of preservation, although the top part had eroded away. Another set of panels was found in Sennacherib's South-West Palace; although they do not survive, luckily they were drawn at the time of discovery, and the drawing survives in the British Museum, known as Original Drawing IV 77 (see Figure 13). So three pictorial records of palace gardens complement descriptions in cuneiform texts.

While excavations took place at Nineveh, mainly by tunnelling, drawings were made of many of the sculptures. When the originals are preserved in museums, direct comparisons can be made to check reliability. Layard, the chief excavator, himself did much of the drawing, and F. C. Cooper did some; both are rated 'very faithful' to the originals when a drawing can be compared with one.[6] Both men would have used the *camera lucida*, which Layard took from England to Nineveh, to give a clear image in poor light and enable correct spacing.[7] The instrument had been used successfully by Napoleon's artists recording the monuments of Egypt in the previous generation. For a while nobody was sure where the garden scene should be located within the palace, but recent study shows that the panels belonged in a room which showed many scenes of Nineveh, for the glorification of Sennacherib's peacetime achievements, and it was carved in the time of his grandson Ashurbanipal.[8]

The Classical descriptions of the Hanging Garden accord in several crucial respects with the Nineveh panels known from Original Drawing IV 77, and with the stone bas-relief panel found in the North Palace of Ashurbanipal. Those Assyrian monuments are more than a century earlier than the lifetime of Nebuchadnezzar II.

Fig. 13 A garden at Nineveh, drawn from damaged stone panels of bas-relief, now lost, which lined the walls of a room in the South-West Palace. The pillared walkway surmounted by trees is shown top right.

Original Drawing IV 77 shows three very badly damaged panels that represent a park including a lake on which several military-style activities take place. They were located in the South-West Palace, and presumably represent the garden at a very early stage, recently planted and immature. On the left of the main panel, pairs of men propel boats on which horses have embarked; several naked men are swimming, perhaps racing, on inflated skins. A man who appears to swing on a rope above the water perhaps prepares to plunge in. On the upper right a hillside is shown with two streams of water flowing down into a horizontal stream. At least four terraces below that stream are indicated by horizontal lines; and above the stream are two more, less clearly articulated. The right hand panel cannot be directly related to the edge of the main panel, so part of the scene is missing in the gap; this panel shows two pillars, of which one probably has a proto-Ionic capital, with the capital of a third just visible. Above the pillars, horizontal lines show 4 + 4 layers of roofing, upon which are planted evergreen trees interleaved with small bushes or young trees. The pillars, surmounted by thick roofing in which trees grow, comprise a unique feature of the garden, and match the feature of the Hanging Garden as described by Philo, as Layard realized when he excavated the panels, commenting that it showed 'a hanging garden, supported upon columns . . . This representation of ornamental gardens was highly curious.'[9] The artist has shown sloping and flat terrain together without perspective, using only the flow of water to indicate which is which. In the centre of the main panel is a group of three rows of four identical trees which may be saplings, as they are shown much smaller than adjacent trees. The right-angled lines beneath and beside them are probably irrigation channels. As with the sculptured panel of Ashurbanipal, the foreground of the garden is cut off by a stream and by a file of men who perhaps march along the citadel wall.[10]

The lake would have reflected the terraces that surrounded it and the architecture associated with the garden. The trees growing on a roof over a pillared walkway form an astonishing feature of the design which, taken together with Philo's and Strabo's references to screws, give a very specific idea of why the garden was a World Wonder. But no screws are shown on Original Drawing IV 77, nor on the surviving panel of Ashurbanipal.

The panel of bas-relief installed by Ashurbanipal in his North Palace, showing the garden several decades after it was planted,[11] is another major source of information for the appearance of the garden at a more mature stage of growth. It is not a simple matter to understand how three dimensions have been reduced to two (see Figure 14).

To interpret the scene we begin with the arches supporting the aqueduct, mid-right. The arches resemble those found on the remains of the aqueduct at Jerwan, with their pointed tops. The stonework is represented as three or four courses above the peak of the arches. Stonework rather than brickwork is indicated because of the scale of the arches, and because brickwork was not normally shown with courses picked out, according to Assyrian artistic convention. From the left end of the aqueduct the water, which contains fishes, flows down and separates into subsidiary streams, implying steeply sloping ground. This implication is reinforced by the way that trees are shown in the central triangle of the picture, some set behind others. If it is correct to suppose that the lake shown in the Original Drawing

Fig. 14 Part of the garden at Nineveh two generations after planting, damaged stone bas-relief from walls inside the palace of Ashurbanipal. Length 208.3 cm.

described below is out of sight in this picture, at the bottom of the garden, it is possible that there was one or more small waterfalls where the streams ended at the lake. In the top right corner of the panel, terracing above the aqueduct is indicated by the rows of trees, suggesting at least two terraces above the level of the top of the aqueduct.[12] To them water had to be raised by mechanical means because they were planted, at least in part, on vaulted terraces and so their roots could not reach the water table. The pavilion in the centre top of the panel has a cavetto cornice beneath the roof which is topped with small crenellations (also known as merlons). The two central pillars have proto-Ionic-style capitals, smooth columns, and a repeat of the proto-Ionic motif for the column bases. The heavier pilasters that have no separate bases mark the corners of the main building. On the left side of the pavilion an extension to the building with a path leading up to a stela showing the standing king probably follows a convention for showing two sides of a building on a single plane surface.[13] If so, it would be the portico which is a feature of the *bīt hilāni*, a type of residential building with a pillared portico that the Assyrians adopted from Syria.[14] Maybe the stela showing the king stood just outside the front door. Halfway down the path stands a feature that can be interpreted either as an outdoor altar, or as a stand on which a lamp would have been placed, a porch-light for moon-lit trysts and midnight feasts. To the left of the path and the building, upper terraces are again shown,[15] partly matching those on the right side of the pavilion; lower down, the lines of trees slant, implying again steeply sloping ground. Further to the left, a triangle of space is shown empty: at the top left corner of the panel the corner of the roof of a building projects slightly from the damaged edge. This is all that remains of the edge of the South-West Palace, the line of its wall presumably broken away at the damaged edge, and it is clear evidence that the garden was not a park outside the city as has sometimes been suggested. Accordingly the triangle of empty space may represent the forecourt area on to which people coming out of the palace gate would step before entering the garden.

If it is correct to interpret the left part of the pavilion as showing by rabattement the side that in fact faced the palace and the triangle of forecourt space, it follows that the stream did not actually flow across the path.

The trees cannot be identified botanically, and may be stereotypes of deciduous trees and bushes or saplings, interspersed with pine-like evergreens. Some variation, mainly in proportions, may be due to efforts to fit into a particular space without obscuring any other element in the composition. The foreground of the garden is cut off by a band of water, perhaps representing the Khosr river, and a row of men marching. A substantial amount of the top of the panel is broken away.

The adjacent panel shows the palace with pillars placed upon lion bases (see Figure 15). There seems to be a gap between the two panels, perhaps because several inches have been lost from the edges of each. The horizontal lines for the lower register, beneath the garden and continuing below the palace, do not match up exactly, and only the hindquarters of quadrupeds are left on two of the lower registers.

Some parts if not all of the panel would have been painted. The water would have been fairly dark blue (at Khorsabad traces of dark blue remain on the depiction of water), the fishes perhaps silvery. The trunks and branches of the trees would have been brown; the foliage probably in more than one shade of green and greenish-blue. The king's crown and staff would have been covered with gold leaf. The background may have been left unpainted. Since two shades of red and three shades of blue survive on stone panels found at

Fig. 15 Pillared façade, probably depicting part of Sennacherib's South-West Palace, shown on a panel from the palace of Ashurbanipal at Nineveh. The perspective convention is not understood.

Khorsabad, we know that nuances of colour were certainly used to produce subtle effects.

There are so many matches between the Classical descriptions of the Hanging Garden and the scenes sculptured in those Assyrian palaces that it is clearly worth looking to see if the detail about the screws can also be matched from that period. Neither Strabo nor Philo gives the name of Archimedes in connection with the screw, an omission which may imply that their readers would not have associated the man with the invention. Both authors would have known that the garden, if built by Nebuchadnezzar or by one of those Assyrian kings who ruled Babylon, was created long before the lifetime of Archimedes, a well-known historical character of the 3rd century BC, who flourished two centuries before Strabo.

Since most people now think Archimedes invented the water-raising screw, we need to examine in more general terms traditions about inventors, assumptions about how innovations are made, and what economic and social forces promote or inhibit technical progress.

Among some modern scholars the idea is quite entrenched that the ancient Orient endured for centuries—millennia even—without change or new inventions, once cities had come into existence and bronze-working had spread. Partly it arose from a romantic view held by 19th- and 20th-century travellers for whom camels, donkeys and shepherds with their flocks seemed to belong in an unchanging continuum stretching back into early biblical times. And partly it was the result of Marxist theory, that in a slave-owning society there was no stimulus to improvement. This latter view included a rigid understanding of slavery, based upon questionable analogies with cotton and sugar plantations in the New World, and with colonial mining in Africa. Two influential scholars promoted the view of static society: Gordon Childe, especially in his 1952 book *New Light on the Most Ancient East: The Oriental Prelude to European Prehistory*, widely read by archaeologists and prehistorians; and Moses Finley who enjoyed a great following among classicists.[16] Their persuasive prose suggested that there was no need to look for inventors or inventions, because pre-Greek civilization in the Near East was static. They envisaged a society in which the prestige of the elite was the sole motivation for great works and the accumulation of wealth, so that efficiency and productivity were alien concepts. Agriculture and irrigation occupied the efforts of the workforce, which had no incentives for improving technical skills, leading to a stagnant society in which financial credit had not yet evolved.

Evidence to the contrary is now clear from cuneiform texts which show how kings at various times were personally keen on innovation, whether in viticulture, metal and glass alloys, bee-keeping, astronomy or architecture; and the concept of financial credit had already been put into practice.[17] Royal interest and patronage gave the required stimulus to improvements and development. Another part of the impetus came, inevitably, from warfare, where the need to stay ahead of one's enemy, or at least to incorporate his best ideas into one's own armoury, is critical for victory. The intellectual environment of the late Assyrian period with specific royal interest in new machinery opens the way to search for pre-Greek inventions.[18]

In some strata of Greek and Roman society the engineer was actually denigrated, higher esteem being accorded to poets, playwrights and sculptors. According to Plutarch, Archimedes was praised for refusing to contaminate his theoretical and mathematical science with practical applications, although under extreme pressure at the siege of Syracuse in Sicily he did design practical machinery.

He had so great a spirit, so profound a soul, and such a wealth of theories which gave him a name and reputation for a sort of divine rather than human sagacity, that he did not wish to leave behind him any treatise on these matters, but, regarding mechanical occupations and every art that ministers to needs as ignoble or vulgar, he directed his own ambition solely to those studies the beauty and subtlety of which are unadulterated by necessity.[19]

This passage might be thought to support the idea that Archimedes did not invent the screw, although Plutarch called him a 'demiourgos', a flattering term that was applied to gods as creators. One need not necessarily take Plutarch at face value, although it is hard to discount entirely his statement that Archimedes regarded practical engineering as an ignoble and vulgar activity.

Two passages written by Diodorus Siculus which have often been understood to authenticate the connection between the machine and its named inventor Archimedes, are ambiguous.[20] In the latter passage he described them as 'Egyptian screws' which Archimedes had 'found' when he travelled to Egypt:

And what is the most surprising thing of all, they drain out the waters of the streams they meet by means of what are called Egyptian screws, which Archimedes the Syracusan found when he was going round in Egypt. And by the use of such devices they carry the water in successive lifts as far as the entrance ... Since this machine is an exceptionally ingenious device, an enormous amount of water is thrown out, to one's astonishment, with a trifling amount of labour.

He was quoting Posidonius (c.135–50 BC) in the context of mines in Spain. By referring to them as Egyptian screws, he implies that the screws found in Egypt by Archimedes were there before the latter reached the Nile. In Egypt the screw is ideal for raising water over the banks of canals or branches of the Nile delta into the fields lying alongside, and they are still in common use there.

Archimedes wrote in his introduction to *Method of Mechanical Theorems* that he often worked out his theorems by mechanical means, and only later developed the mathematical proofs that were the subject of his published works.[21] Given that he was especially interested in spirals, one can easily imagine how his interest in calculation was triggered by seeing mechanical screws in operation in Egypt during his visit. He wrote his treatise *On Spirals* years after returning from Egypt, so it is unlikely that the practical application arose from his work on the theory and mathematical principles. 'It is not impossible that the machine is of a much older date, and that Archimedes himself became acquainted with it in Egypt. It is also striking that neither Strabo nor Philo of Byzantium nor Vitruvius, who all three mention or describe it, associate with it the name of Archimedes.'[22]

The idea that Archimedes did not invent the screw is nothing new. As long ago as 1684 Claude Perrault wrote that he thought the screw machine was older than the lifetime of Archimedes.[23] The evidence of Archimedes' own writings substantiates the view that his interests lay in the study of mathematics and its abstractions, not in workaday matters of hands-on construction. There are good reasons, therefore, to accept the judgement of those several scholars who suggested that Archimedes did not invent the screw.[24]

Another way to approach the issue is to put Archimedes into the wider context of the Culture Hero. Later tradition, with its inexorable tendency to simplify, conflate, and invent 'culture heroes' from the past, may have considered Archimedes to be the sole inventor of the screw, but it is far from certain that people thought so during his lifetime. Many different cultures make their own claim to inventions by one of their own people which can be refuted on occasion by datable physical evidence, although independent invention by more than one person cannot be excluded. In general the phenomenon is part of the process of building identity in a more or less nationalistic way.

In very early times, claims to invention were not made by individual men. In Mesopotamia as also in early Greek tradition inventions and authorship were understood to belong to a chain of tradition emanating from heaven rather than to single human genius. Human craftsmen attributed their skills to a patron deity or to demigods.[25] Among the Babylonians and Assyrians the god Ea was primarily acknowledged in that role, but also, as part of an invented tradition supposedly of great antiquity from before the mythical Flood, the legendary Seven Sages were said to have brought knowledge of the arts, crafts and institutions of civilized urban life from the god Ea to Mesopotamia. In the *Epic of Gilgamesh* the man who built a boat and survived the Flood, Ut-napishtim, allowed craftsmen and scholars to board the boat when the Flood was imminent.[26] Those men had no natural life-span and were responsible for continuing cultural life after the Flood. Presumably they had descendants. They are referred to as seven counsellors in the prologue to the *Epic of Gilgamesh*, and as seven sages in magical texts.

Those types of knowledge were regarded as abstract ideals, known in Sumerian by the term *me*. They were the archetypes or ideal forms represented on earth by individual examples. After the legendary Flood, mortal sages were linked to famous historical kings, and were occasionally credited with authorship too.

Similarly in Greek tradition there were the Telchines, seven sages, mythical inventors of metalworking skills, associated also with magic and waterworks. In a more individual but still legendary tradition, Prometheus was said to have invented architecture, astronomy and arithmetic, and the shadowy figure of Pythagoras was supposed to have formulated the theorem related to right-angle triangles that often bears his name. In fact the formula was already known in Mesopotamia since at least the Middle Bronze Age.[27] The legendary musician Terpander was said to have invented the lyre, an attribution that can be put alongside the biblical claim that it was Jubal, descendant of Cain, who invented the harp. In biblical writings a special genealogy was reserved for inventors: they are all sons of Cain, among them Enoch who built the first city, and Tubal-Cain the 'inventor' of brass and iron.[28]

A Hellenistic writer who gives Semitic demigods credit for some such inventions is Herennius Philo of Byblos, writing in the 1st century AD his *Phoenician History*, including a technogony in which the hero Chousor, together with another, unnamed hero, supposedly invented iron and iron-working as well as incantations, divination, fishing with hook, line and bait, rafts and sailing.[29] After his death he was deified, and identified with Hephaistos and Zeus. His brothers, the appropriately named hero Technites and another hero, supposedly invented building with sun-dried bricks. These inventive heroes and others like them have names that are in some cases Greek, in others Phoenician.

The Greeks were spectacular in attributing inventions to themselves. Some Athenians claimed that they had invented pottery; that Athena had planted the first olive and invented weaving. The people of the island of Samos in the Aegean claimed the invention of cast bronze statuary, a claim that is easily falsified by archaeological researches in Egypt and the Near East. Not much was left for anyone else, if we are to believe them. Of course, they are divine or legendary characters, unlike Archimedes; but one can understand how he could have been inserted into such a tradition after his lifetime. The expression 'Hippodamian street plan' for a very regular layout of streets is in general use, honouring the name of Hippodamus, a town-planner from Miletus around 500 BC, despite the fact that several much earlier examples have been uncovered by archaeologists.[30]

A claim to independent introduction may sometimes appear to be a claim for primary invention. An introduction wrongly interpreted as an invention may explain why some instances are not to be understood literally even if they were believed to be true at the time, or soon afterwards. We can point to bee-keeping as a clear example: known from the third millennium BC in Egypt on tomb paintings, attested on the site of Tel Rehov in Israel in the 10th or 9th centuries BC;[31] yet claimed to be a first introduction by the ruler of Suhu near Mari on the Middle Euphrates, who wrote in the 8th century BC:

I, Shamash-resh-uṣur, governor of the land of Suhu and the land of Mari, brought down from the mountain of the people of Habhu, bees that gather honey, which none among my ancestors had seen or brought down to the land of Suhu, and I established them in the gardens of the town Al-gabbari-bani. They now collect honey and wax there. I know how to separate honey and wax by melting, and the gardeners know how too. Anyone who comes forward in future should ask the elders of his land: 'Is it true that Shamash-resh-uṣur, governor of the land of Suhu, introduced honey-bees into the land of Suhu?'[32]

Such fame is attached to the person and to his country when he achieves an invention or a 'first' that false claims are sometimes made or implied.

Bearing in mind the tendency to claim culture heroes in late antiquity, it is likely that the name of Archimedes was linked to the screw machine as its inventor because of his mathematical work *On Spirals*, and because of the well-established tendency in late antiquity to ascribe inventions to Greeks.

We now turn to an Assyrian text which shows that the Assyrian king Sennacherib cast water-raising screws in bronze around 700 BC.

4

Sennacherib's Great Invention

Sennacherib the great king, strong king, king of the world, king of Assyria, unrivalled king, pious shepherd who serves the great gods, guardian of justice, lover of righteousness, doer of good deeds who goes to the help of the weak, who seeks for good fortune, ideal man, heroic male, leader of all rulers, bridle that curbs the insubmissive, who strikes the enemy like lightning: Ashur the great god perfected in me unrivalled kingship

Rassam Cylinder inscription 1–4

To make his new palace and its garden as wonderful as possible, Sennacherib made use of a new method of casting bronze,[1] of which he was so proud that he describes it in detail. The casting was designed for two types of object: huge lions and other creatures as architectural elements, and machines to raise water 'instead of a shaduf'. Two copies of the text, both written in cuneiform script on clay prisms, are extant, enabling scholars to check difficult details.[2]

To compose his prism inscription Sennacherib's scholars made brilliant use of a high literary dialect known as Standard Babylonian. With its regular lengths of line, its similes, its occasional archaic vocabulary and constructions, the text is poetry rather than prose. In such a context the technical vocabulary required to describe parts of machinery by metaphors based on natural forms fitted beautifully. Often for new machines and inventions, words are adopted from suitably well-known animals or plants such as the Roman *testudo* 'tortoise/shield', the 'branch' of a railway line, the world-wide 'web',

Fig. 16 Sennacherib in his chariot. This is one of few sculptures of the king on which the royal face was not deliberately disfigured.

the computer 'mouse'. Just as Strabo used the word 'snail' to mean a screw (as well as for a spiral staircase, in another context[3]), so the Assyrians took words for a cylinder and for a spiral from the natural world most familiar to them. To recognize those words as metaphors has been crucial to understanding a technical passage in the inscription (see Figure 17 and Plate 3).

Only gradually has the whole meaning become apparent, thanks largely to progress made by the great dictionary-writers in Germany and Chicago. Thus it has become possible to link the technical part of Sennacherib's text with the descriptions of Strabo and Philo who gave the screw as the machine by which water was raised to the top of the Hanging Garden.

As a result of understanding the crucial terms involved, and with the benefit of the duplicate prism, a new translation can now be offered:

Whereas in former times the kings my forefathers had created bronze statues imitating real-life forms to put on display inside temples, but in their method of work they had exhausted all the craftsmen, for lack of skill and failure to

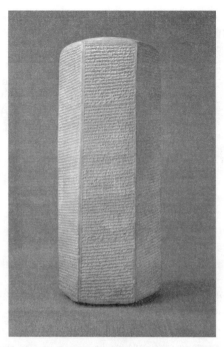

Fig. 17 The Chicago prism of Sennacherib, giving a detailed account of how he created his palace garden. Ht. 38 cm, 500 lines, 689 BC.

understand the principles; they needed so much oil, wax (*iškuru*) and tallow (*nalbaš ṣēni*) for the work that they caused a shortage in their own countries—I, Sennacherib, leader of all princes, knowledgeable in all kinds of work, took much advice and deep thought over doing that kind of work... I created clay moulds as if by divine intelligence for 'cylinders' (*gišmahhu*—tall tree-trunks) and 'screws' (*alamittu*—palm-trees), tree of riches...[4] In order to draw water up all day long, I had ropes, bronze wire and bronze chains made.[5] And instead of a shaduf I set up the 'cylinders' and 'screws' of 'copper' over cisterns. I made those pavilions look just right.[6] I raised the height of the surroundings of the palace, to be a Wonder for All Peoples. I gave it the name 'Incomparable Palace'. A high garden (*kirimāhu*) imitating the Amanus mountains I laid out next to it, with all kinds of aromatic plants, orchard fruit trees, trees that enrich not only mountain country but also Chaldaea (Babylonia), as well as trees that bear wool, planted within it.

There were few ways of raising water in the 7th century BC, but one needs to distinguish between two types of action: lifting it up from far below ground through a well, and transferring it from one ground level to another. For the latter type, in specifying 'instead of a shaduf', Sennacherib mentions the commonest piece of machinery for transferring between ground levels. The shaduf consists of an upright pole planted in the ground, another pole attached to it as an arm that swings with a weight on one end, and a rope attached to the other end of the swinging arm, by which a man can lever a bucket up and down, as shown in Chapter 2, Figure 9. The mechanism makes a characteristic creaking noise, and is highly visible in the landscape; it is most efficiently used to transfer water over a bank of earth or a low wall, for example from a canal to a field. This method is not used to raise water from a well. Many ancient ration texts include an allocation to the shaduf-workers, who were numerous in the canal networks of southern Mesopotamia's flat alluvium. As far as we know neither the water wheel nor any kind of chamber pump was yet in use.

To understand why it has taken so long to recognize the importance of Sennacherib's text, one must look back at the struggle of earlier scholars to make sense of it. The first translation was made, inevitably, without recourse to good dictionaries because none had yet been compiled. The translator simply had to guess the meaning of words according to his view of the context. Not surprisingly therefore, the technical passages did not make sense in translation, and the nonsense was a stimulus to subsequent attempts to understand what it meant. In 1924 the first attempt at a translation, made by Daniel Luckenbill in Chicago, was published:

In times past, when the kings my forefathers fashioned a bronze image in the likeness of their members, to set up in their temples, the labor on them exhausted every workman; in their ignorance and lack of knowledge they drank (*iškuru*) oil and wore sheepskins (*nalbaš šēni*) to carry out the work they wanted to do in the midst of their mountains . . . . I fashioned a work of bronze and cunningly wrought it. Over great posts (*gišmahhu*) and crossbars of wood (*alamittu*), 12 fierce lion-colossi together with 12 mighty bull-colossi, complete in form, . . . at the command of the god I built a form of clay and poured bronze into it, as in making half-shekel pieces,[7] and finished their construction. (Prism inscription VI.80–VII.19)

That daily there might be abundant flow of water of the buckets, I had copper cables(?) and pails made, and in place of the (mud-brick) pedestals (pillars) I set up great posts and cross beams over the wells (*būrtu*). Those palaces, all around the (large) palace, I beautified; to the astonishment of all nations, I raised aloft its head. (Prism inscription VII.45–51)

Thirty years later in a new attempt to translate certain difficult lines, the Danish scholar Jorgen Laessøe made some improvements, replacing 'pails' with chains, 'pedestals' with shadufs, and 'cross beams/bars' with the date palm, but he followed Luckenbill in supposing that Sennacherib had reverted to well-drawn water, hardly an innovation to boast of, and, besides, inappropriate for replacing shadufs. He offered no explanation for why a date palm was set over the supposed wells, nor why the rare word *alamittu* was used rather than the common word *gišimmaru*.[8] He translated a short extract from the prism inscription:

In order that you might draw(?) (well-)drawn water every day, I had ropes, 'cables' of bronze and 'chains' of bronze made, and instead of shadufs I let... beams (*gišmahhu*) and the date palm (*alamittu*)[9] stand over the wells (*būrtu*).[10] (VII.45–9)

In discarding Luckenbill's incorrect reference to buckets and pails, it is notable that no word for 'bucket' is used to describe the mechanism. This eliminates the possibility that a *saqia* or *cerd* is described.[11]

Laessøe's translation of that extract was made just before a duplicate of the prism was published by Alexander Heidel, who realized that the word *iškuru* was not a verb meaning 'they drank', as Luckenbill had translated it, but a noun meaning 'wax'—the form of the word is identical for both. Another ambiguity comes from the word *būrtu* to which both Luckenbill and Laessøe had given the meaning 'well': we now know that the meaning 'cistern' is also applicable—as well as 'waterhole', even 'fish-pond' too: the word has a much wider semantic range than might be expected, and of course the translator chooses according to the supposed context. 'Cistern' is a better choice than 'wells' because of the ground-level type of lifting implied by the phrase 'instead of a shaduf'.

A further ambiguity in the wording is *nalbaš ṣēni* which Luckenbill translated as 'sheepskins'; Heidel translated 'wool', despite its unsuitability in the context. The expression means literally 'clothing/cloak of flocks', and is not found in any other text. Since the common word for sheepskin or fleece was *itqu*, presumably *nalbaš ṣēni* had a different, metaphorical meaning which should fit the context of casting copper or bronze. If one skins a sheep, one detaches the leather-to-be from a whitish layer of fat which clings to the flesh like cloth. By scraping it off and melting it in a pan, one renders it into tallow, a useful and abundant substitute for beeswax in the casting process.

The duplicate prism showed a sign, badly damaged on the first prism, clear enough to show that the 'great tree-trunk' and the 'date-palm' were made of copper or bronze, so they were metal castings, and not, therefore, living trees or timber from a real tree. But the crucial understanding of meanings for the copper objects *gišmahhu* and *alamittu* still eluded Heidel. He thought that the words were to be understood literally as 'great tree' and '(type of) palm-tree', supposing that the castings were purely decorative, designed in some way to embellish whatever water-raising mechanism was involved. He presumably relied by then on the understanding of *alamittu* as *Chamaerops humilis*, the decorative fan-palm (which is now often planted outside hotels and airports around the Mediterranean). The identification of the Akkadian word had been made in 1924 in a study of ancient flora,[12] and forty years later was still favoured by the *Chicago Assyrian Dictionary*. There must have been a very specific reason for the choice of words. *gišmahhu* and *alamittu* are not a matching pair of items—the one used for a general category of large tree-trunks and the other a specific type of palm tree. For these reasons it is very unlikely that they refer to a purely decorative superstructure erected above a water supply.

An understanding of the *gišmahhu*—literally 'tall tree-trunks'— and *alamittu*-palm-trees still requires explanation, based on a metaphorical use of each word. *gišmahhu* is a compound noun, a Sumerian loanword in Akkadian which literally means 'big log, tall tree-trunk' according to its parts GIŠ 'wood, tree' and MAH 'big, high'. It is a rare word, elsewhere found meaning a solid tree-trunk with the type of timber, such as cedar, added to qualify it. In the prism inscription the word *gišmahhu* lacks such a qualification. Its first component *iṣu* (corresponding to Sumerian GIŠ) is used in a much earlier text giving a mathematical problem for calculating the capacity of a cylindrical container, as 'log' with the meaning 'cylinder'.[13]

Since the cylinder is one of the two component parts of the water-raising screw, I decided to investigate whether the '*alamittu*-palm-tree' could be understood as a screw. On discovering that the *alamittu* tree had been identified as the fan palm, I found two mature examples in Oxford's Botanic Gardens, and to my delight their trunks displayed a spiral pattern where the fronds had dropped off as the tree grew taller (see Plate 4). This seemed to be the answer.[14] Later, however, a severe critic wrote to tell me that *Chamaerops humilis* is not native to Iraq; in fact, it is largely restricted to the western Mediterranean. This had not been noticed by the *Chicago Assyrian Dictionary* when its editors accepted the identification. At about the same time I was beginning to understand how few Linnaean classifications corres-pond to ancient ones—naturally enough, since Linnaeus was reforming old systems along different, more analytical lines. Having ascertained from other cuneiform texts that *alamittu* grew on waste ground and had hard, inedible black fruit, I tried again, and estab-lished with the help of John Dransfield of Kew Botanical Gardens in London—a world expert on all kinds of palm trees—that it was almost certainly the wild, male date palm.[15] The date palm is dioe-cious: to pollinate the fruit-bearing female tree, spathes from the male tree are sometimes tied on to the female in order to obtain the maximum of fruit. The Babylonians and Assyrians described this process of pollination with the verb *rakābu* 'to ride' which is also used of human and animal copulation.[16] The relevance of its gender is shown below.

No explanation has been found in previous studies of the word *alamittu* used in this context; the translation 'crosspiece' was given in the G volume (1956) of the *Chicago Assyrian Dictionary*, without justification, based entirely on the imagined structure, but abandoned for the A/1 volume that was published ten years later.[17]

The identification, connecting a type of column to a gendered tree, had an unexpected application which links a feature of early Mesopotamian architecture with a Graeco-Roman concept. Several brick-built Mesopotamian temples of the Middle Bronze Age have a mud-brick façade on which spiral- and scallop-patterned tree trunks alternate as semi-engaged columns. Seldom do archaeologists find mud-brick buildings preserved to a height sufficient to show the external decoration of façades. But there are several examples of well-preserved temple façades of the early second millennium BC which display this feature. Both patterns result from the frond scars that are left when a palm frond drops off the tree as it grows higher (see Plate 4). The patterned façades have been found both in southern and northern Mesopotamia: at Ur, on the so-called Bastion of Warad-Sin,[18] at Larsa on the temple of the sun-god, at Tell Basmusian in north-eastern Iraq,[19] and at Tell al-Rimah in north-western Iraq as well as Tell Leilan in north-eastern Syria (see Figures 18 and 19). The distribution is particularly interesting because it shows that even in the north where the date palm does not produce good fruit, a temple was envisaged as a palm grove enclosing a sacred place.

Fig. 18 A group from the 270 engaged columns of mud brick laid in a spiral pattern in a temple façade at Tell al-Rimah, NW Iraq, early second millennium BC. Similar columns have been excavated on other temples in ancient Mesopotamian cities.

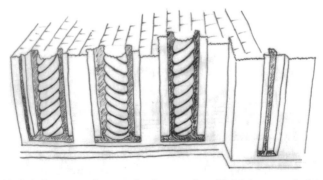

Fig. 19 Spiral-patterned engaged columns of mud brick in a temple façade at Tell Leilan in NE Syria.

If the wild, male palm tree *alamittu* is represented by the spiral, and the cultivated female palm *gišimmaru* by the scallop pattern, that type of architectural façade represents the symbiosis of the wild and the cultivated. And since the tree has separate male and female forms, the two types may also have represented male and female principles, as forerunners of the Classical column types called male and female by Vitruvius, a Roman architect and engineer living in the time of Julius Caesar. He wrote that temples built in the Corinthian order were most suited to gentle goddesses, for the Corinthian column 'imitates the slight figure of a maiden . . . whose ornaments should be unobtrusive', ideal for a temple dedicated to the goddess Diana; whereas the Doric style, which 'obtained its proportion, its strength, and its beauty, from the male figure', is suited to mighty gods such as Mars and Heracles. He compared the fluting on Ionic columns with the folds of a woman's garment, and the volutes on its capital with 'graceful curling hair hanging on each side'.[20] This gender distinction of column types is recognizable 2,000 years earlier on Mesopotamian temples. At Tell al-Rimah in northern Iraq, two stone sculptures were found, the one carved with a bearded male god flanked by spiral-patterned trunks, the other carved with a female goddess flanked by scallop-patterned trunks (see Figure 20). They date early in the second millennium BC.[21] Some designs carved on early stone cylinder seals seem to show the same gender differentiation.[22] Sennacherib's grandson addressed Ishtar of Nineveh in the opening line of a hymn: 'Oh palm tree, powerful one of Nineveh!'[23] These details show that the two types of palm trunk are linked to male and female genders as deities. In other ancient representations of palm trees in their natural habitat—for instance late Assyrian sculptures showing landscape in southern Babylonia—date palms are shown either with spiral or with scallop patterns on their trunks (see Figure 21).[24]

On many archaeological sites throughout the Levant 'proto-Ionic' or 'Aeolic' capitals and column bases have been found, and both Sargon and Sennacherib had a garden pavilion with columns of that kind, shown on the panels of palace sculptures. Careful research of the details has shown that the design of the volutes in that area is based upon the sprouting of shoots at the base of a date palm as well as the upper foliage.[25] This understanding is obviously Near Eastern, and does not preclude a re-interpretation of the form as ram's horns in Greek architecture. But it fits Vitruvius' description of gender in

Fig. 20 (a) Stone sculpture of a bearded god with a palm tree showing a spiral-pattern trunk, impost block from the main temple at Tell al-Rimah, mid-2nd millennium BC. (b) Stone sculpture of a goddess with a palm tree showing a scallop-trunk palm, impost block from the temple at Tell al-Rimah, mid second millennium BC. Ht. of block 58 cm.

column types, because the date palm has separate male and female forms.

Plausibly, then, Sennacherib's wonderful new casting, designed to lift water all day long, was some form of screw which he named with a metaphorical term. However, several problems were pointed out by critics. A screw cast separately from a cylinder and then fitted inside it, as I had understood the inscription, would not be feasible because water and debris would slip through the gap between them. Not until 1999, when I became involved in a BBC television programme *Secrets of the Ancients*, designed to cast a screw in bronze replicating Sennacherib's work, did the solution become plain thanks to a discussion with the bronze-caster Andrew Lacey. He fully understood the practical advantages and the snags of different possibilities. To him it was clear: one made the mould in two pieces, but the casting came out as a single piece with the screw as an integral part of the cylinder. Clay rather than wax was used, extracted by poking and bashing after the firing.[26] There was no need to fit two separately cast pieces together,

Fig. 21 (a) Impression from a limestone cylinder seal showing spiral columns around the temple of the sun-god. The seal may be several centuries earlier than the excavated mud-brick temples with spiral columns. Ht. 2.5 cm.

Fig. 21 (b) Drawing of part of a design incised on an ivory pyxis found at Ashur, showing a tree with spiral trunk, marked as male by perching cockerels. Dated *c.*1400 BC. Ht. (whole pyxis) 9 cm.

with the problems of fitting, attrition and leakage that such a design would entail. The whole machine would have a hollow centre for inserting a pole, probably made of timber, which would take the wear and tear of rotation and could easily be replaced. Our bronze-smith used that method under very primitive conditions to cast a small screw—a modest one metre or so in length—and it worked (see Plates 5–7).

But, argued the critics, a full-size screw cast in this way would be a very different matter, and they suggested that such a casting would have been impossible at that period. Luckily the answer to this objection can be found in Paris, at the Louvre, where a huge pair of cast bronze, cylindrical, hollow 'barriers', rather like modern barriers for road-blocks and car parks, are on display (see Figure 22). They

Fig. 22 Barrier of cast bronze found at Susa, dated 12th century BC from the royal inscription on it.

were excavated in western Iran at Susa, and firmly dated, by an inscription engraved on them, to the 12th century BC, some 420 years before the casting authorized by Sennacherib.[27] The length of each is 4.36 m, diameter 0.18 m, thickness around 1.5 cm, and the weight is estimated at 125–130 kg.[28] This demonstrates that large castings were made successfully long before the lifetime of Sennacherib, and that a huge hollow cylinder cast in a single operation was feasible.[29]

Other objections were raised about difficulties with bearings, but these are obviated when one points to the enormous doors in Assyrian palaces which had no hinges, but were attached to a vertical pole that swivelled in a socket. Administrative records show that doorkeepers were regularly allocated oil to keep the socket well lubricated, allowing the doors to open easily.

The close match of details with various textual sources meets the objections, so it becomes harder to maintain a sceptical stance. The television programme showed that the screw raises water far more efficiently than a shaduf. The screw, which raises water imperceptibly in contrast to other machines, accords with Diodorus Siculus who wrote in the 1st century BC: 'There were machines raising the water in great abundance... although no-one outside could see it being done',[30] and with Strabo who wrote in the same century that there were stairs rising up the slopes of the garden as in a Greek theatre, and 'alongside these stairs there were screws through which the water was continually conducted up into the garden',[31] and Philo who described the screws in a more poetic way:

Aqueducts contain water running from higher places; partly they allow the flow to run straight downhill, and partly they force it up, running backwards, by means of a screw; through mechanical pressure they force it round and round the spiral of the machines.

Sennacherib's new technique for casting bronze improved on the lost-wax process that had sufficed for all sizes of objects for at least 2,000 years, and would continue to be common for centuries to come. With that traditional method, the object required is modelled in wax or tallow, and then coated with clay, then baked so that the wax runs out through one or more holes left in the clay. As a result the mould turns from clay to terracotta. In a second operation, the mould is filled with molten metal and then left to cool before the mould is detached, often by breaking it. Sometimes a mould made of stone in two parts could be recovered intact and re-used; such have been found for small items such as jewellery and arrowheads.[32] In the new technique, however, the inner contours of the desired object were modelled in reverse in clay, and a second clay mould modelled the outside surface, with a gap in between the two moulds which were linked by means of carefully placed pegs. A thin application of oil to the surfaces would help the molten metal to flow smoothly without sticking to the sides of the mould or allowing bubbles of air to form. There are two major advantages to this process: only a single firing is required; and large quantities of wax or tallow are not required.

The method is quite similar to the one which people throughout China had practised since the Shang period, c.1500–1200 or earlier, although there is no suggestion that the beautifully made ceramic moulds of Chinese castings were imitated in Assyria. But news of the casting method, if not independently invented, could have reached Assyria, at least indirectly, by the time of Sennacherib, because soon after the Western Zhou period of Chinese history, c.1150–770 BC, chariotry and archery had become common in China.[33] This was a result of close contact with Central Asian peoples, presumably nomadic, who lived north and west of the Yellow River, and whose activities extended across Central Asia into Iran and the Caucasus. These possibilities of influence make it less likely that the new method of casting in Assyria was really an independent discovery. Sennacherib's adoption of a foreign technique for casting may be an example showing how open the Assyrians were to new ideas and technologies, especially when the king could outdo his predecessors in the size, weight and performance of his own inventive manufactures. Whereas each of Sargon II's cast lions had weighed 17 tons, his son Sennacherib outperformed him with cast lions weighing 43 tons.[34] A characteristic feature of royal inscriptions at that time was the claim that the new ruler was even more successful than his ancestors.

Incidentally, the words which Luckenbill translated as 'I built a form of clay and poured bronze into it, as in making half-shekel pieces' were thought to be evidence that coinage had been invented by this time. But as the next part of the inscription makes clear, the passage is intended as a boast, that the king could cast the metal perfectly whether the casting was huge or tiny. Coinage was a much later invention, as is now generally accepted, although the wrong understanding of Sennacherib's words still lingers.[35]

In any case it is not necessary to deduce that Sennacherib's engineers invented the water-raising screw and shortly afterwards cast it in bronze. It is much more likely that the mechanism was first manufactured in timber, a prototype modified and refined until casting a similar machine in bronze was envisaged as a daring and prestigious imitation of the original, wooden machine. Only then would Sennacherib's bronze-smiths have cast one full-size in bronze.

Excitement in Assyria over the new use of the spiral form may have spilled over into other uses. The most obvious possibility is the design of a spiral staircase or ramp for the ziggurat built by Sargon at Khorsabad (see Figure 23). All other known ziggurats have straight stairways rising centrally up each stage of an essentially rectangular brick structure. But the Khorsabad ziggurat has its rectangular core encircled by a spiral ramp.[36] Two minarets with external spiral ramps encircling a round core were built in the Abbasid period at Samarra in central Iraq, at a time when more of the temple tower at Khorsabad would have been preserved, so imitation is very likely.

Sennacherib's personal enthusiasm for the processes of bronze-casting is evident in a different context, in the inscription that records the building of his temple of the New Year festival in the city of

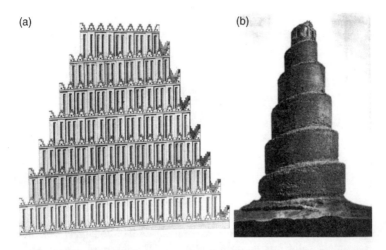

Fig. 23 (a) Reconstruction drawing of ziggurat at Khorsabad with an external spiral staircase. (b) Minaret with external spiral staircase at Samarra, near Baghdad.

Ashur. In an exceptional passage he boasted about his own skill and participation:

I am capable of undertaking the casting of objects in silver, gold and bronze . . . melting from more than 1,000 talents to (as little as) one shekel, fusing them together, fashioning them skilfully. If you do not believe the (account of my) smelting that bronze, I swear by the king of the gods, Anshar, my creator, that I myself smelted that casting where this inscription is written, and the emplacement where the figure of Anshar and the figure of the gods who are with him—they march to battle against Tiamat— are depicted. For the standards (of the gods) let it be known that I smelted that casting by adding more tin to it. Understand from this that I myself smelted that casting.[37]

The passage leaves one in no doubt about the king's personal enthusiasm and commitment to bronze-casting techniques.

Later use of a water-raising screw in the ancient Near East (apart from Egypt) is known from the upper Euphrates region, at Ayni, between Carchemish and Samsat, an area which had long been a part of the Assyrian empire. There a Roman inscription showed that Vespasian and Titus had constructed a screw, *opus cochliae*, complemented by a rock sculpture showing the Euphrates personified; but the method of rotation there is not indicated (see Figure 24).[38]

Fig. 24 Sketch of an eroded rock sculpture at Ayni on the upper Euphrates, set beside a Latin inscription recording the installation of a water-raising screw in the reign of Vespasian. The river-god reclines with a pot from which water flows.

One possible reference to rotating a screw by foot in Egypt may be mentioned. From a Roman wall-painting we know that a screw set at quite a low angle could be rotated by a man standing on the cylinder fitted with foot-holds, and treading it to turn it.[39] This, it has been suggested, is the mechanism behind the image given in the biblical text of Deuteronomy 11:10: 'Egypt...where you sowed your seed and watered it by tread, like a vegetable garden.'[40] There is a more specific and amusing account of the treading process in the writing of Philo Judaeus, a philosopher of Alexandria, who was contemporary with Josephus. He delighted in a reversal of the normal use of hands and feet in the operation of a screw:

Compare the screw, the water-lifting device. There are some treads around the middle onto which the farmer steps whenever he wants to water his fields, but of course he would keep slipping off. To keep from continually falling, he grasps something sturdy close by with his hands, and clings to it, suspending his whole body from it. In this way he uses his hands as feet and his feet as hands, for he supports himself with his hands which are generally used for working, and he works with his feet which normally serve as supports.[41]

But this method of rotation would work only for relatively small, light machines, and Sennacherib's inscription certainly does not refer to treading. In the years since a water-raising screw cast in bronze was understood to make sense of the technical words in Sennacherib's inscription, several suggestions have been made as to how the screw was rotated. Clearly the treading method is not described, for the text speaks of ropes, chains and cables or wires; but whether those words should be taken literally, or whether they are a rhetorical triplet for a single item rather than three separate ones, is impossible to decide. Sennacherib evidently did not try to describe a mechanism with a pulley—for which evidence is described below—nor did he attempt to describe a wheel-type of mechanism with cogs. The word for the wheel in Akkadian is well known to be *mugerru*; as for cogs, which are required to alter the direction of force from an awkward angle to one that maximizes strength, one would expect to recognize the word for teeth in conjunction with the word for wheel; but neither word is there. To the objection that cogs are known only from much later times—the chance discovery of the Antikythera mechanism, described below, pushed back the date for the invention of differential gearing by many centuries—one may point to the discovery by excavation in north-west Iran, in two tombs at Marlik, of what appears to be parts of a gear mechanism, described by the excavator as 'Bronze Gears(?)', datable to between 1250 and 883 BC.[42]

A word of explanation is in order, to give some background from the astounding Antikythera mechanism. Although wooden gears in the form of 'teeth' cut from the radius of a disk were certainly known by the 3rd century BC,[43] sophisticated, differential gearing was thought to come very much later, until a clump of bronze, badly encrusted and corroded, was found by sponge divers underwater in a shipwreck off the Aegean island of Antikythera. It was dated to the 1st century BC. Retrieved at the beginning of the 20th century, it could not be investigated until new techniques, especially high resolution X-ray tomography, were developed to reveal its 30+ gears, a crank, and inscriptions amounting to a manual with an astronomical, mechanical and geographical section. Machines of similar complexity are not known from elsewhere for the next 1,000 years.[44] The level of complexity in the machinery took everyone by surprise, and has shown that scholars had underestimated the possibilities of complex gearing in antiquity. We simply do not know how far back in time it may go. Therefore we cannot say for certain that a simple cog was *not* known in Sennacherib's time, but we can be sure that it is not mentioned in his inscription in connection with the rotation of the screw. It is unlikely that the ropes and chains of Sennacherib's text were linked to a cog mechanism that was not explicitly mentioned in the prism passage.

After the television documentary on the Hanging Garden was shown,[45] various people wrote in with suggestions for the method of rotation, but all of them involved cogs or pumps. However ingenious their proposals, they cannot be adopted because there is no support for them, neither in the inscription of Sennacherib nor in the Greek sources, nor in the technologies known to have existed at that time. In the case of the water wheel,[46] not only is the lack of the word for a wheel significant, but even more telling is the objection that such machines are eminently visible in the landscape; they would surely be shown on Assyrian sculptures just as shadufs are, and would have been mentioned by the Classical authors; their high visibility is impossible to reconcile with the words of Strabo: 'raising the water . . . although no-one outside could see it being done'. My own early suggestion of a crank handle, shown in the drawing I published in 1994, incited derision and is likely to be wrong: there is no evidence for that mechanism at such an early date, and no support for it in Sennacherib's inscription. Despite several ingenious speculations the mechanism for rotating the water-raising screw remains unknown.

Some scholars have suggested other ways of understanding the technical passage in the prism inscription, since from their point of view there is no question of using Classical sources, which they considered to be legendary and fictional, to understand the mechanism described in the cuneiform text. They turned back to earlier attempts to extract a meaning solely from the words used in Sennacherib's prism inscription, and envisage, rather non-specifically, a framework of beams and pillars with ropes and chains, perhaps resembling the *cerd*. The two flaws in such an argument are as follows. As already mentioned, the shaduf, like the screw, is used to raise surface water from lower to higher ground, not to raise water to the surface vertically from a deep well. By contrast, the *cerd* is used to raise water from a well, and requires buckets.[47] The phrase 'instead of a shaduf' implies that the new mechanism does the same job as a shaduf. Besides, to bring water up from a deep well was a familiar task on the citadels of Mesopotamian cities, and not a matter for description in a royal text. As physical evidence for drawing well water, a well-head with a pulley and rope is shown on the Assyrian panel of stone bas-relief found at Nimrud;[48] and pulleys were retrieved from a deep Assyrian well, also at Nimrud.[49] Thus there was no reason to invent anything for drawing well water.

A potential difficulty in the prism inscription arises from the disjointed nature of the text where mention of the castings and the garden occurs. This is the incoherent sequence given in the relevant part of the text: quarrying of stone and making colossal sculptures; casting of bronze by the new method to make 'cylinder and *alamittu-palm*' and pillars and colossal bronze sculptures; details of metal sheathing on cedar pillars, inlay on wooden pillars, bas-reliefs around walls and calling them a wonder; provision of water from cables, ropes and chains and setting up 'cylinder and *alamittu-palm*' over cisterns instead of shadufs; making 'those palaces' beautifully; raising the surrounds of the palace, calling it a wonder for all people; creating a garden to be like the Amanus mountains, planting it with exotic plants. Thus the mention of castings and machines for raising water is not adjacent to the mention of the garden. The disjunctions are due to the cut-and-paste method used for compiling long inscriptions of that kind. Similar disjunctions have been recognized in other inscriptions, and are discussed in detail in Chapter 7.

One might expect that the technical terms used by Sennacherib in connection with the water-raising device would be found in one of the great lexical lists of cuneiform tradition. Those lists are forerunners of dictionaries, in which words are grouped in several different ways. We have sections dealing with ropes and chains; with the parts of a shaduf;[50] and *alamittu* is found in several sections on date palms.[51] Since many such lists were not updated in the first millennium, we would not expect them to list machinery that was invented after the time they were compiled.[52]

Luckenbill's translation 'park' for *kirimāhu* led to the suggestion that the garden was in fact a hunting park, which would have required too much space to be located on the citadel, and as we have seen, the famous garden was on the citadel. The usual word for a hunting park is *ambassu*, which Sennacherib did not use. He selected *kirimāhu*, a rare literary word derived from Sumerian, which can be understood to mean 'high garden', according to its setting high up on the citadel, or metaphorically 'great garden' in the sense of important rather than large. Sargon was the first to coin the word for his palace garden, whereas hunting parks are known much earlier from the inscriptions of previous Assyrian kings. Therefore the word 'park' has been replaced by 'high garden' in this book.

The term KIRI.MAH had great prestige in Sumerian, which is doubtless one good reason why Sargon and Sennacherib chose to use it in its Akkadian rendering. Way back in the third millennium BC it had been used to described a garden attached to a temple of the sky-god of Uruk, built by the Ur-Nammu who founded a great dynasty at the southern city Ur.[53] Even earlier it was used by king Nanne, father of Mes-kiag-nunna, legendary king of the earliest dynasty at Ur, to denote a temple garden associated with the great goddess Ninlil at her cult centre Tummal, close to Nippur, a city regarded as the point where the umbilical cord that attached earth to heaven was located.[54] By choosing to use the word, the two Assyrian kings were associating themselves with three of the greatest Sumerian cities of very ancient times. Alas, we know nothing about those two gardens, but we may suggest that they were set high up on citadel mounds, since that is where great temples were located at that time.

The design and planning of Sennacherib's South-West Palace and the garden are likely to have taken place simultaneously so that the required levels of terrain could be laid out to take into account the inflow of water from the aqueduct, its supply to the palace (with appropriate pipes) and its drainage through the lake at the bottom of the garden, and into the river Khosr at the foot of the citadel wall. By the late 8th century BC Assyrian palaces were provided with a comprehensive system of pipes and drains laid beneath floors and walls according to a design that would have been installed while the foundations were being laid, before floors and walls were put in place. Sennacherib would have inherited from his father the expert survey-ors, engineers and builders whose experiences gained at Khorsabad were invaluable to him (see Figure 25). In all three of the main requirements—creating an artificial hill, bringing water from a far distance by diverting and linking several mountain streams, and installing terracotta pipes and baked brick drains—Khorsabad had been a brilliant testing ground for a work of architectural genius.[55]

Sennacherib the king alone takes the credit for his palace, his garden and his water supply. A key ingredient for the inspiration and success of the project was royal patronage with the king in person taking a close interest, and probably playing a part in both general and detailed discussions. But the identity of the architect is unknown. In modern times the architect is separate from the quantity surveyor, the engineer and the clerk of works, owing to increased specialization which particularly divides theory from practice. Even among architects nowadays one speaks of 'concept architects' as different from 'delivery architects'. Assyrian texts, whether public

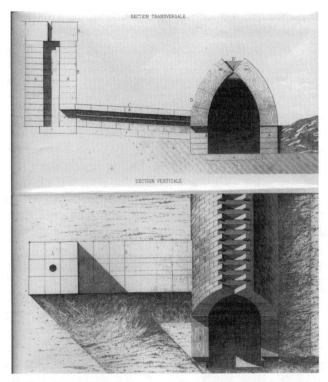

Fig. 25 Brick-built drains in Sargon's palace at Khorsabad.

royal inscriptions or administrative records with restricted circulation, hardly ever mention those professions, let alone the individuals who practised them. Exceptional, therefore, is the mention of some of those professions in the royal inscriptions of Sargon and Sennacherib. In the context of his palace and garden at Nineveh, built 'through the craft of clever master builders',[56] Sennacherib mentions the 'master builder' (*šitimgallu*). A long tradition of water engineers in Mesopotamia is represented by the profession *sēkiru*, who had his own seal, an indication of centralized authority, and was also known as 'builder of watercourses' ŠITIM ID.DA. The 'man in charge of pipes/qanats' (*ša eli qanâte*)[57] was different in being a new profession introduced in Sennacherib's time. There would have been a close relationship between architects, builders and water engineers, matching the need to plan the integral water supply and drainage systems for the public buildings on citadels.

Ground plans for major buildings and canals could be drawn out on plaster or on stone; the famous example is part of a statue of Gudea, ruler of Lagash in the late third millennium BC, who held on his lap the plan of the temple described in the accompanying inscription. Occasionally one finds a sketch of fields and canals on a clay tablet.

To judge from the often rather irregular lines and angles of walls uncovered by excavation, much large-scale building was done by eye from a schematic understanding that was structured loosely around a cosmological symbolism. The symbolism is known from the vocabulary used in the inscriptions of the royal builder.[58] Often modular units were repeated, with standard types that seem to imply the use of a pattern book;[59] and the discovery in different cities of several palace courtyards paved with alternating black and white squares of river pebbles,[60] precursors of mosaics, seems also to imply a centralized approach to design (see Plate 8). A metrological tablet of late Assyrian date gives the measurements of two cross-sections of a temple from gate to gate; other, later tablets show that the arrangement of a complex pilaster was described in terms of the number of standard bricks needed for shallow and deep pilasters, and for the stepped framework of a gateway (sometimes called rabbeted jambs), if the technical vocabulary of the cuneiform text has been understood correctly.[61] The dominant requirement was to order enough bricks of appropriate sizes and shapes for an operation, which implies an arithmetical rather than a geometrical approach. We possess no manuals, no templates, no drawings of moulding profiles. It is likely that some of the rather rough mathematical tablets with multiplication tables found on clay tablets were intended for scaling up from a small sketch, but many other uses are possible. Much of the design would have been worked out on site for individual buildings, but far more planning would have been needed for the whole complex of Sennacherib's palace, garden and aqueduct.

For those critics who have suggested that the water-raising screw to which Strabo and Philo refer was a Hellenistic or Roman improvement, a late installation introduced into a revived version of the famous garden, it must be emphasized that the interpretation of Sennacherib's inscription shows that the screw was part of the original design, and part of the reason why the garden was a World Wonder both in Sennacherib's day and centuries later when Hellenistic authors wrote about it. The water-raising screw is miraculous in appearing to reverse gravity, to overcome the natural imperative of water to flow downhill.

5

Engineering for Water Management

Consider Assyria, a cedar of Lebanon,
Of beautiful branches, a shading wood, and of lofty stature;
Whose crown was among the clouds.
Water made it grow, the Deep made it tall;
Her rivers she made flow around her planting,
But her canals she sent forth to all the (other) trees of the field.

Ezekiel 31: 3–4[1]

More than 2,000 years of accumulated expertise lay behind the engineering required for the supply of water to Nineveh, its orchards and its citadel with the Hanging Garden. An effective control of water was always crucial to the growth and continuity of cities and agriculture in Mesopotamia. Although much of the know-how must have been local, improvements over the course of many centuries were sometimes adopted from foreign practices and expertise; the Assyrians were eclectic and appreciative of foreigners' skills which they encountered in their far-reaching expeditions for trade and conquest, and had no inhibitions about importing experts from other countries or adapting anything foreign that was better than their own.

In the case of Nineveh, the city had long played host to kings. There Tiglath-pileser I (1114–1076 BC) completed a palace which his father had begun to build, probably on the site where Sennacherib later built his South-West Palace, and made a garden on the citadel:

beside that terrace I planted a garden for my royal leisure. I dug a canal from the river Khosr and [directed its water] into that garden. I brought the rest of that water into the outskirts of the city for irrigation. Within that garden I built a(nother?) palace....'[2]

As conqueror of Babylonia, Tiglath-pileser I had a huge labour force at his disposal, 'prisoners without number', so much of the landscaping of the citadel was already in place when Sennacherib undertook to replace the old palace, garden and canal on a more ambitious scale.

When the canals, weir, tunnel, dam and bridge-style aqueduct with corbelled stone arches, all designed and constructed by Sennacherib's engineers, were traced and published in 1935, scholars in the field of Assyriology were amazed that such an extensive and well-planned scheme existed in the early 7th century BC (see Plates 11–13). It was not then fashionable to be concerned with the economics of ancient Mesopotamian cities; art and architecture, alongside texts, were the

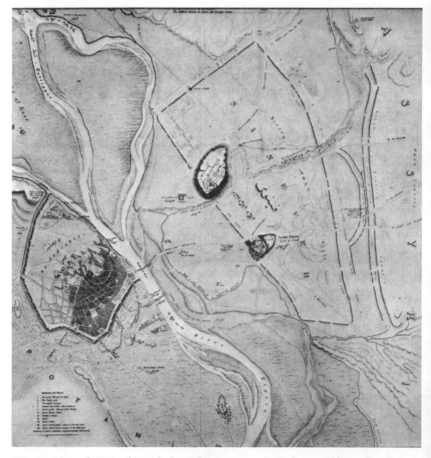

Fig. 26 Map of Nineveh made by Felix Jones in 1852 showing the walls, the two citadels, and modern Mosul across the Tigris.

main focus of study. Since then new emphases on town-planning and supply have raised awareness of water engineering in early times, so that Sennacherib's achievement can be set against a wider background of knowledge. A few installations dated earlier than his time are briefly described here, in order to show that certain advances can no longer be credited to Achaemenid Persians, or to Romans, as they have been in the past.

Part of the reason that the subject was neglected for so long lies in lack of explicit cuneiform texts on the subject. Before the days of printing and of technical university education, the knowledge required to practise such a field of expertise as water management was gained through the apprenticeship of a family member, natural or adopted. A man would thus be responsible in the most personal way for handing on his own knowledge and skill and that of his colleagues. Almost all of it would be done without a need for written manuals or records of projects. There are two exceptions: the basic mathematical exercises written by schoolboys who learned to calculate, for instance, the man-days required to build a dyke of particular dimensions; and the detailed reports to the king by regional governors concerning the regulation of river flow and maintenance of canals, weirs and sluices. The former are known mainly during the early second millennium BC, and are barely relevant. Of the latter, the most extensive is the correspondence of the governor of Saggaratum, a town on the lower Habur river, around 1800 BC.[3] He served under king Zimri-Lim of Mari, a city on the Euphrates just downstream from the Habur, which depended on the regulation of water flow from Saggaratum for the irrigation of its crops, and for the safe passage of boats; a long canal ran alongside the Habur and bypassed the mouth of the river where it joined the Euphrates. His letters contain many poorly understood technical terms for weirs, sluices, dykes and the activities associated with them, so that accurate translation is impossible; but a sharp sense of urgency for getting the right labour force in place is often expressed with the fear of dire consequences for failure. Letters of a similar kind must have been written throughout the centuries in every great city of Mesopotamia. The only royal inscription known to us that describes engineering for water management at length is Sennacherib's *Bavian Inscription*. It was chiselled into a rock face overlooking the headwaters of the new scheme.

Most of the early progress in water management can be traced only by archaeologists, and can be hard to date with precision. Several centuries before the lifetime of Sennacherib the *qanat* system had

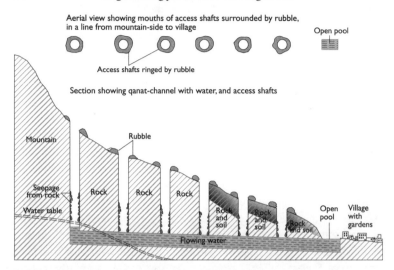

Aerial view showing mouths of access shafts surrounded by rubble, in a line from mountain-side to village

Open pool

Access shafts ringed by rubble

Section showing qanat-channel with water, and access shafts

Mountain

Rubble

Seepage from rock

Rock   Rock   Rock

Water table

Rock and soil   Rock and soil   Rock and soil

Open pool   Village with gardens

Flowing water

Fig. 27 Diagram to show a qanat: aerial view and side section.

been developed in the region now in modern Oman and Abu Dhabi,[4] where it allowed a sudden expansion in the size of settlements (see Figure 27). *Qanat* refers to the system of collecting water that seeps from rock through a long line of tunnels leading from near the foot of a mountain to a settlement far beyond the mountain. Each tunnel was perforated at intervals with vertical shafts for access. Relieving people of the need to haul water up from deep wells, or fetch from a distance, the system is likely to have originated where rivers were rare and ground water deep. In an area where shaft mines were sunk into rock, observation of seepage through underground rock and soil is likely to have stimulated the invention. Such an environment is to be found in modern Oman, where the Hajar mountain range—ancient Agarum— was exploited for its copper over many centuries. Where mountain water drains down underground to supply the great oasis of Al-Ain– Buraimi (now on Oman's border with Abu Dhabi), *aflaj* have been traced with their dependent settlements, dating from around 1000 BC. The term *qanat* in Iraqi and Syrian Arabic, derived from Akkadian *qanû* 'reed; pipe', is known as *falaj* (plural *aflaj*) in Oman, a word derived from Akkadian *palgu* 'ditch, water channel', and it is signifi- cant that both words have close links with the Assyrian language used in the time of Sennacherib. The Assyrians of the 7th century were in contact with that distant area: Sennacherib's grandson Ashurbanipal received tribute from Izki in Oman, a town which still bears that name.[5] The *qanat* system was eventually adopted by the Achaemenid Persians, who are erroneously credited with its invention.[6]

Contrary to assertions (based on the misinterpretation of an Akkadian text) that the Urartians of eastern Anatolia used *qanat*s in the 9th to 7th centuries BC,[7] the *qanat* is not found among Urartian waterworks. Nevertheless, the 50 km-long 'Semiramis' canal built by their king Menua (*c*.810–785) bears testimony to how the Urartians were able to expand their settlements by ingenious and energetic management of water in other ways. In western Iran another 50 km-long open canal, now known as the canal of Darius, was not built by him, for we can now read an inscription on it: its actual builder was an Elamite king of the 14th century BC.[8]

Ashurnasirpal II in the 9th century BC used a construction largely comparable to the *qanat* for his tunnel at Negoub, tunnelling through intransigent conglomerate rock with vertical access shafts from the surface at intervals (see Plate 2).[9] But it was not a true *qanat*, for by this method river water, rather than seepage through rock and soil, was diverted to his palace and garden at Nimrud. Sennacherib made a similar construction at Arbela, probably also to bring river water to an appropriate point. Only the entrance to this tunnel has been found, bearing his inscription:

Three rivers which (flow) from Mt. Hani, a mountain above Arbela, (and) the water of the tributaries that are to the right and left sides of those rivers, I channelled and incorporated them. I dug out a canal and caused its flow to go straight through Arbela, residence of Ishtar, the exalted lady.[10]

As discussed in the previous chapter in connection with Archimedes and the invention of the water-raising screw, the phenomenon of the named inventor or culture hero in Greek tradition stands in sharp contrast to the anonymity of non-royal inventors and high achievers in the Ancient Near East. In Assyrian tradition we do not know who engineered Sennacherib's aqueduct and adjacent watercourses, but in Greek tradition we do know that an engineer named Eupolinos constructed a tunnel and water system for Polycrates on Samos less than two centuries later, which shows how recognition for individual achievement in Greek society was different from that of the ancient Near East. Only by archaeological research can we be sure of identifying prior invention: recent discoveries of a tunnel with shafts, to supply water in Bronze Age Troy, dated to the third millennium BC,[11] and an elaborate system for controlling water around Lake Copais near Thebes in Mycenaean Greece,[12] dated to the mid second millennium BC, show that we have underestimated the ingenuity and achievements of anonymous people in earlier times.

What instruments were used? Quite precise survey work is required to construct long watercourses over uneven terrain. Neither texts nor sculptures offer information. The Assyrian king, whose prerogative was the building, beautifying and repair of temples, is sometimes shown standing before a god who holds out to him a rod and a ring of coiled rope, as if to emphasize the duty, divinely ordained, of the ruler to his god in the matter of surveying and measuring land. Much can be done with a measuring rod (Akkadian *ginindanakku*) and a long string of specified length (*ašlu*), and there is no evidence for the existence of more sophisticated devices. However, to make the alignment required for the *qanat*-type of tunnel with shafts made for Nimrud by Ashurnasirpal in the 9th century, and the similar tunnel made for Arbela by Sennacherib in the early 7th, it is likely that the suspended sighting tube was used.[13] The ideal gradient for which the engineers aimed has been reckoned at one metre per kilometre.[14]

Stone aqueducts in the shape of long bridges for carrying water over a valley are commonly associated with Roman engineering. Bridges built to span short widths of water, as opposed to pontoon bridges made of rafts strung together for wide rivers, were probably a feature of many Mesopotamian cities at earlier periods. Sargon had built a bridge with a single arch on his citadel at Khorsabad, though not crossing a river bed,[15] and there are examples of ancient bridges that are older still, such as stone bridges with arched culverts, of Mycenaean date.[16] Where Sennacherib's watercourse guided water across the wadi (a valley down which water flows intermittently) at Jerwan, it passed along a stone aqueduct supported by a row of pointed arches and buttresses. Its width without the buttresses is 22 m, and the total length more than 280 m (see Figure 31 and Plate 12).[17]

Sennacherib would have benefited from the experience of his father's schemes to supply the new capital at Khorsabad with water. Sargon described his installations with extreme brevity, using ambiguous and rare vocabulary that can be translated in different ways according to the preconceptions of the translator.[18]

(Sargon) the clever king, who thinks of good things, who put his mind to settling people on uncultivated ground and opening up neglected land for planting orchards, at that time over a spring (*namba'e*) at the foot of Mt Muṣri, a mountain above Nineveh, built a city and called it Fort of Sargon. A high garden (*kirimāhu*) in the image of the Amanus mountains in which all the aromatic plants of northern Syria, fruits of the mountains, are planted, I built beside it.[19]

Another inscription adds:

to open up springs (*innī*) in an area without water-sources (*kuppī*) as *karattu* (unknown word) and to raise up the waters of abundance above and below like the gushing of flood-water.[20]

Sargon used the word *kirimāhu* for the first time. As already discussed in the context of Sennacherib's prism inscription, it referred to a landscape garden, set upon the high citadel alongside the palace. In Sargon's case the whole citadel was an entirely artificial construction, imitating an ancient city, towering above the level of the surrounding fields. His phrase 'to raise up the waters of abundance above and below' must refer to methods by which he supplied the citadel with water. The drains built for the buildings on the citadel at Khorsabad are so magnificent that one supposes a vast amount of water was anticipated. One system collected water from roofs, upper storeys and courtyards through vertical pipes, then led it through under-floor piping, made of interlocking terracotta sections, away from the building. Another system collected sewage from comfortable lavatories consisting of a stone or brick seat with a central hole; the effluent fell down a pipe into a sewer, big enough for a man to walk upright along its length. It was vaulted with baked brick, and waterproofed with bitumen (see Figure 25). Presumably this great sewer collected from many sources and led the sewage outside the citadel wall.[21] The whole system must have been planned coherently before the buildings were begun. These remarkable installations show that daily comfort and convenience were just as important as ostentation and superficial grandeur.

Whether Sargon's engineers succeeded in matching the water supply to the drainage system may be questioned; one wonders whether Sennacherib decided to set up Nineveh as his capital because only there could he access the water of the river Khosr and its many tributaries. Sargon credited the god Ea–Nishiku with the power to

provide water, as did his son, and he wrote a prayer on the threshold
to the temple he built to Ea on the citadel:

O Nishiku, lord of wisdom, creator of all and everything, for Sargon king of
the world, king of Assyria, governor of Babylon, king of Sumer and Akkad,
builder of your shrine: Open up for me your depths, bring for me its water-
sources, make the waters of abundance and prosperity irrigate for me in its
environs! Decree for his destiny broad understanding and wide intelligence,
perfect his works and may he achieve his desire.[22]

Whereas Sargon had built up terraces for his new citadel at Khorsabad, Sennacherib took over a citadel already high from the debris of
more than 2,000 years of building. The South-West Palace of Sennacherib, built on top of the old citadel at Nineveh, stood beside its
garden which was elevated on a series of artificial terraces, with an
aqueduct bringing in water halfway up the garden.[23] Those great
building works were one end-product of a tremendous feat of engineering and water management which was executed in four phases.[24]
The various inscriptions do not acknowledge the extent to which
Sennacherib relied on the work done by previous kings, but he
supplies an unparalleled wealth of detail. All the texts are remarkable
for the detailed interest shown in engineering, a characteristic so
striking that it can only mirror the king's personal predilections.
When one considers the huge scale of operations, one can only
admire the fact that the king, beginning as soon as he came to the
throne, had completed all four phases within fifteen years (see
Figure 28).

The river Khosr flows through the middle of Nineveh so that the
city is divided into two separate parts, each with its own high citadel:
Kouyunjik on which the great palaces were found, and Nebi Yunus
(see Figure 34b). It joins the river Tigris on the western side of the
city.[25] At most seasons the water in the Tigris is quite clean and
drinkable, but in spring and early summer, when the snows in the
mountains are melting, the turbulence of extra water stirs up dirt,
causing temporary unpleasantness. Moreover, the bed of the Tigris on
the western side of the city lies many metres lower than the neo-
Assyrian citadel, and the difference in height makes it very hard to
raise water to the citadel, too high even using banks of shadufs. The
water of the river Khosr is always fresh and clean, having made a
fairly direct journey from the mountains some 80 km away, and
tumbles down quite steeply into the Tigris. But the advantage of

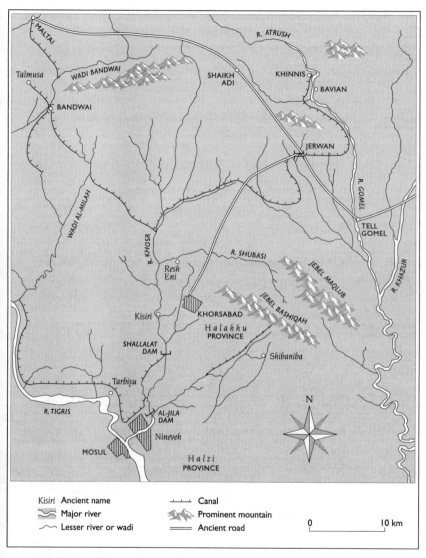

Fig. 28 Sketch map to show rivers, canals and roads to the north-east of Nineveh.

purity is coupled with the disadvantage that it is prone to violent spate when snows melt fast or when rain falls torrentially. In that condition it threatened the very walls of Nineveh, especially the part of the Kouyunjik citadel where the South-West Palace was situated. The king explained how such floods in the past had damaged the palace of his predecessors and had washed away some old royal tombs. If harnessed carefully, using the height of its upper courses to lead off canals, the river water could be used to create gardens and orchards around the city, and to provide good drinking water for the citizens.[26]

During the past century several different scholars have contributed to the complicated task of understanding these networks, through surface survey and, most recently, the use of satellite photographs.[27]

On rock faces at the head of the main systems, sculptured panels of bas-reliefs showed the king and processions of gods, the best preserved being at Maltai and Khinnis (see Figures 29, 30, 32, and Plates 11, 13). For lesser canals an occasional niche in a suitable expanse of rock contains the figure of the king. At least 13 such places with niches or panels have been located; 18 canals are referred to in the first stage of the project, 16 in a later phase. The long but damaged Bavian inscription, engraved into the rock high up overlooking the first stretch of canal, gives an overall account of all the different networks.[28] Each scheme had reservoirs, dams, weirs and sluices associated with it for regulating the flow and making the best possible use of the water at different times of year, at seasons of excess and seasons of shortage.

In the first project a canal about 13.4 km long was cut from the village of Kisiri to Nineveh, to control the flow of the lower course of the Khosr. Designed to water orchards to the north of the citadel mound, it may have run from the Shallalat dam, which still survives today, and was a favourite picnic spot for Agatha Christie and the British archaeologists excavating at Nimrud in the mid 20th century.[29] It was one of Sennacherib's earliest projects, carried out around 705–703 BC, and is often known as the Kisiri canal.

In a second phase another canal was constructed to the south-east of the first one, controlling the flow of water that drained from Mt. Muṣri (modern Jebel Bashiqah), and it joined the Khosr just outside Nineveh. This canal, often known as the Muṣri canal, was about the same length as the first one, and may have incorporated canals built by Sargon.

In a third, and far more ambitious phase, referred to as the 'northern system', a channel may have begun at Maltai, and perhaps joined a huge canal located near the village of Faida, then possibly joining up with the Bandwai canal, eventually flowing along a terrace beside the Tigris and bringing water to the town Tarbiṣu north of Nineveh. This was built some time after 694, following the building of a new city wall and ditch around Nineveh in c.696.

The fourth system, created around 688, is the one best known because of the work of Jacobsen and Lloyd. The source is in the mountains at Khinnis, on the Gomel river, where water is channelled into a dam and flows out alongside the river but at an ever higher level, skirting a mountain to leave the Gomel river and cross a different river at Jerwan, collecting more and more water from joining streams and springs at many points, eventually joining the Khosr (see Plates 9, 10). By the time it reached Nineveh, the water had flowed along man-made channels for some 90 km. Because the beginnings of this last canal are quite remote, the remains are still visible and can be traced rather better than the earlier canals.

The author visited Bavian–Khinnis in 1967. There the natural river comes out from a gorge and begins a steep descent in the direction of Nineveh. It is a place of great beauty, with marvellous views to the south-west across patches of meadowland bright with flowers and delicate grasses. On vertical rock faces the Assyrians carved panels of sculpture showing the king, stately and dignified, facing the many great gods who favoured and supported his enterprises. On some panels he holds the rod and ring of kingship, or extends his arm towards a deity who offers those symbols to him (see Figures 29, 30, Plate 11). A square, rock-cut cistern with statues of lions on opposing sides allows water to collect and to spout through the mouths of the lions, a fountain providing a convenient and elegant drinking-place for the sculptors and engineers who spent weeks there working on the project. The long inscription, devoted

Fig. 29 Drawing of a great rock sculpture at Maltai, showing Sennacherib in the assembly of gods.

Fig. 30 (a) Large panel of sculpture on a rock face at Khinnis, showing Sennacherib facing the great deities.

Fig. 30 (b) Reconstruction drawing of the panel.

to details of construction of all four projects, was chiselled on another rock face.[30] In accordance with traditional procedure for composing royal narratives, highlights from the text were copied for re-use in subsequent inscriptions, and edited for different locations.

The canal which led out from the sculptured area was 7 m wide, with parapets built out of stone blocks on each side, to channel the stream at its maximum. One large sculptured square block stood at this point with the canal flowing on one side of it and a weir at the other, so that the natural bed of the river continued to receive water, necessary for the villages and farms along its course. After running for about 300 m the water entered a dam with sluices, and at that point the canal altered its course and cut through a rock, so that the water flowed through a tunnel some 2 m high (allowing easy access for maintenance). The canal was named Sennacherib's Canal.

This change from one river catchment to another involved the need to cross a shallow but nevertheless inconvenient wadi at Jerwan, a valley hyperbolically described in the rock inscription as a deep ravine. To overcome this difficulty, Sennacherib had an aqueduct constructed, so magnificent that much of it survives to this day (see Figure 31, Plate 12). From the air it looks like a stretch of motorway: using more than two million blocks of smooth limestone, it stood 9 m high at its maximum, and had buttresses to strengthen the sides at regular intervals. The gradient was finely managed, and the surface over which the water flowed consisted of a thick layer of concrete some 40 cm deep, laid over the courses of stone. Supporting arches were corbelled, with pointed tops, and the piers were boat-shaped to allow flood water to pass through with minimal resistance. The model for this was the pontoon bridge consisting of a row of boats linked together, with wooden planking on top forming a pathway.

So fine was this marvel of engineering that the transformed landscape gave rise to a local legend telling how it was built by one of two suitors for the hand of the king's daughter. One suitor did the work most energetically, while the other bided his time until the work was finished, and then, while the exhausted man rested, the idle one tricked the king and his daughter into believing it was his own work, by laying linen sheets along the surface of the aqueduct to make it appear, from a distance, as if water was flowing. He won the princess.[31]

At certain intervals stone blocks in the aqueduct bore a nine-line inscription which reads:

Fig. 31 (a) Aerial view of the Jerwan aqueduct.

Fig. 31 (b) Perspective restoration drawing of the Jerwan aqueduct.

Sennacherib king of the world king of Assyria. Over a great distance I had a watercourse directed to the environs of Nineveh, joining together the waters of two streams of the Khosr river,—flood-prone waters—and the waters of Hanusa town and Gammagara town, and the waters of springs of the mountains to right and left. Over steep-sided valleys I spanned an aqueduct (bridge)[32] of white limestone blocks, I made those waters flow over it.[33]

This left no doubt that the aqueduct was built in the 7th century and was not a later construction.

As we saw in the Introduction, the group of seven World Wonders by Greek authors can be traced back at the latest to the time of

Alexander the Great through his historians whose works were used by Roman writers. It is highly significant that the battle of Gaugamela, where Alexander defeated Darius III to win the world, took place only a few kilometres from Jerwan. The great aqueduct spanned a main road known from Assyrian times.[34] Although the battlefield itself has not been identified, it takes its name from the river Gomel and from the modern village Tell Gomel which lies just south of Bavian on that river. In the words of Layard, one of the earliest European travellers to describe the area:

The rock-sculptures of Bavian are the most important that have yet been discovered in Assyria . . . on the right bank of the Gomel, a brawling mountain torrent. The Gomel or Gomela may, perhaps, be traced in the ancient name of Gaugamela, celebrated for that great victory which gave to the Macedonian conqueror the dominion of the Eastern world. Although the battlefield was called after Arbela, a neighbouring city,[35] we know that the river Zab intervened between them, and that the battle was fought near the village of Gaugamela, on the banks of the Bumadus or Ghazir, the Gomela of the Kurds.[36]

As Alexander's 47,000 men marched from the north-west along the road past Jerwan to face the Persian army at Gaugamela, he and his scouts cannot have failed to notice the great aqueduct. They would have marvelled at the scale and detail of its construction, and would have discovered from local knowledge that this was part of the grand design for the gardens and orchards of Nineveh. By direct experience of an element so crucial for the Hanging Garden, and from reports gathered in the vicinity, they would have become aware that the royal garden at Nineveh (whether or not it still flourished) was linked to a very impressive feat of engineering, greater than anything known at home in Macedonia. The location of Gaugamela, therefore, is a key to understanding how the garden became known to Greeks long after the fall of Assyria. Knowledge of the garden, and of the water management linked to it, was associated with Alexander's most triumphant victory. His historians found it a worthy subject for their accounts, which were taken up in turn by Roman writers.

Later, when Roman troops marched into northern Mesopotamia, they would have taken the same road. The aqueducts both at Jerwan and at Nineveh would still have featured prominently in the landscape. Soldiers and travellers would have seen the aqueduct, the rock-cut canals and tunnels, and the rock carvings of Sennacherib, for which the relevance to the Hanging Garden would still have been understood locally.

There are other reasons why Greeks and Romans would have admired the building work that they saw in Assyria. It is a common preconception that the true arch (with a key-stone) was invented by the Romans, because early Greek architects did not build with arches. In fact, pre-Roman arches, both corbelled and with key-stones, are attested both in Egypt and in Mesopotamia from the time of the very earliest rulers. When Sir Leonard Woolley found evidence in Sumerian architecture at Ur for all kinds of arches built in mud brick, he suggested that the technique remained restricted to brickwork until the Hellenistic period, when the construction was transferred from brick to stone.[37] The aqueduct at Jerwan shows that the Assyrians around 700 BC had already made the transfer to stone.

It is often thought that concrete was not developed until the Roman period. As recently expressed, 'One of the most renowned of the Roman contributions to building technology was the development of concrete.'[38] It is lucky for our understanding of Assyrian technology that the archaeologist Seton Lloyd, who explored the Assyrian ruins at Jerwan, was an architect by training. On finding what he thought was Assyrian concrete at Jerwan, he submitted samples for analysis to the British Building Research Station's department of scientific and industrial research, who reported that the samples 'consisted of a mix made up of a magnesian limestone aggregate and muddy river sand, cemented by a magnesian lime made by burning a magnesian limestone'. He included the full analysis in his detailed report of 1935.[39]

More can be said about the passage mentioned above in which Herodotus referred to the network of canals that brought water down from the mountains on the approach to Assyria and the border with Media.[40] While describing Babylon, Herodotus digresses with a description of installations that cannot refer to the real Babylon because the topography in Babylonia and the lower Euphrates valley is not suited for the works as he describes them; and besides, he mentions Semiramis, Nineveh, and Assyria in the passage. Having made it clear that there were two queens, 'the earlier, Semiramis, preceding the later by five generations', he goes on to separate their two contributions (I have added inverted commas to highlight confusion in names, and italics to highlight names that indicate the relevance to Assyria rather than Babylon):

It was 'Semiramis' who was responsible for certain remarkable embankments in the plain outside the city, built to control the river which until then used to flood the whole countryside. The later of the two queens, 'Nitocris', ... having her eye on the great and expanding power of the Medes and the many cities, including *Nineveh* itself, which had fallen before them, ... changed the course of the 'Euphrates', which flows through 'Babylon'. Its course was originally straight, but by cutting channels higher upstream she made it wind about with so many twists and turns that now it actually passes a certain *Assyrian* village called Ardericca three separate times ... The purpose ... of the diversion of the river was to cause the frequent bends to reduce the speed of the current ... Moreover, these works lay in the neighbourhood of the approaches to *Assyria* and on the direct route to Media.

Note that the text has 'cutting channels' rather than 'digging canals', and that the purpose expressed, to reduce the speed of the current, is reminiscent of Sennacherib's own words in his rock inscription at Bavian:

Above the towns Dur-Ishtar, Shibaniba and Sulu I saw streams and enlarged their narrow sources ... I cut through difficult places with pickaxes and directed their outflow ... I strengthened their channels, heaping up their banks ... to arrest the flow of those waters I made a swamp and set out a canebrake within it ...

The name of the village called Ardericca by Herodotus has not been identified in the Bavian inscription or any other Assyrian source.

Exactly how the water came into Nineveh at a level high enough to reach the aqueduct in the royal garden may be deduced from another of Sennacherib's inscriptions:

In order to bring the outflow of the river Khosr within the city and a course of water above and below, I built twin(?) bridges with kiln-baked bricks. Below it, facing the city gate of the citadel, I had a bridge made of baked brick and white limestone for my royal chariot to pass along.[41]

This description allows the interpretation that an aqueduct, whose course cannot now be traced, brought mountain water into the city at a higher level than a lower bridge on which the king entered the citadel on his chariot.

To inaugurate the installations that brought water to Nineveh, yet prevented damage from uncontrolled flow, a ceremony was derived from traditional rituals performed for beginning a new building. It was carried out at the source of the water. Not only was there a great panel of sculpture carved into the high rock face overlooking the headwaters both at Bavian and at Maltai (and perhaps elsewhere), but also offerings were cast into the water, equivalent to foundation deposits laid in a new building.

For the opening ceremony of that canal I instructed an incantation priest (*āšipu*) and a *kalû*-priest, and I presented as gifts carnelian, lapis lazuli, *mušgarru*-stone, *hulālu*-agate stone, alabaster, choice gemstones, a turtle, a carp figurine in the likeness of [a sage?] made of gold, aromatics, perfumed oil for Ea the lord of sources, springs and the meadows of Enkimdu the divine canal-overseer, lord of channels and ditches. I prayed to the great gods and they heard my prayers, and prospered the work of my hands. The sluice-gate of that canal opens without a spade or a shovel and lets the waters of abundance flow: its sluice gate is not opened by the labour of man's hands, but by the will of the gods.[42]

Here Sennacherib shows his enthusiasm for a new, automatic mechanism for opening and closing sluice-gates. We do not have any detailed information about the invention, but it is interesting to note that one of the transmitters of Berossus attributed to 'Nebuchadnezzar' an echo of the same idea:

sluices which on being opened irrigated the plain (around 'Babylon'). They called these sluices *echetognōmones*, just as if they have the will or the ability to comply on their own.[43]

Nearly two centuries earlier, the 9th-century king Ashurnasirpal II (or a later improver) had put sluice-gates into the rock-cut Negoub tunnel, but they were almost certainly operated manually.

Sennacherib's inscription continues:

When I looked upon the canal and directed its work I made offerings of fat cows and plump sheep and pure libations to the great gods who go at my side and make my reign secure. I clothed those men who had dug that canal with multi-coloured garments, and I put gold rings and pectorals on them.

This is an unusual passage for declaring publicly that the king rewarded the men responsible for the successful completion of the work. It is comparable with his expression of concern for the exhausting conditions under which huge castings were made in the time of his predecessors, before a new, less exhausting technique was introduced, to the benefit of his workforce.

Sennacherib's offerings presented at the opening ceremony would have been tossed into the water in an act of sacrifice that is widely known in other cultures. The outlet of a water course marks a cosmological boundary that requires protection by the gods. In England, at the site of Roman bridges and Saxon causeways, votive offerings have been recovered, both accidentally and by excavation, some of them representing fish and other aquatic creatures especially appropriate to the setting. Similar offerings were cast into water during Sennacherib's campaign to the marshes of southern Iraq, when a sudden flood endangered the king and his encamped army:

A surge of high water from the sea rose and entered my tent, and it completely surrounded me while in my camp, causing all of my men to camp in strong boats as in cages for five days and nights . . . To Ea, king of the Apsu,[44] I offered pure sacrifices, and together with a gold boat, I cast into the sea a golden fish and a golden crab.[45]

Sennacherib claimed to have constructed his canal works from Bavian to Nineveh with a mere seventy men. That number cannot represent the entire workforce—the Jerwan aqueduct alone required two million smoothed, close-fitting stones—but may refer to the management team, perhaps for only one of the four phases; or it may be a schematic number.

Several centuries later it was a matter of some astonishment to Greeks to learn what a personal interest Near Eastern kings took in basic work, even to the extent of getting their hands dirty and raising a sweat. Their stereotype of the foreign tyrant, secluded and effete, conflicted with reality. In a fictional conversation Xenophon composed this dialogue:

Critobulus: Do you really believe, Socrates, that the king of the Persians is concerned at all about farming?

Socrates: If we look at it in the following way, Critobulus, perhaps we may learn whether he is concerned at all about it. We agree that he is seriously concerned about military matters, because he gives orders to each man who is in charge of the countries from which he receives tribute to supply provisions . . . Furthermore, he himself examines all of the land that he sees as he rides through it . . . When Lysander came to him (Cyrus) . . . Cyrus had personally shown him the *paradeisos* at Sardis. When Lysander had expressed amazement at the beauty of the trees in it (for they were planted at equal intervals in straight rows and all at regular angles), and many sweet fragrances wafted about them as they strolled around, he exclaimed, in amazement, 'Cyrus, I certainly am amazed at all these things for their beauty, but I admire even more the man who measured out each of the trees for you and arranged each one of them in order.' When Cyrus heard this, he was pleased and replied, 'Lysander, I myself measured and arranged everything and I even planted some of the trees myself.'[46]

Two titles taken by the Assyrian king in his official inscriptions reflect his responsibility for cultivating land: *ikkaru* 'ploughman' and *iššakku* 'steward, farmer'. Just as the title 'shepherd of his people' represents the duty of the king in promoting the pastoral side of the economy, so 'ploughman' and 'farmer' represent his promotion of agriculture, in which horticulture plays its part. Symbolizing the king's engagement with down-to-earth activities, a plough, a plant, and a sheep, goat or cow in Assyrian art are sometimes used to mark the ideology of royalty. But not only in pictures. Ceremonially the king in person must perform actions appropriate to the titles he claimed. When kings claimed to have formed the first brick, it was no idle boast but a genuine ritual act that linked the king to the gods as primeval builders.[47] Just as Sennacherib's grandson showed himself as builder carrying a hod of bricks on his royal head,[48] so Sennacherib's role as a cultivator is demonstrated in the garden beside his palace. His claim that people made cloth from the cotton plants he had introduced,[49] and used olive oil from the olive trees he had planted, shows that his horticulture was not simply an extravagant prestige project, but benefited the people whom the gods, by choosing him for kingship, had entrusted with their welfare.

The royal wonder-garden at Nineveh was the show-piece of an extensive scheme which brought great benefits to other parts of the city. The copious supply of water allowed all kinds of orchards to be planted around the city, improving the supply of fresh food to its inhabitants. Good drinking water reached north, south and east of the city walls. Fresh mountain water would have flowed into the palace as well as watering its garden, and then flushed through the drainage systems of the South-West Palace.

Nineveh was now the finest city in the world,

the exalted metropolis, the city beloved of Ishtar, in which all the ceremonies of gods and goddesses take place, the eternal base, the everlasting foundation whose plan was drawn in the writing of the firmament at the beginning of time, whose structure was then made known; a clever place where hidden knowledge resides for every kind of skilful work.[50]

Sennacherib transformed Nineveh together with its surrounding orchards, irrigated all year round by the network of canals, into a garden city. Whether quite such an elaborate work was required for the city's practical needs has been doubted, giving rise to the suggestion that the projects were intended to demonstrate the skill of Assyrian engineers and the king's power, and to give the city the image of the canal-entwined landscape of Babylonia. Against the background of early competence in water management, we can set the extraordinary accomplishment of Sennacherib in bringing mountain water to irrigate his wonderful garden, set high up on the citadel of Nineveh beside his palace.

So sturdily constructed were its canals, dams and aqueduct that they were able to survive the disasters of conquests by Medes, Babylonians and Persians. During the Achaemenid period, around the time when Herodotus was writing, the great satrap Arshama owned estates near to Nineveh and collected revenue from them.[51] There continued to be a great incentive to repair and maintain the canals, dams and aqueducts of that region so that the flow of water for irrigation in general was not diminished.

Such a grand scheme linking a major hydraulic project with a superb palace garden can be linked to the king's perception of himself as god-like (see Figure 32, Plate 13). Very early kings in Mesopotamia had occasionally presented themselves as gods by wearing the horned crown of divinity and by putting the cuneiform sign for 'god' in front of their written name. Much later, in the two centuries before the reign of Sennacherib, it was normal practice on monuments to show the Assyrian king standing with symbols of the great gods, such as sun-disc and lunar crescent, above and beside his head. At Maltai and Bavian, however, Sennacherib stood in the assembly of those same great gods who were there depicted in human form no larger than himself: king and gods stood side by side, although the gods were standing upon animals. This blatant style of self-promotion had a near-precedent in images of Ashurnasirpal II in his magnificent North-West Palace at Nimrud, a marvel of the 9th century. Since Ashurnasirpal was especially distinguished for having engineered a project for water supply with a fabulous palace and a garden, the achievements of those two kings are closely comparable, both exceptional, and may be seen as qualifications for claiming god-like status through the subtle use of images.[52]

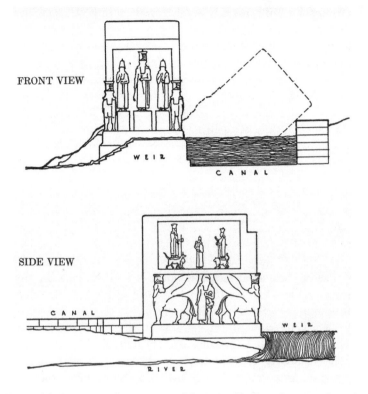

Fig. 32 (a) Tentative reconstruction of the stone block at the weir where the canal led off, showing Sennacherib in company with deities, front and side views.

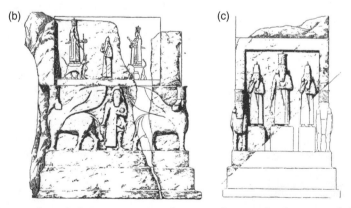

Fig. 32 (b and c) Reconstruction drawings, front and side views of the sculptured block that stood between the canal and a weir at Khinnis, showing the king in the company of great gods.

Subsequently tourists of late antiquity would have viewed the same installations in the vicinity of Jerwan, just as we still can today. The canals, dams and aqueduct were part of the wonder. The fame of the Hanging Garden, dependent on such brilliant works of engineering at the heart of Assyria, helped to disseminate to distant lands tales based essentially on the deeds of Sennacherib and his family.

Postscript

In the summer of 2012 the Italian Archaeological Mission to Assyria directed by Daniele Morandi Bonacossi reported the discovery of six unknown Assyrian rock relief sculptures. They represent a procession of deities along a stretch of canal probably built by Sennacherib at Faideh, a modern village located 10 km south of Maltai (see Figure 29). The remains of five aqueducts along the Khinnis canal were also identified.

6

Confusion of Names

> ... Assyria, a country remarkable for the number of great cities
> it contained, and especially for the most powerful and renowned
> of them all—Babylon, to which the seat of government was
> transferred after the fall of Nineveh
>
> Herodotus, *History* I.179

> And in ancient time Babylon was the metropolis of Assyria
>
> Strabo, *Geography* XVI.1.16

Several confusions have been identified. It would be satisfactory if we
could account for them, to strengthen yet further the argument that
the Hanging Garden was built by Sennacherib in Nineveh rather than
by Nebuchadnezzar or Semiramis in Babylon. Four distinct pairs of
names are relevant for tracing the story of the legendary garden:
'Nebuchadnezzar' named for Sennacherib, the city name 'Babylon'
used for Nineveh, the river 'Euphrates' named instead of the Tigris,
and 'Semiramis' confused with other queens and with 'Nitocris'. For
each of them an explanation can be given.

At the most fundamental level, the confusions can in part be
understood from an ancient Mesopotamian concept known chiefly
from mythology. In Sumerian myths the Sumerian word *me* represented the timeless notions of powers, arts and crafts, archetypal
functions which the gods had bestowed on mankind. Among them
was kingship. The *Sumerian King-list*, beginning with the words
'When kingship descended from Heaven', gives a specific example
of how the concept of kingship comes from heaven and is then
exemplified in the rulers of the different cities. Each one of the *mes*

was regarded as a concrete object, an item of insignia which could be handed over physically from one person to another.[1]

The Sumerian myth *Inanna and Enki* gives a half-humorous account of how kingship, as an item that could be stolen, passed from one city to the next.[2] Although it was transferred from one city to another according to changes of power, it was also available in every city—a paradox typical of many aspects of Mesopotamian thought which saw strength in multiplicity, in the liberality of ideas and possibilities. Among 110 or so abstract concepts including kingship are the many institutions of city life. Each king was a manifestation of the archetype of kingship. The concept exists outside time, independent of individual kings, but the name of a superlative example of the archetype could come to stand for the archetype itself. No doubt the much later Greek concept of ideal forms to which Plato refers in many of his works had something in common with the Sumerian expression for archetypes. In Mesopotamia the notion that more than one city could be a 'Babylon', or more than one queen could be a 'Semiramis', is never discussed in a philosophical context, but it can be teased out from various strands of information.

Sennacherib was evidently confused with Nebuchadnezzar in several late texts. In the opening words of the Book of Judith the two kings are confused: 'It was the twelfth year of Nebuchadnezzar who reigned over the Assyrians in the great city of Nineveh.' When Josephus named Nebuchadnezzar as builder of the garden, both he and his readers would have been confused between Nineveh and Babylon, and between Sennacherib and Nebuchadnezzar, because at the time they were reading his account, the Book of Judith was already in circulation. The Arab writer Tha'labi called Sennacherib 'a king of the kings of Babylon'.[3] One reason for confusion in Hebrew and Arab tradition is the result of military action: that both kings attacked Jerusalem, and so it was easy for later tradition to merge the two events, which were a mere century apart. Although Sennacherib did not in fact sack Jerusalem in 701, for he managed to collect punitive tribute without the need to do so, he had besieged the city. It was Babylon in 689 that he sacked, so in later times people conflated the two events because they fitted the wicked reputation of both kings. Also the name of Nebuchadnezzar was used by two pretenders in the time of Darius I presumably because they wished to associate themselves with an archetypal great king. Seleucid kings too deliberately associated themselves with him, promoting themselves with the promise of past glory restored. This reputation comes from the opposite polarity for Nebuchadnezzar's fame. As a good king and a great builder he was comparable also with Sennacherib. In these ways both kings could stand as archetypes for the exceptional bad ruler and the exceptional good one.

How did Nineveh come to be known as Babylon? This seemed at first to be a question that defied a satisfactory answer, leaving only the feeble resort to a scarcely convincing explanation: muddle. Greek authors, one might argue, were so far away from Mesopotamia that they confused both its cities and its rivers, and had no particular interest in distinguishing between them. In the case of the cities this would be more plausible if the terrains of northern and southern Mesopotamia were not so very different, as would have been obvious to travellers, soldiers and administrators. Much better reasons can be suggested.

There are many occasions on which the reader of a Classical text suspects that Babylon and Nineveh have been confused. For instance, Xenophon wrote of Babylon as the capital of the Assyrians.[4] The story of Sardanapalus dying in the flames of Nineveh, told by Ctesias, is generally reckoned to have taken some details from the death of Ashurbanipal's brother in the flames of Babylon, thus confusing Nineveh with Babylon.[5] This can now be identified as one of several events which Ctesias deliberately and mischievously transposed. Another example of ambiguity is found in the description Diodorus Siculus gives of how 'Semiramis' decorated her palace in Babylonia,

> decorating them with scenes of a hunt, complete in every detail, of all sorts of wild animals, and their size was more than four cubits. Among the animals, moreover, Semiramis had also been portrayed, on horse-back, and in the act of hurling a javelin at a leopard, and nearby was her husband Ninos, in the act of thrusting his spear into a lion at close quarters.[6]

This fits the style known from hunting scenes in several Assyrian palaces, especially the lion hunts of Ashurbanipal's North Palace at Nineveh which include beardless horse-riders brandishing spears. By contrast the throne-room of Nebuchadnezzar at Babylon has a static, heraldic design of lions and stylized palm trees, devoid of narrative content (see Figure 33).

Some of the arguments for Nineveh as a Babylon are derived from Sennacherib's inscriptions. One approach is to compare the naming of the city gates in the two cities. The earliest writing of the name Babylon shows that the city was understood to mean 'gate (*bāb*) of the

Fig. 33 (a–c) Decorative scheme of colour-glazed brick in the main court of Nebuchadnezzar's palace in Babylon: a continuous band of stylized plant motifs over long pillars; below the pillars, a continuous row of striding lions between bands of stylized plant motifs.

god (*ilim*)' or, in some ways of writing it, 'of the gods'. The city gates were originally named along traditional lines of a kind that can be found in many of the world's great cities, such as Westgate, Northgate, Eastgate and Southgate; King's Gate, Great Gate and Little Gate. Babylon certainly had a King's Gate, an East Gate and a Great Gate in early times. Almost as common are gates named after the speciality of their area: Market Gate, Canongate, Watergate, Smithgate, Bishopsgate. Babylon is known to have had a Market Gate. Also common is the gate named after the destination of the road that passes through it: London gate, Damascus gate, and so on. Babylon had its Akuṣ Gate, leading to the town Akuṣum. Most old cities have a mixture of such names.[7] But Babylon had another set of names for the same gates, presumably more ceremonial than vernacular, named after deities: Ishtar Gate, Marduk Gate, Zababa Gate, Shamash Gate and Adad Gate. Those names are related to the understanding of the city's name as 'Gate of the Gods', a name particularly appropriate for a city that played host to all the great gods of other ancient cities. The name implied that Babylon was the world centre of worship. Babylon's gates had been named after gods since at least the 12th century, and very likely much earlier.

At Nineveh, imitating Babylon, Sennacherib rebuilt the city walls and named its new gates after the great gods, yet mostly retained an older name (see Figure 34). Once again he followed in the footsteps of his father, for Sargon had named his city gates at Khorsabad after the chief deities: Shamash, Adad, Enlil, Mullissu, Anu, Ishtar, Ea, Bēlet-ilī, Ashur and Ninurta.[8] As at Babylon, the naming implied that each Assyrian royal city in turn laid claim to be a world centre where all the gods had dwellings.

To signify that a city and its cults were adopted by a royal capital, it is likely that a particular ceremony would mark the introduction. Models of cities shown on wall sculptures at Khorsabad are carried as tribute by foreign emissaries, showing a ceremony which may be linked to Sargon's policy for making Khorsabad a world centre (see Figure 35).

Sennacherib gave ceremonial names to eighteen of the gates. Of the several listings known, the fullest put the divine names before the traditional ones that related to topographical features.[9] Some of the gates or their names shifted as the work of construction and reshaping took place at Nineveh, as plans were modified and new walls and ditches constructed, but the general plan modelled on Babylon is

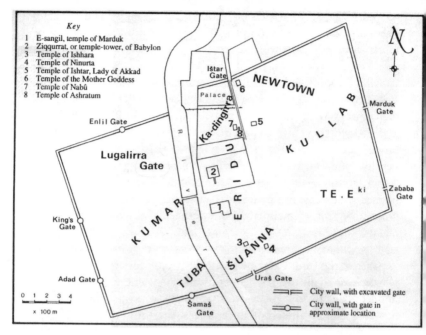

Key
1 E-sangil, temple of Marduk
2 Ziqqurrat, or temple-tower, of Babylon
3 Temple of Ishhara
4 Temple of Ninurta
5 Temple of Ishtar, Lady of Akkad
6 Temple of the Mother Goddess
7 Temple of Nabû
8 Temple of Ashratum

Ištar Gate
Palace
NEWTOWN
Marduk Gate
Enlil Gate
Ka-dingir-ra
Lugalirra Gate
KULLAB
King's Gate
KUMAR
TE.E ki
Zababa Gate
Adad Gate
TUBA
ŠUANNA
Uraš Gate
Šamaš Gate

0 1 2 3 4
x 100 m

City wall, with excavated gate
City wall, with gate in approximate location

Fig. 34 (a) Sketch plan of the citadel of Babylon showing names of city gates.

clear. This would have made it appropriate for Nineveh to be known as a Babylon, a 'Gates of Gods' city. Sennacherib must have been aware of that, and is likely to have renamed the gates as a deliberate act to match his capital city with Babylon. The lists include a gate named after the god of gardens, Igisigsig 'Green-green Eye'. Only Nineveh has a garden gate.

Another argument is based on a mythological interpretation of Sennacherib's most literary, hyperbolic inscriptions. One of them is written on the rocks above Bavian; another is inscribed on a clay cylinder. Sennacherib adapted a motif used by much earlier kings who described how an old regime had been swept away by a Flood, making way for a new and better order that rose up from the devastation.[10] He contrasted Babylon, where he had caused a deliberate inundation, reducing it to bare, flooded ground after sacking it, with a new era in Nineveh after it too had been damaged—recently, by an accidental flood—as if Nineveh would take the place of

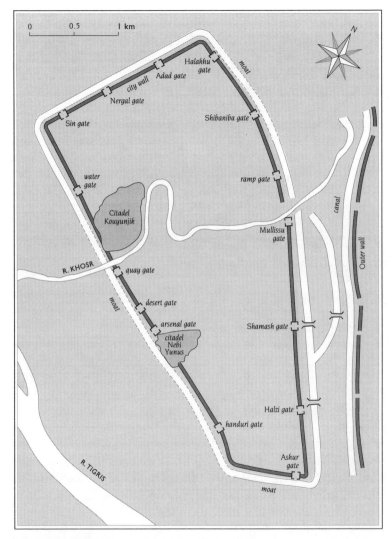

Fig. 34 (b) Sketch plan of the citadel of Nineveh showing names of city gates in the time of Sennacherib.

annihilated Babylon in the centre of the world, a pivotal place of royal power and worship. His texts include passages that mythologize flood damage done to Nineveh by rivers in the recent past. By this manipulation of real events, Sennacherib portrayed himself as the refounder

Fig. 35 Drawing from a sculpture panel from Khorsabad showing models of cities carried as tribute.

of Nineveh, superseding earlier foundations. Babylon sank into the waters of chaos as Nineveh arose from them.[11]

In early Sumerian mythology and history the city regarded as the cosmic centre of religious power was Nippur which lies to the south of Babylon. A myth told of a visit to its patron god Enlil from his son Enki, the god of water and wisdom, when a grand occasion was celebrated in the temple Ekur by all the great gods with a huge drinking competition.[12] In another myth Nippur was the place where Enlil first created mankind.[13] The city was also known as Duranki, the 'bond of sky and earth' where an umbilical cord linked the divine and mortal spheres. Those two spheres were themselves named as primeval deities, An-shar 'sky-sphere' and Ki-shar 'earth-sphere', and the main temple complex at Nippur had the name E-duranki, 'House of the bond of sky and earth'.

Nippur was exceptional for being a leading religious and educational centre of Mesopotamia even though it had never held temporal power. Priests in temples, rather than kings in palaces, held sway there. It did not boast conquering kings, nor is it found in any version of the *Sumerian King-list*. Yet it lent its Sumerian temple name Ekur to temples in other cities, and Ekur became a loanword in Akkadian, *ekurru* meaning any temple, with a change to a generic sense. Its god Enlil and the powers he exercised, *enlilūtu*, became the epithet and attribute of other great gods, notably Marduk and Ashur, who raised themselves to greater eminence by means of this association. The Babylonian language easily formed abstract nouns according to a standard pattern *šarru* 'king'—*šarrūtu* 'kingship', *Enlil* 'the god Enlil', *enlilūtu* 'the power of Enlil'. In this way we see the archetype put into use.

Any other city which hoped to add the religious prestige of Nippur to its own aura of power would make use of imagery that originated there. As a relative late-comer in an early developing civilization, Babylon took its cue from that more ancient city. One of the titles and epithets bestowed on Marduk when he had built Babylon in the *Epic of Creation* was 'Gilimma who established the cosmic bond of the gods'. With allusive subtlety the title implies that Marduk has taken over the power of Enlil, and that the world's umbilical cord is now located also in his own city Babylon. Following the tradition established in Nippur, any great city such as Babylon, and eventually Nineveh and Nimrud, could lay claim to be the centre of the universe, but the claim was not exclusive.

The primeval traditions of Nippur were adopted and adapted in Assyria too. Ekur became used as a name for the temple of the Assyrian national god Ashur in his city Ashur.[14] Enlil's consort was Sumerian Ninlil, whose name in Assyrian, Mullissu—itself an esoteric play on the name of Enlil[15]—was a name for the consort of the god Ashur from quite early times, connecting with his title as 'the Assyrian Enlil'. The great hymn to Ishtar, found in her temple at Nineveh, calls her 'the one who holds the bond of the holy firmament'.[16] Not only Babylon, therefore, but also Assyria took various traditions of Nippur as a model to enhance their standing in the world. As we have seen, Sargon and Sennacherib adopted the term 'high garden' *kirimāhu* from the famous temple garden of Ninlil at Nippur, and the latter described Nineveh as the bond of sky and earth emanating from its patron goddess Ishtar, 'the city beloved of Ishtar in which all the ceremonies of gods and goddesses take place, the eternal base, the everlasting foundation whose plan was drawn in the writing of the firmament at the beginning of time'.

Any city claiming to contain the cord linking heaven and earth could reinforce the claim by using the god Anshar 'sky-sphere' as a kind of catalyst. In Assyria a syncretism between Ashur or Ishtar and Anshar was plausible because their names were so similar. Such a similarity was regarded as significant, an innate meaning that scholars could discover by applying their own cleverness.[17] The earliest spelling Anshar for Ashur is known from the 13th century BC, but became common during the reign of Sargon II. In his reign it is particularly significant because it is attested only in his inscriptions from Nimrud which he made his capital city while he was building Khorsabad. A hymn of Ashurbanipal to Ishtar of Nineveh makes the equation of Ishtar with Anshar clear: 'Just like Anshar she wears a beard and is clothed with brilliance!' despite the difference that she was a goddess and he a male god.[18] This association means that Anshar would have had an important shrine within her temple at Nineveh; and some writings of Ishtar's name imply that she too was regarded as a form of Anshar who symbolized the link, the point of attachment between heaven and earth, allowing the temple of Ishtar of Nineveh to claim that the sphere of heaven touched the sphere of earth there. Such subtle indications, expressed through minutiae of language and writing, are only beginning to emerge as more clay tablets are edited by treating different versions separately instead of listing variants as minor deviations from a supposedly fixed text: variation reveals the manipulators, reformers and modernizers at work.[19]

Following the sack of Babylon by Sennacherib, the New Year festival was not celebrated, as is stated laconically in the *Babylonian Akītu-Chronicle*:

For [8] years during (the reign of) Se[nnacherib], for 12 years (during the reign of) Esar[haddon]—20 years altogether—Bel (Marduk) stayed in Baltil (Ashur city) and the *akītu*-festival did not take place.[20]

Instead, the ritual was performed in Assyria. Quite overtly, an Assyrian version of part of the *Epic of Creation* used syncretism with Anshar to put an Assyrian deity, whether Ashur or Ishtar, as the hero-god in place of Babylon's patron god Marduk, making appropriate changes in the early genealogy of the primeval gods. At the culmination of the epic in its Babylonian version Marduk supervised the building of Babylon by the gods; but with Babylon out of the question and an Assyrian version with Marduk replaced by an Assyrian deity, the city name too must have been altered in the revised text. Presumably Ashur city took that role when Ashur was the hero-god, and Nineveh when Ishtar of Nineveh took the leading part. Written in the reign of Sennacherib, the small part of the Assyrian version that is extant shows that he made deliberate modifications to the composition as part of his policy to elevate Assyria to supreme status, using techniques that were already in use. Although the wording changed in those particulars, the myth was essentially the same and had the authority of past scholarship.[21]

The change was associated with the building in Nineveh of an *akītu*-house, a temple of the New Year festival, for Ishtar of Nineveh in her city.[22] In this instance the manipulation of a traditional text shows clearly a central plank in Sennacherib's policy of making Nineveh supersede Babylon. With his new version recited at the New Year festival in Nineveh, and with that adaptation reflected on the great bronze doors of his New Year festival temple at Ashur city, there was nothing surreptitious about his reform. It allowed Ashur to take the place of Marduk as Bēl 'Lord' at the city Ashur, and Ishtar of Nineveh to take the place of Marduk as Bēl 'Lord' at Nineveh. The change was visible to the public, not just embedded in text, and is no longer thought to indicate a short-lived or unsuccessful reform.[23]

A different kind of explanation, not linked directly to the reign of Sennacherib but pointing to a tradition that he would have known, comes from evidence that various Babylonian cities in southern Mesopotamia could be called 'Babylon'. It was an indigenous tradition dating from at least the 12th century BC, and perhaps even earlier. The first inkling came from several lexical texts—the dictionaries of ancient Babylonia—dated to that time or earlier. In two of them the city of Borsippa, which lies quite close to Babylon on the Euphrates, was called 'Babylon the second' or 'another Babylon'. Also, a lexical text which listed gates, temples and quarters of Babylon city gave the information that the city of Eridu, located near the sea in the far south of the country, was likewise a 'Babylon'.[24]

This phenomenon can be explained through a historical development. More than a millennium before Sennacherib lived, king Hammurabi of Babylon conquered powerful rivals and became master of the lands from the Arabian Gulf to the borders of Assyria. He was sixth in a dynasty that had been until then quite parochial, but nevertheless had succeeded in establishing a reasonably stable line of city rulers, whose patron god Marduk was hardly important beyond his city. Hammurabi's conquests, and his ambitious programme of law and education that accompanied them, enabled him to promote his city. Even before then he had associated his kingship with the oldest city, Eridu, by holding his coronation ceremony there. Either then or later in his reign he manipulated the theology of Babylon to assimilate Marduk with the god of Ku'ara, a city near

Eridu, in the deep south. This god was Asalluhi, a god of magic and of the powers of healing closely connected to magic in the world of that time. In this way a powerful new dimension was added to the character of Babylon's agricultural god. At that time or a little later, Babylon began to incorporate the gods of those cities into its own walls, by setting up branch temples. This move allowed the area of Babylon in which a branch temple stood to bear the name of the parent city, so that districts in Babylon were named 'Eridu', 'Ku'ara', and so on. In exchange the parent city might be called a 'Babylon'.

This strategy for promoting Babylon and securing the goodwill of older cities is particularly clear if we look at variation in the *Sumerian King-list*. A century or so before the lifetime of Hammurabi several rather different versions were composed. The aim was to show an unbroken line of kingship bestowed by the gods, securing legitimacy for the current ruler, so each version of the list was slanted towards a particular city. One version gives Eridu as the city which first received kingship from the gods, and another gives Ku'ara as the place to which kingship first descended from heaven. A third variant maintained that Babylon itself was the first city with a king.

Eridu, as a name for a district of Babylon, was the most sacred area which encompassed the great temple and ziggurat of Marduk. We do not know if this happened in Hammurabi's time, for our evidence comes from later in the second millennium. What is certain is that Babylon incorporated 'Eridu' and 'Ku'ara' into its innermost citadel area as districts bearing those city names. The great *Epic of Creation* refers to this tradition of incorporation in the portentous declaration of Marduk, whose words celebrate the building of Babylon as the first city to be built, following the defeat of chaos:

> The Lord invited the gods his fathers to attend a banquet,
> In the great sanctuary which he had created as his dwelling.
> 'Indeed, Bab-ili ("gate of gods") is your home too!
> Sing for joy there, dwell in happiness!'

Eridu and Ku'ara are not the only two city-names that were given to districts in the heart of Babylon city. Another is Kullab, the name of a part of Uruk, ruled by the legendary hero-king Gilgamesh. In the case of Uruk, we know for certain that cultic rituals appropriate to that city were replicated in Babylon.

From a lexical text and from variants of a king-list, as well as the names of areas within the city, it is certain that Babylon enfolded those other great cities: Borsippa, Eridu, Ku'ara, and Kullab-Uruk. The declaration spoken by Marduk in the *Epic of Creation* had a solid basis in the temples and rituals of Babylon, to which the names of its districts refer. This situation was a source of ambiguity which occasionally needed to be clarified by special emphasis in expressions of Babylonian kings: 'The land of Babylon which is within Babylon', and 'the land of Kumar (Ku'ara) which is within Babylon'.

An example of a name given to more than one city as a result of reforms comes from Egypt. Several centuries earlier than the time of Sennacherib, it dates from the New Kingdom, and is linked to the changes made in the time of Akhenaten when not only the city he built at Amarna, but also Thebes and probably Memphis too, were referred to in the same period as 'Horizon of the Aten'.[25] This was an epithet that did not replace the traditional name of each city. As a deliberate act, the naming would have given a sense of cohesion to an even more extenuated kingdom than that of Assyria and Babylonia. By analogy we may suggest that 'gate of gods' *bab-ilī* was an epithet for certain cities in Babylonia and Assyria, although there is no direct evidence for its use in any Assyrian inscriptions from the time of Sargon and Sennacherib onwards.

Unexpectedly specific evidence that a 'Babylon' was located in Assyria came to light very much later, from medieval texts on astronomy. An astronomer named Azarqiel,[26] working around AD 1070, incorporated much older information into the 'Toledo tables'. His text referred explicitly to ancient observations taken from Mesopotamian astronomical data, supposedly still available in the Middle Ages, giving a standard figure for the longest day of the year, claiming it came from 'Old Babylon'. Such a figure is specific to the latitude on which the observations were originally taken, and it is demonstrably not that of Babylon but somewhere in Assyria, in the vicinity of Nineveh. The records showed that three sets of observations attributed to Old Babylon, 'Other/Second Babylon', and 'New Babylon' respectively, were made on different latitudes. 36.06 degrees for 'Old Babylon' suits Nimrud, 33.04, 32.32 and 32.04 for 'Other/Second Babylon' suit Sippar, Babylon and Borsippa respectively, 31.18 and 30.56 for 'New Babylon' suit Uruk and Ur respectively.[27]

Cuneiform sources showed that Azarqiel's information could be correct. However enticing this may be, it has its weaknesses. An exact match for Nineveh is not found there, neither for Nineveh nor for Babylon. Promising though these latitude-linked observations are, the gap in time between the earliest mention of the Hanging Garden in the 2nd century BC and the Toledo tables of the 11th century AD was a huge one, and one could argue that the observations were attributed spuriously to Babylon to give them the authority of great antiquity, and that the latitudes were either coincidental or faked.

As for the confusion of rivers: in Babylonia it was relatively easy to confuse the Tigris and Euphrates because they had many branches, and were linked by an extensive network of canals bringing slow-moving water across flat and featureless land. To an Ionian, a Greek or a Hebrew for whom swift, separate rivers between hills or moun-tain ranges were normal, the terrain would have been quite alien. But in the north of the country, where Nineveh lay on the Tigris, irriga-tion canals are not part of the scenery, and the Tigris is easy to distinguish. Since the two regions are so different, it is almost certain that Herodotus made reference to the channelling that leads from Bavian through Jerwan to Nineveh when he described the changes that 'Nitocris' made to turn a straight watercourse into a winding one which passed an Assyrian village three times. He misleadingly attrib-uted it to 'Babylon',[28] as described above, just as Diodorus Siculus wrote that Ninus founded on the Euphrates (not the Tigris) the city to which he gave his own name, Nineveh.[29] It was the confusion of naming Nineveh as a Babylon that caused the confusion between the two rivers.

Why should more than one queen be called a Semiramis, in addition to her own name? The answer to the question lies, as with confusion in naming kings, in the concept of the archetype, repre-sented by that Sumerian word *me*. Queenship, like kingship, was a concept represented by insignia, an ordinance sent to mankind from heaven. The name of a very famous example of a historical queen came to be identified with the archetype, and could be used for later famous queens, as we have seen for Nebuchadnezzar. An accretion of legends is attached to the name 'Semiramis' in Greek texts, and the use of the name for more than one woman can be explained through that concept. She was variously credited with leading campaigns with her husband 'Ninus', and with building works in Babylon, among them the famous Hanging Garden: Diodorus Siculus wrote that she founded a large city in Babylonia on the Euphrates including the temple of the Babylonian Zeus and the Hanging Garden (he does not actually name the city), and Quintus Curtius Rufus wrote that Se-miramis, not Bel, founded Babylon.

The original 'Semiramis' was a historical queen at a time when Nimrud, not Nineveh, was the main royal residence. If you were an Assyrian early in the 8th century BC you would have known about Sammu-ramat, daughter-in-law of Shalmaneser III, wife of Shamshi-Adad V, and mother of Adad-nirari III, because she was the most powerful woman in the world of that time. You would know that she in person, contrary to the custom of queens at that time, joined her son in a campaign to Arpad in the vicinity of modern Aleppo with the result that her own name was inscribed on a royal stela, as partner in heroism with her son the king. That stela was set up on the border of Assyrian territory on the upper Euphrates, and was discovered in recent times.

Boundary stone of Adad-nirari, king of Assyria, son of Shamshi-Adad king of Assyria (and of) Sammu-ramat, the palace woman of Shamshi-Adad king of Assyria, mother of Adad-nirari, strong king, king of Assyria, daughter-in-law of Shalmaneser, king of the four quarters.

When Ushpilulume king of Kummuh (Commagene) incited Adad-nirari king of Assyria, and Sammu-ramat the palace woman, to cross the Euphrates, I fought a pitched battle with them: Atar-shumki son of Adramu from Arpad, together with 8 kings who were with him, at Paqarahubunu. I robbed them of their camp. To save their lives they dispersed.

In that year this boundary stone was erected between Ushpilulume king of Kummuh and Qalparunda son of Palalam king of Gurgum.[30]

The term 'palace woman' meant 'queen, official consort' at that period because the word normally translated as 'queen' was reserved for goddesses. The inscription shows without a doubt that Sammu-ramat campaigned with her son, which suggests that the campaigns later ascribed to Semiramis by Ctesias and others may have had some link, however tenuous or garbled, with a genuine event.

The extent of her fame during her lifetime is confirmed by the existence of another stela, inscribed only with her name and titles, found during excavations in the city of Ashur on the Tigris, and first published in 1913:

Statue[31] of Sammu-ramat the palace woman of Shamshi-Adad king of the universe, king of Assyria, mother of Adad-nirari, king of the universe, king of Assyria, daughter-in-law of Shalmaneser, king of the four quarters.[32]

The stela lacks any kind of human image. It stood in a forest of similar stelae, in a space between two city walls, perhaps as a result of clearing out a temple in much later times; the other stelae bore the names of kings and high male officials.

Sammu-ramat is also named alongside her son in a dedicatory inscription for a new temple to the god Nabu, composed by the governor of Nimrud (ancient Calah).[33] The text was written on a pair of life-size statues of divine attendants which were found in their original positions in the temple of Nabu:

To the god Nabu, heroic, exalted son of Esagil, wise, splendid, mighty prince, heir of Nudimmud, whose command is supreme, skilled in the arts, trustee of all heaven and earth, expert in everything, wise, holder of the tablet stylus, learned in scribal art, merciful, judicious, who has the power to depopulate and resettle, beloved of Enlil lord of lords, whose might has no rival, without whom there can be no order in heaven, the merciful, compassionate, whose benevolence is good, dweller in Ezida, which is within Calah, great lord, his lord: For the life of Adad-nirari king of Assyria his lord, and the life of Sammu-ramat the palace woman his lady, Bel-tarṣi-iluma the governor of Calah . . . had (this statue) made and dedicated for his lengthy life, that his days might be long, his years many . . .

This inscription and the two statues mark the promotion of a major Babylonian god in the heart of Assyria. They were still standing there when the temple was used during the Hellenistic period.[34]

The epithet 'son of Esagil' links Nabu directly to Marduk whose temple in Babylon was called Esagil. At that time the kings of Assyria were on good terms with the kings of Babylon, a cordial relationship epitomized by a scene sculptured on a throne-base,[35] showing Shalmaneser III clasping hands with the contemporary king of Babylon (see Plate 14). Therefore the historical Sammu-ramat would not have been involved in building work in Babylon.

Those monuments recording the exceptional fame of Sammu-ramat are the ones that we know of; there may have been others. Long after her death, traces of her presence would still have been visible, even if the literacy required to read the cuneiform inscriptions was no longer available. Nimrud is the site where the memory of the great queen would have taken root, for Nineveh had not yet become the capital city; and the temple of Nabu at Nimrud was the main focus for memory, not least because of the statues that remained there until modern times. The 'roughly carved limestone altar' erected in one of its courts; 'a considerable succession of potsherds' found in another court, 'the latest of which are Hellenistic';[36] and fine pottery beakers imitating the late Assyrian palace ware in the same building, show that the building had not been abandoned; its residents would have seen the statues every day. In this way the archaeological evidence supports the inference that legends based on the real Semiramis survived into Seleucid times.[37]

In at least one of several 'universal' histories of Hellenistic times, written in Greek, the history of empires began with Ninus and Semiramis, and it was Semiramis who conquered the first world empire alongside her consort, the eponymous founder of Nineveh.[38] Hers was an empire that was to endure, according to the understanding of those historians, for 1,300 years. For that reason Alexander the Great was inspired 'with a wish to rival Cyrus and Semiramis',[39] the first great empire-builders,[40] for her fame outlived the downfall of Assyria and the following centuries of neo-Babylonian and Achaemenid rule.

The name Sammu-ramat in the form Semiramis—by which the Greeks knew her—was used also for later historical Assyrian queens of great repute, causing much confusion among Greek historians who tried to trace the history of Assyria at a time when stories had already merged.[41] The most significant of the great queens lived about a century later—Naqia the wife of Sennacherib, mother of Esarhaddon, and grandmother of Ashurbanipal and Shamash-shum-ukin who became kings of Assyria and Babylonia respectively. Naqia recorded her own building of a new palace at Nineveh for her son;[42] and at Nimrud she made sacrifices in the temple of Nabu founded by her predecessor Sammu-ramat, where she associated herself with the historical queen in dedicating a statue of herself, decorated with gold. She placed it in close proximity to the inscription of Sammu-ramat, which would have been a century old at that time.[43] She contributed publicly to the restoration of the great temple to Nabu in Borsippa near Babylon, supplying gold for making a crown for the god's statue.[44] Thus she was associated with acts normally acknowledged as deeds of the king alone. She owned estates east of the Tigris, on the border with Babylonia, in her own name.[45] She made public donations for work on temples in Harran, and is known from a bronze sculpture in low relief to have shown herself as a public figure with her royal son (or grandson)—perhaps the 'bronze likeness of Ninus and Semiramis and their officers' which Diodorus says graced the palace walls (see Plate 15).[46] The panel has an inscription engraved on it identifying her, and may well be the very work of art that lies behind his account.[47] Such panels may be the kind of relic of past glory that evokes new stories, reinterpreting antiquities in the visible landscape to create new versions for local tradition.

Naqia was closely associated with Nineveh because her husband built two palaces there and made the city his capital. Many letters were written directly to her, or mention her, and we have a document recording the loyalty oaths that she imposed on members of her family, requiring them to support her two royal grandsons. Another text particularly relevant here is that which records the building work she undertook at Nineveh on behalf of her son Esarhaddon, who ruled vast territories including Babylonia. The introduction to the inscription puts her at the head of the text where the name of the king would normally be found.

Naqia, the palace woman of Sennacherib king of the universe, king of Assyria, daughter-in-law of Sargon king of the universe king of Assyria, mother of Esarhaddon king of the world, king of Assyria . . . a palace befitting royalty for Esarhaddon my beloved son . . . [48]

Here, then, we have a group of material that indicates attachment of Naqia's deeds to the name 'Semiramis'. As second wife of Sennacherib, she bears comparison with the historical Sammu-ramat for having her name on inscriptions written during her lifetime, and for supporting publicly first her husband and then her son, both as kings. There was every reason, therefore, to conflate the two great queens, two great builders. Naqia would be the wife of the later Assyrian king to whom Diodorus referred when he wrote: ' . . . the Hanging Garden, as it is called, which was built, not by Semiramis, but by a later Syrian king . . . ' His account that 'Semiramis' alongside a Ninus founded 'Babylon' on the Euphrates gives details that are applicable to Nineveh: two palaces, technical details of water supply, walls adorned with hunting scenes.

Another archetypal 'Semiramis' is Stratonice. Like the original Sammu-ramat and like Naqia, Stratonice was the wife of a king, Seleucus I, and continued her rise to fame when she was then transferred as wife to his son Antiochus I 'Soter'. Her own name is publicly joined with that of Antiochus on the cylinder inscription from Borsippa, recording rebuilding work on the great temple Ezida dedicated to the god Nabu—Naqia had also been involved in refurbishment there, some four centuries earlier—and referring also to building work in Babylon (see Figure 36).[49] She rebuilt the temple of

Fig. 36 Cylinder inscription of Antiochus and Stratonice recording the restoration of the temple of Nabu in Borsippa near Babylon. Length 19.1 cm.

Fig. 37 (a) Panel showing Semiramis with Gordis, labelled as legendary founders of Aphrodisias–Nineveh-on-Meander, SW Turkey, from the Late Roman basilica. Ht. 99 cm, length 235 cm.

Fig. 37 (b) Showing Ninos as a founding father of Aphrodisias–Nineveh. Ht. 98 cm, length 229 cm.

Atargatis in Hierapolis (Membidj in North Syria) which had previously been built or restored by 'Semiramis'.[50] Whether Stratonice and Antiochus played a role in the revival of Nimrud and Nineveh is not known. But Roman citizens at Aphrodisias on the Meander had 'Ninos and Semiramis' sculpted in stone, labelled and displayed among the legendary founding fathers; and that city even took the name Nineveh for a while.[51] Ninos and Semiramis were the first rulers in the *World History* written by the Roman writer Pompeius Trogus, so the original Nineveh and its namesake at Aphrodisias could lay claim to being the first great cities in the civilized world (see Figure 37).

Heroes and heroines of the past were positive or negative models for behaviour. The use of Semiramis' name shows how particularly outstanding queens were transformed into heroines of the distant past. Traces of her fame were still visible in late antiquity.

The evidence falls short of proving that Nineveh was called Babylon at the time when the Hanging Garden was built. But a strong case can be made for Sennacherib's distinctive reforms to make Nineveh into a city that superseded the original Babylon, showing the traditions on which he drew in order to make the new regime acceptable. Taking each one of the confusions, it is possible to explain why Sennacherib was mistaken for Nebuchadnezzar, why Nineveh became known as a Babylon, why the Euphrates was mistaken for the Tigris, and why Semiramis was credited with building Babylon and the Hanging Garden.

7

The Unrivalled Palace, the Queen and the Garden

> And blest is he, who tir'd with his affairs
> Far from all noise, all vain applause, prepares
> To go, and underneath some silent shade,
> Which neither cares nor anxious thoughts invade,
> Do's, for a while, himself alone possess
>
> René Rapin (1621–87), *Of Gardens*[1]

Sargon's wide-ranging interests extended beyond the chief preoccupations of Mesopotamian rulers in conquest and building, and he inspired his son Sennacherib with his enthusiasm (see Figure 38). Just to take one example, Sargon took a personal interest in the mining and smelting of minerals from a new source in the mountains of Syria. It was unusual for a king to record such a particular interest in his public inscriptions, but he was not restrained by lack of precedence, and wrote:

At that time, during my reign, they brought to me hidden treasures of the mountains of northern Syria, and I heaped them up as possessions: refined minerals fit for a palace (from) Mt. Laris'u, Mt. Shuruman; the creation of the god Nudimmud, shining bronze,[2] was created in Mt. Tushanira and Mt. Elikudurini; iron of Mt. Lammun (located) in between [. . .], lead which brightens their dullness he revealed (to me); pure alabaster from Mt. Ammun . . . choice multicoloured stone, fit for royalty, . . . mountain of Baʿal-Ṣapuna the great mountain,[3] bronze together he created, and I mixed the heaped ores of those mountains, and I put them in the furnace and watched them heating.[4]

Fig. 38 Sargon II with his son Sennacherib.

In Sargon's official letters too we find references to the energy he devoted to metalwork when planning his new palace at Khorsabad (which is the modern name of the site). Around 717 BC his treasurer wrote:

As to what the king, my lord, wrote to me: 'When are they going to cast the gateway column-bases for the portico of the *hilāni*-palace?'[5] I have asked Ashur-shumu-ke'in and the craftsmen, who told me: 'We are going to cast four column-bases of bronze for two *hilāni*-palaces in the 8th month; the small lions for the *hilānis* will be cast together with the large lions in the Spring.'[6]

Many grand rooms in that palace were lined with stone panels on which scenes of war and peace were sculpted with far more grace and beauty than those of his father Tiglath-pileser.[7] Unlike earlier Assyrian monarchs, he used light-coloured limestone alongside black marble to great effect both internally and externally. This was one of several striking innovations in the architecture of Khorsabad, for which the inspiration came from palaces he had seen in Syria, where alternating black basalt and white stone panels had long been fashionable. But Sargon's panels were much larger and better carved, and the rooms they enhanced were bigger. Owing to limitation in the length of roof-beams, rooms were characteristically quite narrow but long, providing plenty of wall-space for the creative artist. Colossal animals in stone were recovered in excavations, mainly from doorways, but none of his bronze-cast figures survived, so they are known only from texts.

Sargon chose a virgin site for his new capital city, situated unusually far from the river Tigris. Built upon land which the king purchased legally at the market rate (as he took care to record for posterity),[8] it lay to the north-east of Nineveh where water fresh from mountain springs could be channelled directly to the city. To display his mastery over nature in this respect, he built a garden with an artificial wooded hill and a lake for boating from a charming pavilion-like boat-house. It was his declared aim to imitate a beauty-spot in the Amanus mountains of northern Syria with shade, fragrance and flowing water.[9] Where this delightful 'high garden' (*kirimāhu*) was located is still uncertain, but it was certainly visible from the great palace and easily accessible to the king. He named his new city Dur-Sharrukin, 'Sargon's Fort', and called his new palace 'Unrivalled Palace', the epithet revealing his ambition to reach a pinnacle of fame as a brilliant builder. Although the palace is described in texts as an ideal building, and the garden is shown finished and mature, neither was likely to have been completed before Sargon's unexpected death in 704 BC, so we may envisage the king and his son sharing the excitement of planning and constructing a whole new city while standing amid the dust and noise of building works. On his sculptures Sargon showed scenes from the building of his city and its garden.

Both enterprises would have had a formative influence upon the taste and interests of his son. Sargon was generous to his family, and built a great residence for his brother, Sin-ahu-uṣur. This man was the grand vizier who had accompanied him on his successful eighth campaign against Urartu, a triumph culminating in the sack of a wealthy city.[10] Included in the loot were many large animals cast in bronze.

Such was the father whose influence on Sennacherib was deep: a generous man, wide-ranging, fascinated by the challenges and innovations of technology, in particular in metallurgy, keen to promote fashion, and proud to express his enthusiasm in public inscriptions.

Early in his own reign Sennacherib embarked on a huge project at Nineveh: to build a fabulous palace, which we now know as the South-West Palace, and, beside it, an extraordinary garden (see Figures 39, 41). We have many details of the work because he described the craftsmanship that went into it in his long prism inscriptions, and because quite a large part of his palace has been excavated.

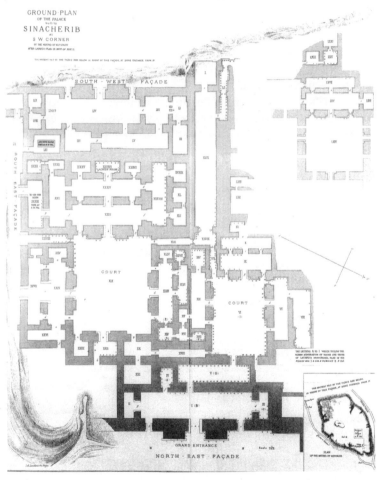

Fig. 39 Plan of part of Sennacherib's South-West Palace at Nineveh, as excavated by the end of the 19th century. Defensive main gates, internal courtyards and long rooms are characteristic.

Even better, the description of the garden has its visual counterpart in the sculpture designed later for his grandson Ashurbanipal.[11] Peacetime achievements were at least as important as conquests in demonstrating the power and wealth of the king, and Sennacherib manifested his power on a stupendous scale.

The palace was built high up on the northern citadel of Nineveh, in the south-west part of the citadel mound, and so was called the South-West Palace by the first European excavators (see Figure 40). The terrace on which it stood was built of brick, about 24 m high, so the palace looked down at the junction of the Khosr river with the Tigris. Inscriptions, written on clay prisms hidden within its walls, revealed that the Assyrians knew it as the Unrivalled Palace, named exactly as the new palace which Sennacherib's father Sargon had built at Khorsabad. Together with its garden Sennacherib declared it 'a wonder for all peoples'. Only a small proportion has been uncovered, but the original whole probably measured around 242 m wide and about twice as much in length, with an eastern extension adding perhaps another 100 m.[12] On two sides the palace lay close to the massive walls of the citadel, and it is likely that there were upper

Fig. 40 Aerial photo of Nineveh taken in 1932, showing the citadel mound Kuyunjik and the bed of the river Khosr winding beside it.

storeys looking out over the walls. The building was raised up on a huge platform of solid brickwork, allowing spacious paved terraces outside. On the ground floor the walls were up to 7 m thick, so the potential exists for several upper storeys. From the roof, views would have stretched over to the Tigris to the west, across the Khosr river and adjacent second citadel to the south-east. One might look across to the Hanging Garden on the north-eastern side (if the suggestion for its exact location is correct), and northwards to the great temple and ziggurat of Ishtar of Nineveh rising above the roof-tops of other buildings on the citadel (see Figures 41, 34b).

Sennacherib described how this palace replaced a smaller, much older one:

At that time I enlarged the settlement of Nineveh greatly. I had renovation work carried out upon the outer and inner walls, . . . and made them moun-tain-high. As for the open land outside the city walls, which had become desolate for lack of water and were festooned with spiders' webs—for the people there had no knowledge of irrigation and relied upon rain that fell by chance from the sky—I provided it with irrigation. The previous palace was 360 cubits long and 95 cubits wide, and so its accommodation was too meagre . . . I pulled it down in its entirety. I diverted the flood-prone river from the city centre, and directed its outflow into the land that surrounds the city at the back. On half an acre beside the water-course I bonded four layers of great limestone blocks with bitumen, and laid reeds from reed-beds and canes over them. I gained extra land from the Khosr river and the outskirts of the city, a stretch of ground 340 cubits long and 289 cubits wide. I added it to the bulk of the earlier terrace and raised the top to a level of 190 courses all over. To prevent the foundation of the terrace weakening due to the strength of the current as time went by, I surrounded its substructure with large blocks of limestone, and so I strengthened its earthwork.[13]

Less than twelve years elapsed during which the building work was planned, and carried out, using thousands of foreign captives as the labour force, assembling clay and chopped straw for making the bricks and plaster, and laying them in position. Huge timbers were brought from mountain-sides far away for the construction of ceil-ings, roofs and doors. For threshold slabs and other ornamental masonry the king took a personal interest in stone-quarrying, first finding new sources of supply, and then transporting back to Nineveh the colossal slabs needed.

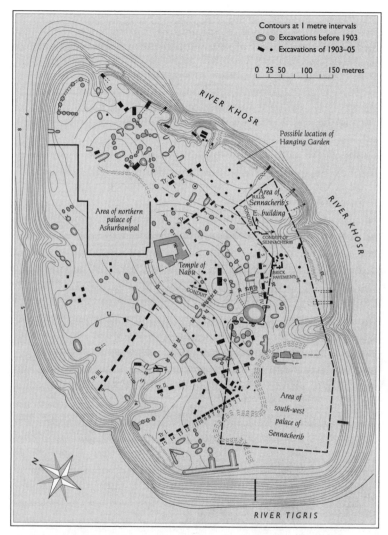

Fig. 41 Sketch map of the citadel mound at Nineveh, to show possible location of the garden next to the palace.

At that time Ashur and Ishtar who love my priesthood and named my name revealed to me the place where gigantic cedars grow, such as have been growing since ancient times and have become quite massive, standing in secret within the mountains of Sirara. They opened up to me access to alabaster, which was prized for dagger pommels in the days of the kings my forefathers . . . Near to Nineveh, in the region of Balatay, white limestone was revealed in large quantities in accordance with the gods' will, and I created great winged bull-colossi and other limbed figures of alabaster, made out of a single block of stone, perfectly proportioned, standing tall on their own bases.[14]

Erosion from weather and surface activity, and looting, whether for second-hand building materials or as works of art, have taken a devastating toll on the most magnificent palace of early antiquity. But marvellous sculptured stone panels survived in some of the rooms, great winged bull-colossi with human heads still stood at many of the doorways when the first excavators arrived, and carved stone thresholds gave extra magnificence to the entrances.[15]

Entering through the grand main portal, the visitor passed between two colossi which reached to the imposing height of 7 m, and weighed between 40 and 50 tons. Those composite creatures marked a transition from the ordinary world to a place of reverence for divine authority, impressing upon the visitor that the royal residence was the home of no ordinary mortal. Huge double doors of fragrant timber were mounted on a pair of gigantic posts each of which pivoted in a well-oiled stone socket. They had elaborate bolts, and were decorated with bronze bands showing scenes of the king's glories. The great thresholds, decorated with a geometric, floral pattern of lotus, palmette and rosette, imitating a carpet, would have been cast, or plated with silver or bronze (see Figure 42).

Fig. 42 Pattern carved on a stone threshold slab from the South-West Palace. Compare the pebble mosaic shown on Plate 6.

Passing through into the great throne-room, one viewed the magnificent sculptured panels lining the walls. They were originally painted in colours of which only faint traces of red and black remain. A few details of the design probably gleamed with gold leaf. Essentially the scenes shown in that room depicted the king's main successes in extending areas under Assyrian control, presented on horizontal registers of low relief. But Sennacherib improved on the artistic conventions of his predecessors, showing details of landscape background so as to give a sense of perspective to subsidiary figures and to turn the bare narrative into fuller pictures of lifelike events. Often actions were shown almost in cartoon form, with, for example, the march towards an enemy city shown on the left of a long series of panels, the siege of the city shown at the centre, and the subsequent procession of tribute and prisoners shown on the right. The king, who in earlier times was usually depicted in the heat of battle enacting a deed of bravery and triumph, was now shown in a more peaceful and benevolent role, receiving homage on the battlefield (see Figure 43). This change is so marked that it can be interpreted as showing a change of policy, persuading the dignitaries who viewed the scene that Assyrian power was not simply inevitable domination but also one of beneficial control. Another change of style is noticeable: whereas former kings had inscribed their deeds, engraved across the

Fig. 43 Sennacherib presiding over the capture of Lachish, south of Jerusalem, detail. His face was chiselled out deliberately after the fall of Assyria. Max. Ht. 178 cm.

narrative scenes in cuneiform, Sennacherib initiated a new tradition of neat captions, briefly recording the place and event without reference to the gods or to his own heroism. The long accounts of his campaigns and building works he restricted to the stone bull-colossi, and to clay prisms and cylinders which were put inside the palace walls for the instruction of posterity.

Some of the symbolism embodied in these sculptures can be inferred. The use of horizontal registers and captions, reminiscent of cylinder seal design, implies the stamp of legal authority, the imposition of law and order which was one of the great benefits of Assyrian rule. The throne-room sculptures show seven different campaigns successfully conducted in different parts of the empire, symbolizing Sennacherib's right to the top title, claimed no sooner than his eighth year, namely 'king of the world'.[16] As we have seen, the word for 'world', *kiššatu*, was equated with seven, the significant number which represented completion to the Assyrians. The winged bull-colossi represented the aeons of time when creation was still young and the forms of living things had not yet settled into their modern species; when unusual combinations including the scorpion-man, the fish-man, the bull-headed man and the man-headed bull still roamed the earth until they were subdued by a later generation of gods in human form, and were sentenced to serve them. At the entrances to royal suites within the palace they are a reminder that the king lived apart from lower beings as if in another realm where he and his family were guarded by fantastic creatures from the past. Those creatures, after their subjugation, were designated by the great gods to protect the forces of justice and order.

In other rooms Sennacherib was keen to record his innovations in architecture and garden planning. His artists composed scenes which broke free from the monotony of severely horizontal registers, showing how huge stone slabs were dragged from quarries for new buildings, and they displayed in great detail the labours of his workforce. Just as important as the depiction of triumph in war, the sculptures of building works and the garden show his pride as patron of the arts, brilliantly devising departures from tradition in which a focal point, such as the siege of Lachish in Palestine, transformed the field to give a complex, triangular arrangement, allowing the action to take up the whole surface of the stone from top to bottom (see Figure 44). Some changes from earlier tradition suggest insights into Sennacherib's own character. Unlike his father and his grandson, he seems not to

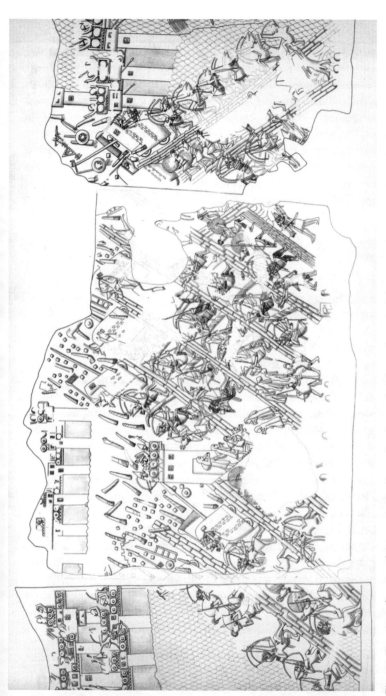

Fig. 44 Drawing showing the innovative triangular design for the sculpture of the siege when Sennacherib captured Lachish. Length of central panel 190.5 cm.

have taken a part in hunting, although it is possible that there are hunting scenes in parts of the palace that have not been excavated.

The royal throne took the form of a high-backed chair with lion's claw feet, decorated with panels of carved ivory on which the motifs signified divine support for the king's reign. The ivories were coloured with inlays of enamel-like coloured glass and with gold leaf.[17] A footstool matched the throne in its design, and both were raised upon a carved stone throne-base which had scenes of royal triumphs around the side, and a floral or geometric pattern on the top, perhaps plated with silver like the threshold slabs. The remains of Sennacherib's throne were discovered by George Smith:

There was part of a crystal[18] throne, a most magnificent article of furniture, in too mutilated condition to copy, but as far as it is preserved closely resembling in shape the bronze one discovered by Mr. Layard at Nimrud.[19]

Over the throne was erected a canopy, a baldachin hung with fabulous textiles, embroidery and tassels. Some of the wall sculptures show details of the king's clothing, clearly elaborate and heavy, but details of workmanship and colour can only be guessed at, for the textiles themselves are never preserved. We know that there were knotted carpets at this time, from evidence of a much earlier period.[20] Tiny coloured glass beads were sewn in patterns on to leather and textiles, especially favoured for ceremonial occasions, shining and resistant to rain and dust, and the man in charge of such work was a top courtier.[21] Another decorative use of glass took the form of very thin rectangular plaques, each roughly 4.2 × 3.5 cm, with a slightly concave surface painted with Phoenician-style sphinxes, or a tree-of-life, or a winged figure. The transparency of the glass would have produced the effect of a shining, multicoloured surface, with some addition of gold leaf.[22]

Glass inlays, beaded fabrics and leather, glass plaques and glazed brick panels, all had the advantage of staying clean, colourful and bright in a dusty place, but only the most miserable fragments have been found to give us a glimpse of former glory.

Rich in symbolism and magic properties, various types of stone were used purposefully in different parts of the palace. Two texts illustrate this, the first of which refers directly to the palace:

Fossiliferous limestone, . . . a charm-stone efficacious for winning acceptance (from the gods) when speaking, for making bad weather pass by (without damage), and for keeping diseases from attacking a person . . . breccia, which looks like dragonflies' wings (i.e. with iridescent inclusions), efficacious for

1. View from Nebuchadnezzar's Summer Palace at Babylon, 1967.

2. The Negoub tunnel, made in the 9th century BC, part of an extensive scheme to bring water from the Upper Zab river to Nimrud, ancient Calah.

3. The Chicago prism of Sennacherib, giving a detailed account of how he created his palace garden. Ht. 38cm.

4. Chamaerops humilis, a type of palm tree, showing where fronds have dropped off leaving a spiral pattern of scars on the trunk. The same pattern is found on other types of palm.

5. Andrew Lacey's casting of a mini-screw in bronze, for the BBC documentary *Secrets of the Ancients*.

6. Wooden full-size screw under construction for the BBC documentary.

7. The wooden screws set up over cisterns for the BBC documentary *Secrets of the Ancients.*

8. Pebble mosaic floor from the courtyard of an Assyrian provincial palace preserved at Tushhan, modern Ziyaret Tepe. Similar designs are carved on palace thresholds of limestone.

9. The river at Khinnis where diversion and control of water began, directed towards the garden at Nineveh looking upstream.

10. Looking downstream at Khinnis.

11. Large panel of sculpture on a rock face at Khinnis, showing Sennacherib facing the great deities.

12. Ruins of the stone aqueduct at Jerwan, where diverted water in a canal crossed a wide valley.

13.
The sculptured
block of rock
at the weir at
Khinnis.

14. Shalmaneser III clasps hands with the king of Babylon on the front panel of the throne-base at Fort Shalmaneser, Nimrud. Assyria and Babylon were on good terms in the time of Sammu-ramat.

15. Cast bronze panel showing Sennacherib's widow Naqia with her son or grandson, from Hilleh near Babylon. Ht. 33 cm, W. 31 cm.

16. Gossypium arboreum, and Gossypium herbaceum, the cotton-bearing tree and its shrub form.

17. Statue of Heracles Epitrapezios 'sitting on a table', found in the South-West Palace at Nineveh. Ht. 54 cm.

assuaging throbbing in the brow, and which brings joy of heart and happiness of mind as a charm-stone . . . *girimhilibû*-stone, beautiful and pleasing to behold, and with the ability to prevent plagues infecting a person . . . [23]

The other text was inscribed on horse-troughs made by Sennacherib and found at Nineveh:

Horse-troughs of white limestone which will not deteriorate in times to come: I had them made, and I filled the area in front of these horse-troughs, to go beneath my horses' hooves, with pieces of agate, banded agate and onyx, including chippings from precious stones, of jasper, breccia, . . . fossiliferous limestone, *alallum*-stone, *girimhilibû*-stone, *engisu*-stone, alabaster, *sabu*-stone, *haltu*-stone, trimmings from the steps of my palace.[24]

From this extraordinary text we learn that the steps of Sennacherib's palace were made with many different semi-precious stones, probably inlaid (as they were in contemporary Urartian palaces), reminiscent of a description in the Hebrew Book of Esther: 'a pavement of red and blue and white and black marble.'[25] Some of the great internal courtyards were carefully paved; in provincial palaces there was a fashion for patterned flooring using black and white river pebbles. The choice of materials was made not just on aesthetic grounds, but to ensure the health of the king and his family was protected. Where vents or air ducts came down into rooms, a panel of bas-relief showing a protective demonic demigod would be placed purposefully to prevent evil forces making an unauthorized entry (see Figure 45).

Fig. 45 Demonic gods who guarded palace entrances, windows, and airshafts from snakes, sneak-thieves, and sicknesses.

Occasionally the excavators of Nineveh have found stone pedestals for sculptures of stone or bronze, or for columns of timber that would have been overlaid with bronze. The statues have almost all gone; but Sennacherib was proud of their lifelike quality and their personal charm: '22 colossal female sphinxes invested with joyous allure, plentifully endowed with sexual attraction' which he cast, some in bronze and coated with electrum, others in a special alloy with a high tin content so that they would have a very shiny surface. His description reminds us of the legendary Pygmalion, king of Cyprus, who fell in love with the statue of a woman which then came to life and bore him a child, or the tale of the lover who left a stain on the thigh of Aphrodite of Cnidos, sculpted by the incomparable Praxiteles. Those attractive sphinxes were probably restricted to the private wings designed for Sennacherib's immediate family, recognizable as groups of chambers forming an architectural unit within the overall building, each unit within the whole building being referred to as a palace, which gives a certain ambiguity to parts of his inscription. In Sennacherib's own words:

I increased the outline of the palace to 700 large cubits at the side, and 440 large cubits at the front, and enlarged its dwelling space. I built other palatial pavilions of gold, silver, bronze, carnelian breccia, alabaster, elephant tusk, ebony, boxwood, rosewood, cedar, cypress, pine, *elammaku*-wood, and Indian wood (sandalwood?) for my royal abodes, and I constructed 'a building with a pillared portico' (*bīt hilāni*) like a North Syrian palace, opposite the gates. I laid over it beams of cedar and cypress whose fragrance is sweet, grown on the mountains of Amanus and Sirara. I bound door-leaves of cedar, cypress, pine and Indian wood with bands of silver and copper, and fix(ed) them in the door-frames. In the upper rooms within the private apartments I open(ed) up latticed (?) windows. I placed feminine protective statues in their doors, fashioned from alabaster and ivory, carrying flowers and holding hands (?), they radiate poise and charm, they are so beautiful that I have made of them a wonder. As for the ceilings inside the main rooms (?), I lightened their darkness and made them as bright as day. I made silver and copper pegs with knobs encircle their interiors. I decorated with baked brick glazed with blue the arches (?), friezes, and all of their cornices (?), in order to make the work in my palace splendid, and to perfect the touch of my hands.

In building a *bīt hilāni* type of palace, Sennacherib once again followed his father's lead. The architectural feature that Assyrian kings admired during their expeditions to the Amanus mountains in North Syria was one characterized by a pillared portico leading into a wide entrance hall.[26] This type of entrance connects the outer landscape with the interior of the building, in sharp contrast to the traditional Mesopotamian palace with its forbidding exterior, and its internal courtyard gardens secluded from the outside world. Sennacherib's South-West Palace is thought to have had that type of entrance, with pillars resting on lions cast in bronze. The entrance, perhaps set out as a terrace, presumably faced the famous garden, so as to give a direct connection between the royal palace and the royal garden, as if the palace was a villa out in the countryside (see Figure 46).[27]

The pillars were marvellous too. From inscriptions of Sargon we know that eight colossal lions, cast in bright copper, each weighing some 17 tons, guarded in pairs the entrance to his palace doors.[28] They served as bases for pillars, as shown on a panel of sculpture. If there was an upper storey, a staircase to the left of the entrance hall would have led up to private rooms with windows such as are depicted on ivories, set in a triple frame, fronted by a balustrade which allowed the person looking out to stand at the very edge and lean upon it (see Figure 47). Alternatively window openings may have contained a panel of lattice-work, of a kind known from Syria, where they were occasionally represented in carved stone. Sometimes the

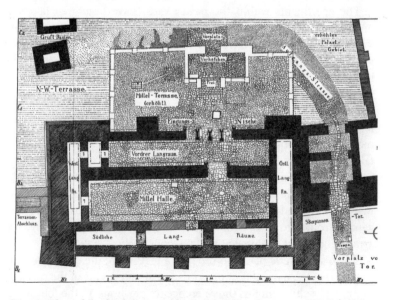

Fig. 46 Plan of the *bīt hilāni*, a palace with pillared portico at Tell Halaf in N. Syria. The city became an Assyrian provincial capital.

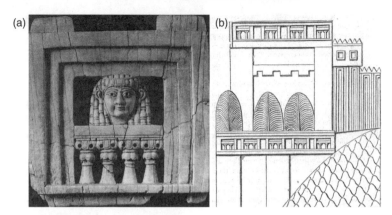

Fig. 47 (a) Ivory furniture ornament showing a woman at a window with a balustrade, from Nimrud, 9th/8th century BC. Ht. 8.2 cm. (b) Drawing from a sculptured panel showing architectural details including windows with balustrades.

panels were solid though carved with the pattern of a window grille, allowing no light or air to pass through, so as to bar demons of disease and pollution.[29]

The apartments within the palace must have been well lit even on the ground floor, to allow the decoration to show to advantage. There would have been clerestory light from the great internal courtyards, when these were adjacent, and the upper storeys may have had framed and balconied windows. Very tall and elaborate lampstands radiated artificial light, as well as plainer, little lamps placed upon furniture or stone 'altars', sufficient to justify the king's boast: 'As for the ceilings inside the main rooms, I lightened their darkness and made them as bright as day.' The timbered ceilings were almost certainly painted and perhaps also carved. Braziers of elaborate bronze work provided movable heating in cold weather,[30] and men with sprinklers kept the dust down in hot weather (see Figure 48). It is likely that the king and queen could walk on to the uppermost tier of the garden from one of the rooms of the top storey of the palace, an arrangement that is hinted at in the reconstruction drawing.

There are several places in the prism text where the careful reader notices that the natural flow of words is disjointed. One of the clearest examples of this contains the reference to 'pavilions' in the following passage:

Fig. 48 Reconstruction drawing of a portable hearth with wheels, made of iron and bronze, for heating a palace at Nimrud. Width *c*.80 cm.

In order to draw water up all day long I had ropes, bronze wires and bronze chains made, and instead of a shaduf I set up the great cylinders and *alamittu*-palms over cisterns. I made those royal pavilions look just right. I raised the height of the surroundings of the palace to be a wonder for all peoples. I gave it the name 'Unrivalled Palace'.

There is nothing in the sentence preceding the reference to the pavilions that informs us what 'those pavilions' were. There is, to put it in a grammarian's terms, no antecedent. An explanation is needed, not least because we need to know whether to connect the water-raising machinery and the pavilions.

Using examples from various other royal inscriptions, scholars have deduced that 'cut and paste' is an ancient technique in writing a text. Initially Assyrian scribes would write a long, detailed and coherent inscription to be displayed in the most public and prestigious location such as a throne-room, using passages from more detailed inscriptions elsewhere. Then they would make other shorter versions for less public and less prestigious places, and they might swap one passage for another that was particularly suitable for a subsequent location. Conversely, they would incorporate short texts or extracts into a longer or more general narrative.[31] During the course of a king's reign new deeds had to be accommodated by including them in earlier texts that were modified. Different reports had to be compacted into a single text.[32] The method is observable from a draft of a long text of Esarhaddon, in which gaps of up to eight lines were left at several places, to be filled in at a later stage.[33] A caption inscribed on a stone panel with bas-relief of Ashurbanipal reads: 'Mr (*blank*) and Mr (*blank*) spoke great insults against Ashur the god my creator'.[34] Such gaps were not always filled appropriately. In an inscription of Nebuchadnezzar II the phrase 'I surrounded the city with mighty waters like the expanse of the sea' was extracted from an inscription concerning building the outermost city wall of Babylon, which had a moat, and was transferred inappropriately to an inscription about building two cross-country walls, in which no water was involved.[35] In a few instances a grammatical error occurred because the insertion was not harmonized with the surrounding words: the Assyrian scribe who composed Sennacherib's *Walters Art Gallery Inscription* failed 'to add subordinated markers to passages imported from other sources as required by the new grammatical context'.[36]

Thus there would have been an inscription tailored for display in the queen's suite, with its dedication to her, and another for the *bīt hilāni* describing its special design. At Bavian, from a very long and detailed rock-cut inscription—describing the construction of all the engineering works of canal, bridge, weir and aqueduct—sentences or passages might be re-used in composing more general accounts such as the one we have found on the prisms. As the rebuilding of Nineveh progressed, updated versions were written, to celebrate and record each stage of the project. As far as the palace garden is concerned, the most detailed and coherent description of the garden may have been put in room XXII of the South-West Palace containing the bas-relief from which we now have only the Original Drawing IV 77 (see Figure 13), or at an appropriate location in the garden itself.[37] Excerpts from it would have been pasted into the prism inscription. Some of the passages quoted are known from more than one text, occasionally with details modified. With such procedures for producing a myriad of similar texts, each adapted for its particular location, it is hardly surprising that some disjunctions were not ironed out.

Assyrian royal inscriptions are of two kinds: for immediate display, such as on internal wall-panels, and for concealment. The prisms are the concealed kind: they were bricked up within the walls of the palace so that one day in the distant future, when the walls crumbled, the fame of the king would be known once again. How excellently our two prisms—one in Iraq, the other in Chicago—have fulfilled their purpose!

One of Sennacherib's own inscriptions confirmed that a part of the palace was lovingly dedicated to his first wife Tashmetu-sharrat, mother of his favoured eldest son Ashur-nadin-shumi who became king of Babylon. Following a North Syrian custom, Sennacherib broke with the normal Assyrian tradition of near-anonymity for queens and dedicated to his chief consort the queen's private apartments, leaving us with a strong sense of a happy first marriage, with these words only recently retrieved from the basement of the British Museum:

And for Tashmetu-sharrat the palace woman, my beloved wife, whose features the Mistress of the Gods has made perfect above all other women, I had a palace of loveliness, delight and joy built, and I set female sphinxes of white limestone in its doorways. At the command of Ashur, Father of the Gods, and of Ishtar the Queen, may we be granted days of health and happiness together within these palaces, may we have our fill of well-being, may the favourable protecting deities *šēdu* and *lamassu* turn to these palaces and never leave them.[38]

It was not to be. Sennacherib abandoned this wonderful building and built a new one, the North Palace, presumably when Tashmetu-sharrat was supplanted by Naqia who ensured that her own son Esarhaddon ousted the crown prince, son of her displaced rival in love.

Although this inscription, proclaiming the king's love, is unparalleled in Assyria, precedents are found from other countries adjacent to Assyria. In the 9th century a king of Carchemish had recorded his dedication of a building, perhaps the queen's private apartments, to his wife: 'for Anas my beloved wife';[39] and around the same time the Urartian king Menua had written a formal dedication of a vineyard to his wife, queen Tariria.[40] The dedicatory inscriptions of Carchemish and Urartu may have passed into oblivion as those countries became vassals of Assyria, but that of Sennacherib, attached to the finest palace in the world, would have coloured the gossip and enriched the legendary fame of 7th-century Nineveh.

This may be the reality that lies behind Diodorus Siculus' claim that the Hanging Garden was built for 'a Syrian Queen', or the 'Median queen' in the account given by Josephus.

Sennacherib's wife may have been involved in the creation of the gardens, giving a romantic angle that would have been taken up with enthusiasm by Greek writers who adapted the theme to suit different purposes. Sennacherib's second official wife Naqia, however, would have taken over from Tashmetu-sharrat as possessor of the garden, so the legend may have been transferred to her. The analysis of her name shows that she came from the west, but probably not from the Amanus area.[41] Naqia was one of the queens who conformed to the archetype 'Semiramis', as we have seen.

Festive occasions allowed foreign emissaries and local dignitaries to view the marvels of the Unrivalled Palace (see Figure 49). Inevitably

Fig. 49 (a) Palace attendants bringing cakes, grapes, pomegranates, and locusts in the South-West Palace.

Fig. 49 (b) Palace attendants bringing drink, drawn from a panel found in Sargon's palace at Khorsabad.

there would have been a splendid feast of dedication when the palace was completed, with thousands of guests eating and drinking from sets of drinking vessels: great mixing-bowls of wine, lion-headed rhyta, and fluted drinking-bowls without handles, vessels of gold and silver balanced on carved ivory stands.[42] Every year a great ceremony was held, at which vassals brought tribute and renewed their oaths of loyalty. For all of them the sculptures around the walls more than any other features would serve to reinforce the message of conquest and diplomacy, assuring native Assyrians as well as foreigners that supremacy could not lightly be challenged; that they served the richest, most powerful man on earth, with all the benefits that obedience could bring: law and order, peaceful trade, and the inspiration of greatness. Many of the palace sculptures show the details of exotic feasting: trays of crunchy locusts, attractively shaped cakes, files of finely clothed attendants supplying every taste and every need.

As in Josephus' account, so in Sennacherib's own description, it is clear that the garden was set out beside the palace on the high citadel, contradicting any suggestion that it was located in another part of the city or outside it.

I raised the height of the surroundings of the palace, to be a Wonder for all peoples. I gave it the name: 'Unrivalled Palace'. A high garden imitating the Amanus mountains I laid out next to it, with all kinds of aromatic plants . . .

Like his father Sargon, who had created an artificial landscape for his entire new citadel at Khorsabad, Sennacherib raised the ground level, in order to create an artificial landscape that looked as if it was natural, and with that level established, he could engineer the aqueduct, screws, lake and drainage, to ensure the success of the exotic plants transferred there, many of them uprooted from very different environments far abroad. The collection of foreign plants showed the king's mastery over the landscape, not just adapting and making the best of what was available, but changing it to make it even more desirable than it had been in its natural state, and yet the end-product was to appear natural, like the superb Amanus mountains with their cloak of fragrant trees. In collecting exotic plants abroad, he was following a tradition that went back in time to the reign of Tiglath-pileser I (1114–1076) who ended a long account of his conquest of '42 lands and their rulers, from the far side of the lower Zab river in distant mountainous regions, to the far side of the Euphrates, people of Hatti (northern Syria), and the Upper Sea in the West (Mediterranean)' with a brief passage that betrays his personal interest in botany:

I took cedar, box-tree, Kanish oak, from the lands over which I had gained dominion—such trees which none among previous kings my forefathers had ever planted—and I planted them in the orchards of my land. I took rare orchard fruit which is not found in my land and filled the orchards of Assyria.[43]

The drawing shown as the Frontispiece, made by the late Terry Ball who had worked as reconstruction artist for English Heritage, made careful use of as much information as possible (see Figure 50 (a)). It combined what was known from Classical texts and the prism inscription with an understanding of the sculptured panel of Ashurbanipal and Original Drawing IV 77 (see Figure 13), according to an interpretation of their perspective. Key features consisted of its shape 'like a Greek theatre' interpreted as a three-dimensional shape with appropriate size, and its location beside the palace, which meant that it had to be on top of the main citadel. Exactly where on the citadel

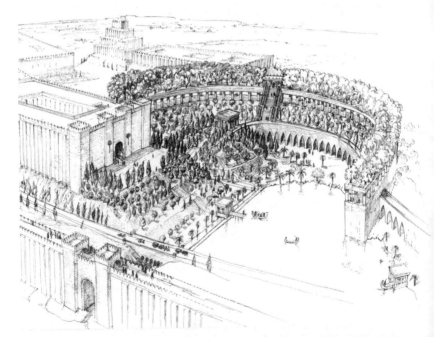

Fig. 50 (a) Reconstruction drawing by Terry Ball of the palace garden at Nineveh.

Fig. 50 (b) Draft reconstruction drawing by Andrew Lacey. Note the water-fall on the right-hand side.

was dictated by two considerations. The direction from which water flowed along the aqueduct was shown on Ashurbanipal's panel, having come from Jerwan. This excluded the west side of the citadel. More speculatively it was envisaged precisely where a set of contours on the side of the mound in recent times, adjacent to the South-West Palace, indicated a theatre-like depression of the right size, steep-sided, overlooking the Khosr river. That position meant putting an entrance to the palace facing the garden, which is not known from that part of the building since it is unexcavated. The placing also allowed us to show the ziggurat of the temple of Ishtar of Nineveh rising up behind the garden, bearing in mind also that the South-West Palace was connected with the temple by a passageway. The topmost level of the garden had to be level with the top of the city walls. The terraces above the level of the water on the aqueduct could be reconstructed from the remaining but damaged top of Ashurbanipal's panel and the pillared walkway from Original Drawing IV 77 combined with the descriptions of Strabo and Philo. No specific evidence supports the way in which the pillared walkway appears to join an upper storey of the palace just out of sight behind the palace; other junctions are possible. The shape of the arches supporting the aqueduct is known both from Ashurbanipal's panel and from existing remains of the Jerwan aqueduct. The lake at the bottom of the garden is taken from Original Drawing IV 77; it meets the need for drainage of water to the bottom of the garden, and thereafter presumably out into the Khosr river, to avoid stagnation. A road runs between the city wall and the bottom of the garden with a bridge to allow the water to drain through; the road is shown at the bottom of Ashurbanipal's garden panel. The boat-houses with a landing stage on the left hand one are adapted from the Khorsabad garden panel of Sargon II, on the understanding that the boats shown in Original Drawing IV 77 implied them. The water-raising screws alongside steps are shown as cutaways, and would have been invisible inside their cylindrical casing.[44] The pavilion is shown with its path crossed by the stream without resolving the problem of how to interpret the perspective in this instance. The trees are roughly sketched according to the three pictures. A terrace outside the palace door corresponds to the triangular empty space on the left of Ashurbanipal's panel. In view of my later understanding of the *bīt hilāni* as a portico entrance into a wing of the main palace, I would now suggest that the façade facing the garden had an open aspect with columns rather than the single arched doorway shown in the reconstruction. The columns would have stood on bases in the form of striding lions, as shown on the panel adjacent to Ashurbanipal's garden sculpture, which may represent the portico entrance giving immediate access to the garden.

Was the colossal outlay of labour and materials, luxury and extravagance, ruinous to the economy of Assyria? There is no definite evidence to suggest that this was so. Virtually all the labour was newly imported from conquered lands; many of the basic materials such as stone, mud brick, straw and reeds were local; timbers came through tribute as well as trade, although much was local, for tree-planting and timber management were traditional skills. By increasing the flow of water for irrigation in the fields and orchards around Nineveh, Sennacherib would have made the farmers less dependent on irregular rainfall, and improved the quantity and quality of yields. The building work was of a high enough quality to give employment to great numbers of craftsmen, and to endure, leaving a sturdy infrastructure and a proud heritage for successors. Stimulation rather than exhaustion seems to have been the effect that so much construction had on the economy.

Whether the garden contained fountains is uncertain, for none is mentioned in any of the textual or pictorial sources. The principle of the fountain was certainly known: a thousand years earlier a near-life-size statue of a goddess, holding a vase overflowing with water represented by incised decoration on her garment, has a channel drilled through from the back of her neck to the vase which she holds in front of her, and was able to exude water, but it stood inside the palace.[45] For an outdoor fountain as we have seen at Khinnis, a cistern with lion-heads protruding from the sides is designed so that water pours out from the mouths of the lions.

In conclusion, Sennacherib's own inscriptions show that his Wonder included the magnificent South-West Palace and the garden adjacent to it, along with his use of cast bronze screws for raising water, and the canals and aqueduct that brought water to Nineveh. In each respect—the palace, the garden, the constructions for watering and the expression 'Wonder'—he was building upon existing Assyrian traditions to create a masterpiece.

8

Symbolism and Imitators

God Almightie first Planted a Garden. And indeed it is the Purest of Humane pleasures. It is the Greatest Refreshment to the Spirits of Man; Without which, Buildings and Pallaces are but Grosse Handy-works: And a Man shall ever see that, when Ages grow to Civility and Elegancie, men come to Build Stately sooner then to Garden Finely: As if Gardening were the Greater Perfection

Francis Bacon, *Essay, Of Gardens*, 1597[1]

To build a new palace with a garden was to replicate creation in miniature, to bring control and order to the earth just as the gods had put order into the world according to the Babylonian *Epic of Creation*. By this deed the ruler acted like the highest god. Thus did the unrivalled palace with its marvellous garden mirror the act of genesis, showing to all the world that Sennacherib was as a god.[2] The wisdom of the builder is revealed through the design and its execution, by using the best materials and the best craftsmanship, drawn from the furthest reaches of the empire, for a high value was placed on brilliant workmanship and rare materials. Just as Sennacherib's prism inscription locates the garden alongside the palace, so we can see that the two represent cultural space, the ultimate in civilized use of land, a carefully arranged symbiosis of nature and architecture that encapsulates the ideal of elite existence and the epitome of technical achievements. In microcosm they symbolize civilization itself, contrasting with the disorder of uncontrolled, primitive territory beyond, a spatial metaphor for the power of the king and of Assyria at the heart of a great empire. Landscape and architecture were integrated into a harmonious whole, *rus in urbe*, a rural sanctuary in the heart of a great city.

The monarch played a vital role in assuring the fruitfulness of his own land and indeed all his empire, so fertility in its many aspects was symbolized in the garden. Obviously plants and flowing water represent life-giving abundance, where birds find shelter and nesting-places, havens of peace where predators are largely excluded. A fresh-water lake, such as is shown on Sargon's panel from Khorsabad (see Figure 11), and on Original Drawing IV 77 (see Figure 13), replicated the Apsu, which was the name for the water beneath the earth that supplies rivers and wells, and its personification as a force in nature. In Mesopotamian tradition it was also the place from which the Seven Sages emerged on to the earth, taking the form of pure carp, survivors of the archetypal Deluge, bringing the arts and crafts of urban, civilized life to mankind (see Figure 51). Those arts included kingship, skills in building, and the art of warfare.

An abundant supply of life-giving water was one of the garden's chief attractions. Water had a special association with wisdom. This is illustrated by the opening lines of the great *Epic of Gilgamesh*: 'He who found out (literally "saw") *nagbu*—the depths/all things gained complete wisdom', in which *nagbu* can mean either the depths from which springs of water gush; or the totality of knowledge. The god in charge of fresh water, Ea, was also the god of wisdom and craftsmanship.

Just as chaos was represented by water in the Babylonian *Epic of Creation*—Tiamat and Apsu, brought under control by Marduk—so Sennacherib's redirection of mountain streams demonstrated his ability to bring chaotic turbulence under control. But more than that, in raising water with screws, the natural, chaotic tendency of water to flow uncontrollably downhill is reversed, and seasonal aridity is banished. Normally a garden on the latitude of Nineveh would lose its greenery during the fierce heat of high summer, and would not become verdant again until the winter rains, followed by the warmth of spring, allowed trees and plants to sprout new growth. The palace garden overrode those natural changes, due to the abundance of water supplied throughout the months of summer heat, and kept its greenness as if in perpetual springtime while all around became desiccated, brown and dusty. Philo of Byzantium commented on the year-round greenery: 'it is just like an ever-green meadow.' The

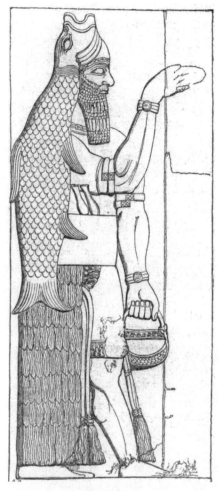

Fig. 51 Fish-man as sage, sculpture found at the entrance to a temple at Nimrud.

theatre-like shape would have afforded protection against the worst of wind and cold, and the evergreen pines would have sheltered adjacent plants from blasts of hot or cold air. Sennacherib's power over nature was apparent in all those ways.

In another way the garden symbolized control, with domesticated plants deliberately set out in an orderly manner, particularly where a rectangular enclosed space gave them special protection. This feature can be seen in the Original Drawing IV 77, where a small part of the garden consists of an enclosure with very regular rows of trees within. A similar arrangement is known from the planting pattern of shrubs or small trees within the courtyard of the temple of the New Year's festival outside the city of Ashur, where careful excavation revealed the root pits laid out in rows.[3] There the king, once a year, replicated the original act of human creation by making love to the great goddess, impersonated by a priestess.[4] In Babylonian mythology the king had been created as a special being, an ideal of masculine strength and beauty according to the command of the great god Ea:

Ea made his voice heard, he addressed Belet-ili, the Mistress of the Gods: 'You are the Mistress of the Gods, you have created the common people: now, make the king as a superior person, clothe his entire being with favour, form his features harmoniously, make his body beautiful'.
    The Mistress of the Gods did indeed create the king as a superior person.[5]

The power of water to transform plants from near-death to life reflects its power to bring a dead god to life, and to satisfy ancestors buried in tombs. In the *Descent of Ishtar to the Underworld* the great goddess of fertility is stripped of her powers, symbolized by her jewellery and her garments, and left for dead in the Underworld. But she is brought back to life by being sprinkled with water, to the fury of her sister the Queen of the Underworld. As a part of traditional custom, deceased members of a family were buried in vaulted chambers, usually beneath the floor of the family house; and it was the duty of the eldest son to ensure that pure water was poured down for them twice a month, often through a pipe which archaeologists occasionally recover in excavations. Therefore the entire scheme of water management, brought to fruition by Sennacherib, encapsulated life-giving and warding off death. As John Evelyn expressed it, writing of the effect of landscape gardens in the 17th century, 'these expedients do influence the soule and spirits of man, and prepare them for convers with good Angells'.[6]

One might suppose that Sennacherib's palace garden attempted to recreate the gardens of the blessed in heaven, or the garden of Eden, but this cannot be claimed from firm evidence. No ancient Mesopotamian myths describe a paradise-garden in which mortals lived happily before their condition changed for the worse. Mesopotamian accounts of man's creation by the gods make it clear that their genesis was intended from the beginning to provide a labour force, expressly to relieve the gods of hard work. Toil therefore was man's way of life from the start, and no primeval garden, no original state of bliss, was involved. However, there was a magical region beyond the known boundaries of the earth which Gilgamesh reached after travelling for ten leagues through darkness, emerging in front of the sun, where bushes blossomed, where 'carnelian bore fruit hanging in clusters, lovely to behold, lapis lazuli bore foliage, bore fruit, and was delightful to the view'. But it was not heaven, nor was it a place of primeval innocence. It is true that the Cedar Mountain, a forbidding place inhabited by 'Something Evil', guarded by the monster Humbaba, is called 'the dwelling of gods' in the *Epic of Gilgamesh*, but variant wording makes it clear that it belongs to the Anunnaki gods of the Underworld.[7] Ideally cedar trees clothed mountains—'On the face of the mountain the cedar proffers its abundance'—and were considered to have been planted by the gods: 'the Lebanon, exuberant forest of Marduk, the fragrance of which is sweet, where mighty cedars, planted by Anu (the sky-god) grow.' Every mountain in lands west of Mesopotamia was the seat of a deity, whether Mt. Cassios in Syria or Mt. Gerizim in Israel, Mt. Zion in Judah, Mt. Olympus in Greece, or Mt. Ida in Crete.

Unfortunately a comparison with biblical Eden stubbornly persists. The Sumerian myth *Enki and Ninhursag* was once described as 'the Paradise myth', but the old association has long been abandoned. The condition of Dilmun (identified as the island of Bahrein in the Arabian Gulf) before the god of fresh water Enki transformed it into a fertile and prosperous place for the island's goddess Nin-sikila caused her to complain that she had been granted a barren, unproductive, 'pure' land. Its primeval state is described in those lines as follows:

In Dilmun no raven yet cawed, no partridge cackled, no lion yet killed, no wolf carried off lambs, no dog knew how to guard goats, no pig had yet learned that grain was for eating, birds did not yet eat the malt that a widow would spread out on her roof, no pigeon tucked its head under its wing, no eye-disease was there to say 'I am Eye-disease', no headache was there to say 'I am Headache', no old woman was there to say 'I am an old woman', no old man was there to say 'I am an old man', no unwashed girl was there to be treated with disrespect in the city, no man dredging a canal was there to say: 'It is getting dark', no herald yet made his rounds in his district, no singer yet sang '*elulam*' there, no wailing yet resounded in the outskirts of the city.[8]

This interpretation has replaced the understanding that Dilmun was a paradise for mortals, a tendentious claim heavily influenced by the desire to show a connection between biblical Genesis and ancient Sumerian mythology.[9] Nevertheless, the idea that Dilmun was a kind of heavenly location is implied by the Sumerian Flood Story in which the survivor of the Flood was set down by the god Enki in Dilmun, to live forever, apart from mortals. Both in the Genesis story, 2: 5–10, and in the Sumerian tale, the term 'to the East' is used; and the condition of the world before the garden was created by Yahweh is expressed similarly to the myth of *Enki and Ninhursag* in this passage: 'At the time when God Yahweh made the earth and the heavens, when no shrub of the field was yet in the earth, and the plants of the field had not yet sprung up—for God Yahweh had not caused it to rain upon the earth and there was no man to till the ground . . .'[10]

The supposed connection was exacerbated by more recent use of the word 'paradise', which in its original Persian usage simply meant a garden, and in Greek (by Xenophon among others) could be applied to various royal parks and gardens in the Near East. Later it acquired a meaning as the Garden of Eden, where the first humans lived in contact with God, and, by extension, as the abode of the blessed. The word 'eden' in its earliest usage was formed from a common Aramaic root meaning 'abundance'.[11] It was understood in that sense by the Septuagint translators of Genesis 3: 23, whose *paradeisos tēs tryphēs* means simply 'garden of delights'.[12] The expression soon took on a new interpretation as a mythological place, which led to the traditional, conservative understanding of the Garden of Eden as a heavenly paradise,[13] and which literally minded interpreters of Genesis sought to locate on earth.

On the other hand Ezekiel must have had Sennacherib's palace garden in mind when he described Assyria as a cedar of Lebanon, with rivers made to flow around the planting and canals sent forth to all the other trees of the field, with roots in abundant water, 'nor any tree in the garden of God was like unto him in his beauty . . . so that all the trees of Eden that were in the garden of God envied him'. Ezekiel began to prophesy nineteen years after the fall of Nineveh, when the fame of the Hanging Garden was widespread. His words show that Sennacherib's creation was regarded as an illustration of excess power, outdoing heaven so as to arouse divine jealousy.

As a celestial paradise inhabited by the blessed, the Garden of Eden was famously promoted by John Milton. Writing *Paradise*

Lost, he sought inspiration, turning to Diodorus' description of the Hanging Garden. As a young man 'he read, it is said, all the Greek and Latin authors', so it is hardly surprising that he chose that passage and modelled the entrance to Paradise after the World Wonder, in a part of the poem that has been recognized as owing a debt to Diodorus for other parts of the description.[14] He envisaged the edge of Paradise as a steep-sided, terraced slope topped by a wall, and even higher, a row of trees:

> ... And overhead up grew
> Insuperable highth of loftiest shade,
> Cedar, and pine, and fir, and branching palm,
> A sylvan scene, and, as the ranks ascend
> Shade above shade, a woody theatre
> Of stateliest view; yet higher than their tops
> The verdurous wall of Paradise up sprung;
> Which to our general sire gave prospect large
> Into his nether empire neighbouring round:
> And higher than that wall a circling row
> Of goodliest trees loaden with fairest fruit ...[15]

This description calls to the mind's eye an image of Sennacherib, the great king like 'our general sire' looking down upon a microcosm of his empire, viewing his domain from a wall crowned with a curving row of trees (see Figure 52). The height of a steep, wooded slope, giving access to Paradise, set the scene for Satan, who journeyed on at first 'pensive and slow', then leaped up and perched 'like a cormorant' to view the wondrous landscape stretching out beneath him. By using the Greek text, Milton forged a new link between the Hanging Garden and the biblical Garden of Eden.

Sennacherib's palace garden sits firmly within an Assyrian tradition that can be traced back at least to the 9th century BC, so we may doubt that inspiration for it as a World Wonder in the 7th century BC was taken from the biblical idea of the Garden of Eden. However, if the story in Genesis was composed before Sennacherib designed his garden (which is a most contentious issue!),[16] one could imagine that the one river flowing out from Eden to branch into four rivers as the biblical account describes: 'And a river went out of Eden to water the garden, and from thence it was parted, and became into four heads', was deliberately depicted as a specific reference to cosmic geography in Ashurbanipal's sculptured panel, for it shows a single stream of

Fig. 52 Milton adapted Diodorus Siculus' description of the Hanging Garden for his poetic depiction of the Garden of Eden, but illustrators did not follow his text.

water flowing down from the aqueduct and then dividing into several streams (see Figure 14). Any such link might derive from a common source rather than being a direct influence.

Certain beliefs current in ancient Assyria would eventually contribute to the transition in understanding from an earthly pleasure garden to a heavenly paradise. One of a pair of divine gate-keepers controlling access to heaven was Nin-gish-zida, whose name can be translated 'Lord Steadfast Tree', and as we have seen in Chapter 3, some temples were designed to represent a sacred grove. The god Nergal had the epithet 'King Poplar' (Lugal-asal); there was also a god 'King date palm' (Lugal-gishimmar); and as we described, the dioecious date palm was pollinated as a recognized act of copulation. The idea that some trees and plants enjoyed sexual pleasure in gardens may have influenced the later image of a paradise in which delectable girls would be available to males as a reward for a virtuous life. In English tradition we refer to 'the birds and the bees' with the implication of sexual activity outdoors amid the beauties of nature.

One of the marvellous features of the Nineveh garden was its greenness throughout the year, so it appeared almost miraculous at times of the year when the rest of the landscape was parched. Eventually the ability to resist seasonal change became an attribute of the heavenly paradise-garden, which, as described in a Manichaean hymn,

adorned graceful hills wholly covered with flowers, grown in much excellence; green fruit-bearing trees whose fruits never drop, never rot, and never become wormed; springs flowing with ambrosia that fill the whole Paradise, its groves and plains; countless mansions and palaces, thrones and benches that exist in perpetuity, for ever and ever. Thus arranged is the Paradise.[17]

Mani, who founded the Manichaean religion and inspired much of its sacred literature, was born in Babylon in AD 216, at a time when the legendary Hanging Garden was still a subject of interest to Greek and Roman authors.

For perfuming temples and the statues of gods, scent was made from the resin of trees, especially cedars and pines, and the exudation of resin was itself referred to as the blood of the tree, as if the tree were an animal. To be in the presence of a deity, to be favoured by him, was to catch the scent of his sweet breath, as we can tell from expressions such as 'the fruit tree on which a god's breath has blown thrives', and, in a prayer addressed to a god, 'your speech is a sweet breath, the life of the lands'. Large quantities of perfumed oil were used in the cults, and emanated from cult statues. Likewise the king was perfumed, so that to catch the scent of his presence was to breathe in royal authority emanating from the gods: 'Let the breath of the Pharaoh not leave us: we are keeping the gate locked until the breath of the king reaches us', wrote the beleaguered ruler of a Canaanite town.[18]

The gods themselves were imagined as making love in a garden full of fragrant resins, fruit, herbs and flowers, which could be related to the understanding that the gods had aromatic breath—no halitosis in heaven!

As a symbol of the king's personal authority the royal stela set up in the garden, as seen on Ashurbanipal's sculptured wall-panel, stands in a commanding position on a path leading to the pavilion (see Figure 14). From there it proclaims that Sennacherib was the king who had created the surrounding wonders, his image a constant reminder of royalty, representing the king when he was absent. It would have been visible from the walls of the citadel. The king would also have been visible when he promenaded along the pillared walk-way at the top of the garden, allowing that architectural feature to act like an Egyptian Window of Appearances[19] from which the king was impressively visible both to his subjects below and to the guards patrolling the walls at the far end of the garden—'the Assyrian equivalent of a political poster'. Some such stelae state explicitly that they were set up as a memorial for eternity, for one of the purposes of reproducing in stone the image of a king was to ensure that the image would outlast him.[20]

Through his buildings and other works of art, the king promoted his own fame. Like modern leaders, he was acutely aware of the legacy that he must try to manipulate for future generations, and his endur-ing monuments and sculptures played a key role. The king's fine royal inscriptions, whether publicly displayed or hidden away for future discovery, served the same essential purpose.

The rare foreign plants in his garden demonstrated the breadth of his conquests abroad, representing the countries through which his armies marched. Thus the plants in the garden symbolized the extent of the king's power.[21] As an empire-builder whose campaigns and trading networks extended to far-flung lands, the king was a pioneer whose travels brought him into contact with exotic plants of which samples were collected and brought back to Assyria for the admir-ation of local people.

On the surviving bas-reliefs from Assyrian palaces of the late 8th and 7th centuries, trees are generally shown as a few stereotypical types that defy botanical identification, apart from date palms. Trees are always shown at the same height, as if a canon of proportions, already proven to exist on those sculptures for the human form, was used also for trees. The two types of tree shown on Ashurbanipal's garden panel may simply be stereotypes for deciduous and evergreen trees. But two scenes suggest a more interesting approach. One is the fenced-off square of trees on Original Drawing IV 77 (see Figure 13), which resembles a tree-nursery within the palace garden at Nineveh. The other is the fragment showing a lion recumbent beneath a vine whose leaves and stems are artistically arranged and naturalistically carved. This frag-ment leads us to believe that there was once a panel showing rare plants, for the vine does not flourish in the vicinity of Nineveh. By juxtaposing a lion with a vine, the sculptor suggests a rustic idyll in which wild animals and foreign plants have yielded happily to the control of the monarch. On Original Drawing IV 69, made from

Fig. 53 Attendants bringing vases of flowers into the South-West Palace.

another bas-relief found in Sennacherib's palace but now lost, men walk in a file, each bringing a large jar containing a big bunch of flowers (see Figure 53).

Botanical knowledge in Assyria is encapsulated in a specialized list, an encyclopaedic compilation which was well known in the time of Sargon and Sennacherib. It describes the features of individual plants in detail: root, fruit, blossom, seed, sprout, stalk, tendril, sap, resin etc.—depending on particular qualities for each plant.[22]

Sennacherib names some of the foreign plants which he cultivated at Nineveh—the world of plants in microcosm. Some of the planting was experimental, and may not have been successful in the long term. Cotton was planted, and traces of cotton textile have been analysed in the tomb of Sargon's queen Atalya, confirming Sennacherib's claim to have made cloth from it.[23] The plant was probably a tree-like form *Gossypium arboreum* which is indigenous to India and Pakistan and was cultivated at a very early date in the Indus valley (see Figure 54 and Plate 16). *Dalbergia sissoo*, also known as Indian rosewood, was introduced into Assyria likewise from lands east of Mesopotamia including modern Oman (see Figure 55).[24] Even though northern Iraq is not an environment suitable for growing olive trees, Sennacherib claimed to have grown them, presumably having brought saplings back from the Levant, and he boasts that he harvested oil for use in a foundation deposit when he began a new building. Similarly date palms from the south of Babylonia were planted at Nineveh, although they would not have produced good fruit at such a northern latitude. But the importance of that tree far outweighed any disadvantages of ecology, for religious connotations of the date palm linked to the cult of Ishtar ran very deep in Mesopotamian society: the significance of

Fig. 54 *Gossypium arboreum*, and *Gossypium herbaceum*, the cotton-bearing tree and its shrub form.

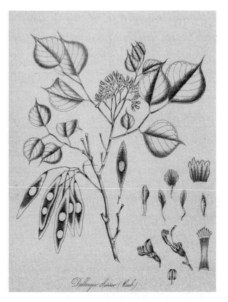

Fig. 55 *Dalbergia sissoo* Roxburgh, a fine hardwood native to Oman, S. India and Pakistan.

the tree is reflected in Sennacherib's extraordinary use for himself of the title 'Date palm of Assyria' instead of the normal 'king of Assyria';[25] and Ashurbanipal addressed Ishtar of Nineveh in a hymn as 'O palm-tree'.[26] An 'indian tree' *sindû* was also introduced, possibly sandalwood. Little detail is available for fruits, but we know from texts on the Middle Euphrates a thousand years earlier that cuttings were routinely taken for planting vines,[27] so we can deduce that Assyrian horticulturalists searched at home and abroad for better stock to improve their produce. These enterprises suggest that Sennacherib, like his predecessors, enriched his country with long-term benefits. Botanical analysis and detailed plantsmanship evidently flourished in 7th-century Assyria.

In two letters which a top Assyrian official resident in northern Syria wrote to Sargon, he assures the king that he has collected 2,800 bundles of cuttings from fruit trees from one town, and 1,000 from another, and that they are on their way to Khorsabad, for planting around his new capital city; another group of people 'are collecting saplings of almond, quince and plum trees, and transporting them to Dur-Sharrukin'.[28] Another letter from the same man mentions plans to prepare saplings of cedar and cypress 'when the time is right'.[29] Not all of them were intended for gardens; panels of sculpture show lines of trees planted alongside Assyrian roads, to give shade to travellers, just as they are in modern times in the Middle East.

In this respect Sargon and Sennacherib stood within an early and long-lasting tradition of introducing new plants into their country. More than two millennia later, when British explorers took a lead in extending their country's influence to new lands they took with them a botanist or biologist, intending to bring back specimens, alive or dead, of hitherto unknown plants, animals and insects. Joseph Banks was one such, travelling with Captain Cook on board the *Endeavour* to bring back plants that were given a Linnaean name celebrating the discoverer—*Banksia*. Charles Darwin was another, accompanying Captain Fitzroy to bring back on board the *Beagle* plants, some of which were named after him, such as *Calceolaria darwinii*. When the plants survived, they were propagated in national gardens such as Kew, or in the gardens of rich men such as at Chatsworth and Heligon. Dutch plantsmen were famous too for searching abroad: Philipp Franz von Siebold, a doctor who lived in Japan for many years, brought back to Leiden, among many other plants, one which was named *Magnolia sieboldii* after him. In the USA the inventor

Thomas Edison collected tropical trees from around the world, using his international network of contacts, for his Tropic Gardens in Florida. These examples illustrate how foreign plants introduced into the home country are trophies which may bring glory to their discoverers and are displayed with pride in the great gardens of the homeland. So it was with the conquering kings of Assyria.

The tradition did not begin with Sennacherib. When Tiglath-Pileser I (1114–1076 BC) campaigned victoriously to the north-west of Assyria, he brought home foreign trees including rare and exotic fruit trees, as already quoted. Ashurnasirpal II (883–859 BC) had set another precedent in his palace garden at Nimrud, by naming more than 39 types of tree in his new garden,[30] to which the Assyrian public was invited to come for the feast of inauguration—47,074 guests, a palindromic number in which 4 (the corners of a square) and 7 (the number of planets that influence human affairs) both symbolize totality.[31] Incidentally this symbolic use of numbers shows how tricky it is to interpret such ancient texts, when our own literature usually lacks such symbolism, and a literal translation is served up plain. Cedars, cypresses, junipers and the incense-bearing *kanaktu* tree afforded shade and aroma; almond, quince, fig, pear, vines and pomegranate contributed blossom in spring and fruit in late summer.[32]

The pine trees that are so much in evidence on Ashurbanipal's sculptured panel have a special role beyond shade and fragrance, for pine-cones and fir-cones, with their attractive shape and their shower of winged seeds, were a special symbol of fertility held by the genies who purified or pollinated the 'tree of life' in Assyrian palaces.[33] Fir-cones were used, alongside tamarisk and date palm, in rituals to dispel evil.

A fashion for collecting rare foreign plants is known from Egypt. The great Egyptian Pharaoh Hatshepsut (*c.*1473–1458 BC) is famous for her expedition to Punt, modern Eritrea, from which she brought back the incense-bearing shrubs illustrated in bas-relief on the walls of her temple at Deir el-Bahri. The stone pictures can still be seen; some of the shrubs would barely have survived the immediate days of triumph, but were nevertheless at least as interesting, if not more so, than gold rings and elephant tusks, which are also depicted there. Rarity creates value and excites attention and admiration. Despite the

Fig. 56 A stone panel of bas-relief with plants, from the 'botanical court' of Tuthmosis III in the temple of Amun at Karnak.

lateral symmetry that is so marked a characteristic of Egyptian gardens, her design may have influenced the design of the Nineveh garden in other ways, for it is striking that the terraces are surrounded by cliffs in the shape of an amphitheatre, and that colonnades on each terrace look down over the garden.

When the Pharaoh Tuthmosis III (*c.*1440 BC) marched from Egypt into the Levant and installed his governors in the main cities, he celebrated his conquests by commissioning a bas-relief for the temple of Amun at Karnak, illustrating foreign plants brought back and planted in Upper Egypt (see Figure 56). Some of them have been identified from the illustrations, but there is no accompanying text to give more context.[34] They are depicted as samples with fruits detached from the main plant, although artistic conventions make modern botanical identifications difficult. Whether Sennacherib and his advisers were aware of those Egyptian collections is not certain, but the idea of separating the different parts of the plant prefigures the Assyrian botanical encyclopaedia mentioned above. The presence of Egyptian emissaries at his father's court, known from the *Nimrud Wine Lists*, makes it likely that there was interaction with lively discussion of garden design. On reciprocal visits Assyrian emissaries may have viewed bas-reliefs at Karnak and Deir el-Bahri as well as existing Egyptian gardens.[35]

Four centuries later, the soldiers of Alexander the Great would bring back botanical information collected by Theophrastus,[36] inspiring the study of a wider range of material than was available at home. In every society people are inspired and excited to see whatever is rare and strange from far-distant lands, whether a platypus from Australia, nutmegs from the island of Rum, or rocks from the surface of the moon.

Fig. 57 Detail of Original Drawing IV 77 showing sporting events taking place in the palace garden at Nineveh.

The king of Assyria frequently led his soldiers on campaign. Horsemanship and charioteering, hunting, wrestling, running, throwing and swimming were all skills required in ancient armies. On other sculptures many of these activities are shown in the course of real campaigns abroad.[37] On Original Drawing IV 77 they are sporting displays held in the royal garden at Nineveh. Naked men swim supported on inflated skins, other men ferry horses across water on boats (see Figure 57). The man who appears to swing on a rope above the water may be practising for scaling a high wall. Like a military tattoo, an exhibition of this kind had the serious purpose of demonstrating prowess useful in warfare. Athletic competitions were held: running races *lismu* were attached to the cults of various deities.[38] An Assyrian road named 'King's Road of the Running Race' allows the deduction that main roads were the venue, as in modern marathons. Such races took place on specific dates in the calendar, and were dedicated to gods; for instance at the city of Ashur a running race in honour of the god Nabu was held in the second month,[39] and a race in honour of Ninurta in the ninth month.[40] Wrestling was a popular sport—wrestlers *ša abāri* are sometimes shown in art, and the acrobat (or maybe juggler) *mubabbilu* contributed to royal entertainment. Other palace sculptures show scenes of hunting with dogs, nets and falcons, chariots and spears, presumably taking place within larger parks outside the city wall, but none of them was commissioned for Sennacherib, who seems to have eschewed hunting, in contrast to his father Sargon and his grandson Ashurbanipal.

In Egypt from the fifth dynasty (2465–2323 BC) onwards sportsmen are known to have competed either nude or very lightly clad in a penis sheath or a short kilt. As a subject for bas-relief sculptures and for painting, their events were popular.[41] Swimming is often shown. The best example of a text comes from the reign of Taharqa, the Pharaoh who ruled at the same time as Sennacherib. Written on a stela set up on the desert road near to the site of Dahshur, it is known as 'the Running Stela of Taharqa', proclaiming that the Pharaoh ordered it to be called 'Running Practice of the Army of the Son of the Sun Taharqa, may he live forever', and it commemorates a great race. He boasted:

There is none among my army who is not toughened for battle . . . they come like the coming of the wind, like falcons who beat the air with their wings . . . . The king himself was in his chariot to inspire the running of his army. He ran with them at the back of the desert of Memphis in the hour 'She has given Satisfaction'. They reached the Fayum in the hour 'Sunrise'. They returned to the palace in the hour 'She defends her Master'. He honoured the first among them to arrive and arranged for him to eat and drink with his bodyguard. He honoured those others who were just behind him and rewarded them with all manner of things.[42]

This text, and its date in Sennacherib's time, provides back-up for interpreting part of the scene in Original Drawing IV 77 as an exhibition of military sports carried out in the king's palace garden.

Some of those physical sports are often assumed to have begun in Greece, linked to the fame of Olympia and the Olympic Games, where recognizable civic architecture helps to show how popular sporting contests were. Around the 8th and 7th centuries BC competitive sports took place at Olympia, Delphi and then spread to Athens and Nemea. Particular gods were the patrons: Apollo, the equivalent to Mesopotamian Nabu, was honoured with the games at Delphi; and Heracles, who was equivalent to Mesopotamian Nergal (who in turn was sometimes equated with Ninurta), was honoured as founder of the Olympic games.[43] Although in Assyria and Egypt there was no equivalent in architecture, there is now evidence that physical exercises were valued there.

In a crowded city, and in homes filled with the busyness of family life, privacy is at a premium, and finding a quiet place for making love is a challenge. A love lyric takes the form of a dialogue between Nabu and his consort Tashmetu who pledge their love in a garden, describing their ecstasy with metaphors of fruit, birdsong and gemstones.

> 'My lord, put a ring on me, let me give you pleasure in the garden!' . . .
>> 'Tashmetu, whose thighs are gazelle in the plain,
>> Tashmetu whose ankles are apple of Siman,
>> Tashmetu whose heels are obsidian, . . .
>> Why, O why are you adorned, my Tashmetu?'
> 'So that I may go to the garden with you, my Nabu.
> Let me go to the garden, to the garden and to my Lord' . . .
> 'May my eyes see the plucking of your fruit,
> May my ears hear the twittering of your birds.' . . .
>> 'Bind your days to the garden and to the lord.
>> Bind your nights to the beautiful garden'.
> 'Let my Tashmetu come with me to the garden . . . .
> May her eyes behold the plucking of my fruit!
> May her ears listen to the twittering of my birds!'[44]

The pavilion, with its façade of columns topped by delicate proto-Ionic capitals, would have given an opportunity for privacy and dalliance within the garden, as well as solitude for reflection, and perhaps also for the king to escape among the butterflies from quarrelsome wives (like Solomon in Rudyard Kipling's story *The Butterfly that Stamped*) and conspiratorial courtiers (like Ahasuerus in the Hebrew Book of Esther). Such a pavilion represented a tent providing comfort and seclusion in the desert, with an ivory couch and luxurious hangings, beautiful textiles, protected against sun, wind, dust, sand, and unwelcome interruptions.

When the Hanging Garden was constructed at Nineveh, outdoor drinking parties in Assyria were occasions for conversation and entertainment with wine and music, presumably also dancers and acrobats, jesters and poets. Wherever courts convened for leisure, courtiers recited wisdom literature, exercising their wit and ingenuity for the king's delight and amusement, and jesters told rude jokes. 'Wisdom' compositions included dialogues that probed the limits of piety and power. In such a setting the wisdom and learning of which Sennacherib boasts in his prism inscription would be associated with the royal garden on some occasions, just as it is in the text. The link suggests that the banquet *al fresco* was the royal equivalent in Assyria of a Greek symposium held in a garden. This linkage is most clearly seen on the sculpture that shows Ashurbanipal and his queen feasting in a garden—its location has not been securely identified—surrounded by the trophies of victory which include an Elamite bow, an Egyptian necklace, and the head of the decapitated Elamite king hanging from a tree (see Figure 58). The king reclines on a couch in the style generally associated with Greek drinking parties, holding his bowl of wine. Outdoor music enchants the air, played on stringed, percussion and wind instruments. From lists of the wine distributed at banquets to the royal family, high officials and foreign delegates as well as musicians, we know that there were several regional types of music: from Syria and Palestine, including specialists from Malatya on the Upper Euphrates, Arpad near Aleppo in Syria, from Jerusalem (sent as part of Hezekiah's tribute); from Luristan, and local Assyrian musicians.[45] Like the plants, the music was international, reflecting the king's far-reaching influence and his appreciation of the skills of his subjects.

Thus the association in Classical antiquity of the garden as a place for philosophers to stroll for relaxed dialogue is a tradition that would lead easily from the garden banquets of Assyrian kings. By the time a Seleucid governor was in control in Nineveh, there was a tradition of philosophers meeting and talking in a garden, sometimes as part of a

Fig. 58 Ashurbanipal and queen with trophies, celebrating with a drink in a garden. The faces and the king's hand were chiselled out after the fall of Assyria. Ht. 56 cm.

more general educational environment. Plato, Theophrastus and Epicurus are all said to have used their own private gardens as meeting places for serious discussion and learning; and Theophrastus bequeathed his garden to the Peripetus school which had the Lyceum as its centre.[46]

Only a few damaged and fragmentary bas-reliefs from the South-West and North palaces at Nineveh bear witness to the importance of the garden in Assyrian art. If Ashurnasirpal II in the 9th century commissioned a sculptured panel showing his garden at Nimrud, it is not extant; but Sargon, Sennacherib and Ashurbanipal in the late 8th and early 7th century certainly did. Three different styles can be identified: first a garden as a landscape without people as in Sargon's garden at Khorsabad, and Ashurbanipal's panel from the North Palace at Nineveh; second, a garden as a scene for activity, as in the Original Drawing IV 77 of Sennacherib's panel showing sports and the pillared walkway; also as a place for leisure the panel showing Ashurbanipal drinking with his consort in celebration of his victories in Egypt and Elam; and third, a garden as a place for displaying particular plants and animals as shown on the fragment from Ashurbanipal's North Palace. (See Figures 11, 13 and 14) These examples from three different reigns are all that survive from what may have been a very much larger number. Such a small proportion of the original number is due to incomplete excavation, to erosion, to accidental loss (many fine panels sank on a raft transporting them to Europe) and to the untraceable re-use of stone in later times.

In the first style, a landscape without people implies a garden as a place for solitude where the beauties of nature are celebrated. Here the emphasis is on the design, the engineering and water flow, imitating a natural landscape, where the trees are of only two stereotypical kinds, probably deciduous and evergreen together. On both panels flowing water is emphasized, but shown in a naturalistic way, despite flowing into the sloping garden on an aqueduct. It is not marshalled into a pond or lake of geometric precision, by contrast with the later, rather rigid form of four channels and a central pond, a flat parterre typical of the Iranian *chahar bagh*. Both panels show the pavilion as a non-urban feature. On Sargon's panel the artificial hill topped by an altar is a metaphor in miniature for the mountain on which the deities lived, as a place in near-contact with the sky, where heaven hovers above. This allows a certain intimacy between man and god, reminding one that the sun, moon, planets and constellations are directly linked to man and earth, where the transcendence of the divine is directly apparent to the mortal recipient. On the Nineveh panel, the king is visibly in control, not quite dominating the scene from his stela but incorporated into it, and his garden is an extension of his palace which is presented on the adjacent slab. Nature is simplified, divine worship is simplified, architecture is integrated into nature: nature and culture are reconciled.

In the second style, the garden is a place for socializing in different ways: a place to recline, drink, carouse with the queen, listen to music, display trophies, and watch sporting events; as a venue for athletic display it serves as an outdoor theatre. This is a function that may have had a deliberate influence on the design, for Diodorus Siculus wrote that the Hanging Garden was like a theatre; and the pillared walkway could be understood as an elevated viewing point, prefiguring the pillars that rose up at the back of many a Hellenistic theatre. In general the encompassing shape of a theatre cocoons people from the intrusions and dangers of life outside, allowing the relaxation needed for contemplation and enjoyable socializing, as well as sheltering the trees from gusts of wind and driving rain.

In the third style, represented only by a single fragment, great care has been taken to show the vine twining around a tree; the daisy-shaped flowers on long, straight stalks, and lilies, well known for their exotic perfume. The lion and lioness are idealized as tranquil and tame, implying that even the animal world is at peace in an

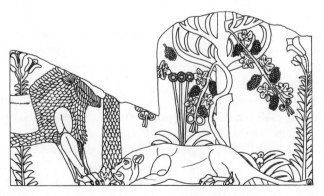

Fig. 59 Idealized landscape on a stone panel fragment showing lions with flowers growing beneath a vine, from an internal wall in the North Palace of Ashurbanipal at Nineveh. Ht. 98 cm, length 178 cm.

environment controlled by the king (see Figure 59). The subject may have been taken from Egypt: a wall-painting beside a palace garden at Tell el-Amarna shows a lion lying under a vine.[47]

All three styles show a tendency to idealize, whether trees, people or animals, showing them as perfect forms in a timeless environment. In sculpture it was possible to show ideal or perfect forms for a garden as well as for humankind. Storm damage, wilting, accidental trampling, were not shown, for perfection was the aspiration of the craftsman whose work would reflect the ideal of kingship and its close relationship to the gods. The ideal of perfection is clear in the way that men are shown on Assyrian sculpture, in the prime of life, distinguished only by garments, hairstyle, jewellery and accoutrements. Likewise the deities shown on the rock sculptures at Khinnis and Maltai are identifiable by the symbols they hold, and the animals on which they stand (see Figures 29, 30). Such models of perfection were later interpreted as dangerous because they imitated divine creation, leading to a periodic avoidance of human forms in art. Even during the late Assyrian period there was a tendency towards non-representational art, especially in showing divinities, but it existed alongside the depiction of ideal forms of gods and men, apparently without tension.[48]

Anyone who plants trees in a garden is aware that future generations will have greater benefit from them than himself. If we accept that Ashurbanipal's panel shows the garden at Nineveh planted by his grandfather,[49] we see that the grandson acknowledged that debt, and linked himself to his famous ancestor. The decision to commission the scene can be understood as paying homage to a great king whose reputation had been so tarnished by terrible deeds: the murder of Sennacherib by one of his own sons, and the damage done to Babylon when he sacked it. Ashurbanipal celebrated the genius of his grandfather in an allusive way.

The World Wonder created by Sennacherib must have had imitators. On a small scale the water engineering of the so-called Siloam tunnel dug by Hezekiah, Sennacherib's contemporary in Jerusalem, may be compared. The tunnel is thought to have been designed to fill the pool of Siloam so that water flowed over into the King's Garden, located in the only part of Jerusalem where a garden could flourish all year round. The inscription carved in Hebrew on the wall of the tunnel shares with texts of Sennacherib a most unusual interest in the work of the labourers. In his prism inscription Sennacherib showed

his interest in the plight of the workers where he wrote of his predecessors: 'in their method of work they had exhausted all the craftsmen', but also many panels of palace sculpture show men at work in
the hard stages of labour to achieve his huge construction projects,
especially the dragging of colossal bull slabs from quarries to Nineveh
on sledges.[50]

Hezekiah wrote:

... [when the tunnel] was chipped through. And this is the story of the
hacking through. While [the quarrymen were still wielding their] axes, each
towards his fellow, and while there were still three cubits to be chipped
through, the voice of a man (was heard) calling to his fellow, for there was an
overlap(?) on the right [and left]. And on the day of chipping through, the
quarrymen struck through each to meet his fellow, axe against axe. Then the
water flowed from the Spring towards the Pool for 1,200 cubits. And 100
cubits was the height of the rock above the heads of the quarrymen.

The King's garden in Jerusalem is first referred to in 2 Kings 25: 4, but
nothing is known of its plan or appearance in antiquity.

The description of the garden of Alcinous in the Odyssey may owe
its inspiration to Sennacherib's garden;[51] the great Church Father
Gregory of Nazianz actually associated them, and it has been nóticed
that they had the same dimensions, about 120 m × 120 m.[52] Whether
the suggestion of influence is acceptable depends upon the disputed
date for 'Homer's' composition: whether a single author completed
the entire work which soon became canonical, or whether revisions
and additions continued to be made to a core narrative over quite a
long period of time. The unitarians propose an 8th-century date—too
early to allow influence from Sennacherib's World Wonder—whereas
the analysts propose additions and revisions down to the 6th century,
which would allow the possibility of influence from 7th-century
Assyria. Alcinous' palace and garden are both described using terms
that apply to Assyrian palaces and gardens, but not to those of the east
Mediterranean at that time.

Outside the courtyard but stretching close up to the gates, and with a hedge
running down on either side, lies a large orchard of four acres, where trees
hang their greenery on high, the pear and the pomegranate, the apple with its
glossy burden, the sweet fig and the luxuriant olive. Their fruit never fails nor
runs short, winter and summer alike. It comes at all seasons of the year . . . .
The garden is served by two springs, one led in rills to all parts of the
enclosure, while its fellow opposite, after providing a watering place for the

townsfolk, runs under the courtyard gate towards the great house itself. Such were the beauties with which the gods had adorned Alcinous' home.[53]

Bronze-clad thresholds, brazen palace walls, silver-plated columns and lintels: these are all known from late Assyrian buildings; the walled garden outside the palace rather than within a courtyard, near the doors, exuberant with pomegranates and figs which are fruits normally associated not with the Mediterranean at that time but with lands further east. These features have been invoked as likely influences from Assyria.

One of the defining features of Sennacherib's garden was the pillared walkway, the peristyle which looked out across the garden to a wonderful view beyond, a combination of features found elsewhere in the Hellenistic Near East. Given that this aspect of the World Wonder is described by Q. Curtius Rufus and by Philo, it would have been the dream of every ambitious ruler to adopt that feature of the Nineveh garden. Owing to its status as a World Wonder, Sennacherib's garden would have been the prototype and the main source of inspiration.

There is an obvious comparison at Pergamum with the Great Altar which is surrounded on three sides by a lofty peristyle overlooking a tremendous view across the Caicus river. The kings responsible for designing and building it were Eumenes II (197–159 BC) and Attalus II (158–138 BC), whose 'Asianizing topophilia' has been emphasized in recent research.[54]

Another likely imitation, also on a spectacular scale, is the winter palace of Herod the Great (c.73–04 BC) at Jericho. Here not only was there a pillared portico overlooking the garden, with a great view beyond across the Wadi Qelt, but also the highly visible viaduct, the artificial hill on which a smaller palace was built; and the semi-circular terraces in the centre of the grand façade of the sunken garden. Although there was a large swimming pool, it was an architectural, rectangular structure within the main palace compound, and cannot be compared with the 'natural' lake of the Original Drawing IV 77 (see Figure 60). It was more closely comparable with Egyptian gardens in which symmetry and axial planning were dominant.[55] Herod was a builder of palaces on an extravagant scale, not only at Jericho, but also in Jerusalem, Caesarea and Herodium, and he had World Wonders in mind, for Josephus wrote that a tower he built in Jerusalem 'was as strong and as extensive a building as the Pharos of Alexandria'.[56]

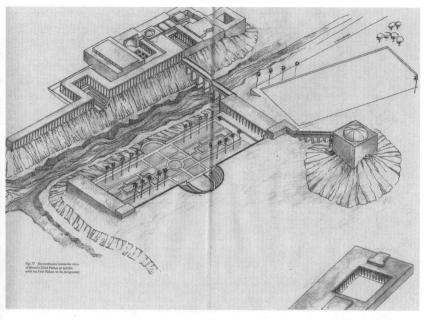

Fig. 60 The third winter palace of Herod the Great at Jericho, isometric re
construction drawing showing colonnade overlooking garden with flowing
water, artificial landscaping, and pavilion.

A further likely imitation was set in the heart of Rome: the Domus
Aurea. Built by Nero (AD 37–68) with its centre on the Oppian hill, a
palatial villa had pillared porticoes looking out across the hills of
Rome. It was set into a garden terraced on an artificially created
landscape. The extensive grounds featured at least one pavilion, and
contained a lake at the heart of an extraordinary arrangement of
monumental buildings.[57] At that time Roman soldiers, stationed in
the Near East to control the growing power of Parthia, would have
brought back to Rome tales of the wonders of Mesopotamia. At that
time too, the poem of Antipater claiming to have seen the Hanging
Garden was in circulation, likewise the descriptions of Strabo and
Diodorus Siculus, and Josephus' account. Nineveh was enjoying a
great revival under the local rule of a *stratēgos*. Most likely, therefore,
Nero had the World Wonder of 'Babylon' specifically in mind when
he designed his complex on such a grand scale, incorporating so
many of Sennacherib's design features. The Domus Aurea was soon
replaced by other buildings; the lake was drained and the Colosseum
was built where it had been.

In conclusion, the Assyrian tradition of a landscape garden set beside a palace continued long after the decline of the Assyrian empire. Distinct from courtyard gardens, mortuary gardens, and temple gardens, it had symbolic value for displaying the king's wisdom, his control over nature, his widespread influence, his ability to override seasonal decay, his role as propagator of fertility, and his dedication to agriculture and horticulture. From Jerusalem to Pergamum, from Jericho to Rome, one finds traces of the influence that came from Nineveh, spreading out widely into distant lands.

9

Defeat and Revival

Nineveh after 612 BC

A ruin—yet what ruin! from its mass
Walls, palaces, half-cities have been rear'd

Byron, 'Childe Harold's Pilgrimage' 143.1–2

Saith the Lord: 'And shall I not spare Nineveh, that great city, in
which there are more than a hundred and twenty thousand
persons?'

Jonah 4: 11

An accepted truth until recent times has been the utter destruction of
Nineveh in 612 BC, total abandonment of one of the ancient world's
biggest and longest-lived cities. Had Nineveh been utterly destroyed
and looted when the Assyrian empire came to an end, how could
Sennacherib's garden with its complex watering system have been a
World Wonder famed in Seleucid and Parthian times? If neither the
garden nor the inscriptions were available to Greek writers, how
would the detailed descriptions of those authors have been possible,
and how would the knowledge that a screw raised water there have
been transmitted? If the garden was ruined, is it possible that the
Classical accounts relied upon the panels of sculpture showing the
garden, if we suppose that they survived the fall of Assyria and
remained visible, at least in Alexander's time, and perhaps for
many centuries afterwards (see Figures 61, 62)?

In theory datable texts referring to a particular city should match
archaeological evidence for the occupation of the site. In the case of
Nineveh, however, around the time of its sack in 612 BC, there was
a hugely significant change in material used for writing: inorganic

Fig. 61 View of Nebi Yunus, the second citadel mound at Nineveh.

Fig. 62 View of Nimrud with winged gateway-colossus in foreground, mound of Ninurta temple and ziggurat on horizon.

clay, which survives only for cuneiform writing, gave way to organic parchment and papyrus, which do not survive. In addition, the city was no longer a royal residence and so it no longer boasted new commemorative inscriptions in stone. Those changes—from solid textual evidence to lack of it—reinforce the impression that Nineveh was utterly destroyed. That impression is strengthened by the survival of ivory ornaments, metal objects and other valuables. It was supposed they would have been looted in the aftermath of the sack unless the destruction had been so complete as to preclude later access.

In the mid 19th century Rawlinson and Layard, both well-educated men, knew the Old Testament thoroughly, and many of their contemporaries still believed that the Hebrew text was the word of God. Indeed, some Europeans still supposed that the Hebrew language was the very tongue that God spoke, the first language of mankind, so that all later languages were derived from it: they had made lists of words in German that sounded like Hebrew words, and interpreted the similarities as proof that German (among all other tongues) was derived ultimately from Hebrew.[1] A French understanding of the same concept had been satirized by Voltaire, who supposedly overheard this pronouncement in the 18th century: 'What a dreadful pity that the bother at the Tower of Babel should have got language all mixed up; but for that, everyone would always have spoken French.' Such a belief allowed a literal understanding of biblical text.

The biblical account given by Nahum described the fall of Nineveh in apocalyptic terms, prophesying that fire, flood, sword, and scattered people would leave the city 'empty, void and waste'. 'All who look on you will turn their backs on you and say, "Nineveh is a ruin".... The gates of your country stand wide open to the foe.... All who hear the news of you clap their hands at your downfall.'[2] A spectacular account of the fall of Nineveh was given by Ctesias a couple of centuries after the event. His words, retold by Diodorus Siculus, were also regarded as essentially trustworthy until recently; having described the last Assyrian king 'Sardanapalus' as an effete monarch drenched in perfumes and drained by sexual excesses, he wrote: 'Because he was a man of this character, not only did he end his own life in a disgraceful manner, but he caused the total destruction of the Assyrian empire.'[3] Ctesias, we now think, had written this in a satirical vein, mischievously transposing events and inventing salacious details.[4] His account transposes the last king of Assyria with the earlier, rebellious brother of Ashurbanipal, who became king in Babylon and lived some thirty-six years before the historical fall of Nineveh. It muddles Nineveh with Babylon.[5] No wonder that Greeks were confused.

Historians in modern times could not resist the temptation to pen purple passages with sweeping generalizations, relying on a literal reading of Ctesias. Sidney Smith, writing in 1925, stated: 'The disappearance of the Assyrian people will always remain an unique and striking phenomenon in ancient history. Other, similar kingdoms and empires have indeed passed away, but the people have lived on . . . No other land seems to have been sacked and pillaged so completely as was Assyria . . . the Assyrians seem to have been unduly devoted to practices (sc. "of a libidinous complexion") which can only end in racial suicide.'[6]

A false certainty that Nineveh was annihilated in 612 BC encouraged the first excavators to preclude the possibility of subsequent habitation there. The primary excavator was Henry Austen Layard, whose popular book *Nineveh and its Remains* was published in 1850, and *Nineveh and Babylon* appeared in print three years later. His declared aim had been to find Assyrian sculptures to enrich the collections of the British Museum, and so he tunnelled alongside the walls of the great palaces.[7] (See Figure 63) In doing so he bypassed evidence for later history contained in layers deposited above the 7th-century buildings. Although Charles Lyell's *Principles of Geology* was already popular, strict observation of stratigraphy and a scientific approach to archaeology had yet to emerge from an antiquarian approach to excavation.[8]

Layard was sure that Nineveh was utterly destroyed when the Medes and Babylonians sacked the city. The plain reading of Nahum was apparently supported by the eye-witness observations recorded by Xenophon when he marched through the area two centuries later.[9] Quoting Xenophon's *Anabasis* as proof, Layard wrote in 1853:

The first ascertained date from which our enquiry must commence, is the destruction of Nineveh by the combined armies of Cyaxares King of Persia and Media, and Nabopolassar, king of Babylon . . . It must, I think, be readily admitted that all the monuments hitherto discovered in Assyria are to be

Fig. 63 Layard excavated at Nineveh by tunnelling to reach the Assyrian buildings, bypassing later settlement.

attributed to a period preceding the Persian conquest ... When Xenophon passed over the remains of Nineveh, its very name had been forgotten.[10]

British excavators at Nineveh in the 1920s shared the same understanding. By the time they published their results, cuneiform texts were being edited in a more-or-less coherent manner, and so it appeared conclusive that no cuneiform texts later than 612 BC contained references to Nineveh.[11] Confirmation of their understanding seemed to come from the cuneiform *Chronicle concerning the Fall of Nineveh*, first published in 1923, which stated categorically that Nineveh was 'turned into mounds and heaps'.[12] They wrote: 'After the sack of Nineveh in 612 BC the site remained deserted until the third century BC, and probably later.'[13] All evidence for destruction in the palaces was assigned to events of the late 7th century BC. No later events were considered to have caused burning in the palaces and temples because they were supposed already to have been reduced to dust.[14] Likewise, when excavations in 1987–90 revealed the skeletons of soldiers lying where they fell in the Halzi gate of the city,[15] the excavator unquestioningly assigned the date of 612 BC to the slaughter.

Nineveh became a byword for utter ruin and desolation. The statement that Arbaces the Mede levelled 'Ninus' to the ground belongs to the hyperbole of triumph.[16] Similarly Lucian (c. AD 115–180) put into the mouth of the ferryman from the Underworld, visiting the upper world to report on the brevity of life and achievement:

Well, as for Nineveh, skipper, it was wiped out long ago. There isn't a trace of it left, and one can't even guess where it was. Babylon is over there, the place with great towers and a huge wall around it, but before long it will be just as hard to find as Nineveh.[17]

Lucian was relaying a stereotype based ultimately on the misunderstood language of destruction, and the fall of tyrants executed by divine retribution.

Research eventually showed that such phrases as 'turned into mounds and heaps' should not be taken literally. For instance the Elamites of Susa in Iran turned the great city of Ur into mounds and heaps late in the third millennium BC, and the town Apqu suffered the same fate around 900 BC, but both places were flourishing soon afterwards. Similarly the Elamite capital Susa, comprehensively looted, demolished and depopulated by Ashurbanipal around 646 BC, nevertheless recovered sufficiently to re-establish an independent kingdom and to receive back its captured gods in 625 BC. At Nineveh the walls of the South-West Palace were some 12 m thick in places, and were protected on each side by high stone facings which were still in place in Layard's day. It would have taken a superhuman and unnecessary effort to destroy more than a part of the buildings. Conquerors at that time would often select a few symbolic targets for devastation. The misleading phrases used in chronicles and Assyrian annals were borrowed from the language and imagery of formal lamentation, a type of liturgical text which we now know was used to promote revival, and so was used on ceremonial occasions when a sacred building was repaired.[18] The favour of the gods' return was implored by exaggerating current wretchedness. And they did return, as the biblical prophet Jonah made clear in his vain appeal to God, begging him to carry out his foretold punishment on a sinful people.[19]

The civil war that preceded the end of empire lasted for about eighteen years, roughly 627–609 BC. This is known because three names were omitted from the list of the last kings of Assyria recorded by the mother of Nabonidus, who evidently had not supported their factions.[20] That period of unrest would have weakened the Assyrian heartland, but would not necessarily have dealt a death-blow to the city.

Recent historians have accepted less readily the description penned by Xenophon and the account given by Ctesias, and looked with a more open mind at archaeological evidence.[21] Although a heavy ash layer was found in parts of the palaces on Kouyunjik[22] from a fire that had badly damaged many of the sculptured stone panels, and a city gate had been demolished, there is no definite evidence to show whether the fire raged in 612 or as the result of a later conquest. A later capture of Nineveh around 538 BC is mentioned by Athenaeus:

Amyntas says in the third book of his *Stages* that in Nineveh is a high mound which Cyrus demolished in raising counter-walls against the city during the siege; and that this mound is said to be the work of Sardanapalus, who had been king in Nineveh.[23]

Another capture took place around 90 BC by Tigranes of Armenia which Strabo recounted,[24] and yet another by Mithridates around AD 50, mentioned by Tacitus.[25]

Layard was sufficiently observant and thoughtful to recognize evidence for later occupation at Nineveh, and eventually had doubts about his earlier assumptions and the dating derived from them. Towards the end of *Nineveh and Babylon* he mentioned that Nineveh had belonged to the Parthian and Sassanian Persians according to the two Roman historians, Tacitus in the 1st century AD and Ammianus Marcellinus in the 4th;[26] and he decided that some excavated material originally ascribed to the late Assyrian period, both at Nineveh and at Khorsabad, belonged to Hellenistic times.[27] In his day it was impossible to make a clear distinction between Assyrian and later, non-Greek art. The most obvious example of such confusion was a carved 'door-lintel' 1.83 m long, which George Smith discovered lying in Sennacherib's palace and considered to be an example of Assyrian sculpture. We now know that the style is Parthian, and so the lintel (if that was its function) belongs to the Roman period. Layard's successor as excavator at Nineveh, Hormuzd Rassam, did not publish

Fig. 64 Parthian lintel found in the South-West Palace at Nineveh, in the 19th century. Its design was thought to be Assyrian. Length 1.83 m, ht. 0.26 m.

an account until several decades later, when he wrote: 'There is no doubt that the main destruction of the palaces was the work of the Sassanians,'[28] for he found that many of the Assyrian palace sculptures had been re-used in 'a large building of some well-to-do Sassanian or Arab' in the vicinity; and he also discovered a hoard of 145 Sassanian silver coins in the North Palace.[29]

The Parthian 'lintel' is not long enough to fit over an original doorway in the South-West Palace; 4 m, 3 m and 2 m are the approximate widths of different original doorways there, so that even the narrowest would not allow for the overlap required to support the ends of the stone (see Figure 64). An original doorway was perhaps narrowed, or the carved stone was designed for a different use. In any case, the existence of such an object shows without a doubt that the site of the South-West Palace of Sennacherib was occupied, in part at least, by a social elite, for mere squatters do not install large, sculptured stones.

Had the palace been utterly ruined for many centuries, the Assyrian panels of bas-relief sculpture would have been buried, hidden beneath metres of debris, and so not available for re-use by that hypothetical 'well-to-do Sassanian or Arab'. A part of Sennacherib's palace was excavated much more recently, in 1968, and in Hellenistic levels were found 'floor and foundations made of limestone and marble', as well as columns and re-used bas-relief panels 'that once graced the Throne-Room'.[30]

Almost a thousand years intervene between Assyrian decline in 612 BC and the Sassanian period, when Ammianus Marcellinus referred to events of AD 359 and when Philo the Paradoxographer was writing. In theory each stratum of occupation should be found in place in between previous and subsequent layers. In practice whole levels are often missing even though texts show clearly that the city flourished during those times.[31] These difficulties are compounded with the much wider problem of dating pottery and other finds. The uncertainty applies when a late addition was made to a panel of sculptures in the South-West Palace, where the surface was only partly rubbed smooth for a new cavalryman on horseback.[32] The figures bear no relationship to the surrounding scene; the horseman bears an intriguing resemblance to figures on the frieze of the Parthenon in Athens, as well as to earlier Assyrian ones. If some access to the palace buildings was possible after 612, a wider range of time opens up for dating the addition.[33] If a pair of figures without an Assyrian context—such as a particular campaign—was added, the alteration suggests a lack of royal engagement or centralized control that might be characteristic of the post-empire period.

Excavators were surprised to detect renovation carried out soon after 612 on the temple of Nabu, not far from Sennacherib's palace. On a paved road alongside it, wall-panels of Sennacherib and Ashurbanipal had been re-used.[34] Campbell-Thompson and Hutchinson, who excavated many decades after Layard, were at a loss to account for what they found just on top of a major destruction level with ash. 'It is not easy to explain the presence of three repairs on the E. corner. All are subsequent to the destruction . . . Indeed, there are many repairs on the SE side.' A similar situation was found for the so-called palace of Ashurnaṣirpal II on the south-east side of the Nabu temple, where the same excavators reluctantly admitted to some apparent restorations that followed the destruction.[35] The administration responsible for repairing the temple of Nabu may not have cleared and repaired every point of damage, but one often visits an old city or an ancient castle to find that some of its rooms and gates have been cleaned and refurbished, whereas others are quite ruined and no longer functional. Four levels of occupation following the destruction, and probably earlier than the Seleucid period, were discovered by later excavators in two other areas.[36]

More recently a fresh analysis of reports and objects found in the great temple of Ishtar of Nineveh suggested that repairs originally assigned to the Parthian period were actually made soon after 612, comparable with those made to the temple of Nabu. Conversely, other signs of repairs or modifications, originally dated to the Assyrian period because so much Assyrian material was re-used there, are now thought to be Parthian in date.[37] Possibly, therefore, the cult of Ishtar of Nineveh was never discontinued but was maintained without a break to Parthian times. Several Roman helmets of Parthian or Sassanian date were found in the Ishtar temple, likely to be dedications made by soldiers, owing to her nature as a war-goddess ('battle is a game for her'), as well as terracotta figurines with erotic themes,[38] stored or dedicated there owing to her nature as goddess of love and fertility.

So little is known about the circumstances of Nineveh's sack in 612 that we are not even sure who kept control of the heartland of Assyria afterwards. But the Babylonians retained some control, for a contemporary chronicle tells that the conquering king Nabopolassar honoured the city after its capture by receiving tribute there, presumably in a palace. He would not have done so if nothing but smoking ruins and dusty rubble had remained, with danger from collapsing roof-beams. At the very least, this detail shows that one part of one building was still in sufficiently good condition to be chosen for a royal ceremony.

The 14th year (of Nabopolassar's reign, i.e. 612 BC—after the siege of Nineveh had been successful for the Babylonians)... the king of Akkad [and his troops] moved as far as Naṣibina. Pillage and banishment... and the Rusapeans were brought to Nineveh before the king of Akkad.[39]

Nabopolassar was distraught at the damage done to the wonderful city. Nabonidus later recorded his predecessor's reaction to the sack:

(As for) the king of Babylon—the work of Marduk, for whom pillage is an abomination—he (Nabopolassar) did not lay a finger on the cult of any of the gods, but went around with his hair unkempt (in mourning), and slept on the ground as his couch,[40]

an admission which shows the intention had been to prevent devastation, and that some cults were still viable in the city. Thus archaeological evidence of repair to the temples may be linked to that confession in a Neo-Babylonian text.

No clay records specifically dated later than 612 BC have been found at Nineveh. However, the Assyrian city of Dur-Katlimmu[41] on the Habur river has recently yielded unquestionable evidence that it remained important, revealing late Assyrian monumental buildings where Assyrian-style administration persisted without a break for the next fifty years, into the reign of Nebuchadnezzar II.[42] Duplicates of Sennacherib's prism and cylinder inscriptions, describing how he created his palace garden, were placed in several different cities, raising their chances of long-term survival.

Fig. 65 Impression from a cylinder seal with a Late Elamite inscription, probably late 7th–6th century BC, found above the temple of Ishtar at Nineveh. Chalcedony, 2.2 × 1.75 cm.

A few undated clay tablets bearing correspondence in the Elamite language were found at Nineveh, and a study made of the seal designs impressed on them suggested that they quite likely dated after 612 (see Figure 65).[43] This suggestion, though challenged,[44] matches a new understanding that the Elamite capital at Susa had recovered by 625 from an earlier destruction, confirmed by new evidence from a rich tomb and the analysis of its contents.[45] Cyrus the Great has proved to be an Elamite rather than a Persian, so his conquest of Babylon reflects the strength of that Elamite revival.[46] On some of the sculpture panels in both the South-West Palace and the North Palace, selective damage done to disfigure pro-Assyrian Elamites and the images of those Assyrian kings who had fought the Elamites implies the rooms were still accessible after the sack, perhaps some time later.[47] It now seems possible that Greek historians implicitly included Elamites when they referred to 'Medes', emphasizing Cyrus' family connection with the Median royal line.[48]

As at Nineveh, so at nearby Nimrud, archaeologists expected to find that the city had been abandoned in 612, for they dug with Xenophon's *Anabasis* in hand.[49] When one reads Mallowan's quite detailed account, one finds a discrepancy and a tension between what was found and what was expected. He found that the 'ruins' of the temple of Nabu were reoccupied between around 500 and 300 BC,[50] and a sequence of six 'not unprosperous villages' arose upon the citadel,[51] around and on top of the temple of Nabu, continuing the ceramic and burial customs of Assyria. Its people built large kilns for the manufacture of glass; they imported the best wine (for strength and bouquet) all the way from Thasos in the northern Aegean,[52] and buried their dead with silver coins and with antiquities such as cylinder seals. From the subsequent period when Seleucid kings ruled, a remarkable hemispherical glass bowl of laced design, mainly clear but with yellow and brown elements, is dated from similar finds elsewhere, as a fashionable item probably imported from Alexandria in the late 3rd or 2nd century BC.[53] Renewed excavations in the 1980s found no less than three levels of post-Assyrian occupation in a large building complex inside the wall of the lower city, and 'all produced pottery identical with that of the latest Assyrian occupation from when they cannot have been far removed in time'.[54] A reasonable level of reoccupation had soon followed the disaster of conquest; in particular, 'an important post-Assyrian settlement is attested by a large house' in which Achaemenid pottery was identified.[55]

Archaeological evidence for the Achaemenid period presents notorious difficulties which extend far beyond Nineveh. Apart from the two ceremonial centres at Persepolis and Pasargadae, in which the Persian kings imported foreign styles along with foreign craftsmen, the new rulers had no tradition of civic architecture to impose upon conquered cities, unlike the Greeks whose theatres, stoas and gymnasia herald Greek presence throughout the ancient world. In Assyria palaces had been built so monumental and durable that it was easy to make them available for a new administration, sweeping aside debris and using local workmen to repair roofs and doorways in the traditional way. Even in Babylon and Uruk, where a high standard of cultural and civic life was maintained, one is hard-pressed to identify a specifically Achaemenid building. As Willem Vogelsang has remarked, the Persian empire 'does not seem to have had much effect upon the material culture of the East', and the old cities, with their grand buildings still more or less preserved, 'often provided the administrative infrastructure for the newly emerging empire'.[56]

When Cyrus II built his ceremonial capital at Pasargadae around 545 BC, it was the palace architecture of Nineveh that he imitated, not that of Babylon or Susa. He could send craftsmen 'to the partly ruined palaces of Sargon and Sennacherib in order to make close copies of the original models'.[57] Likewise when Darius built Persepolis around 515 BC, nearly a century after the fall of Nineveh, 'most of the motifs on the reliefs on façades, staircases and doorways can be paralleled in Assyria ... the overwhelming impression of influence [is] from Assyria', specifically from the South-West Palace of Sennacherib at

Nineveh.[58] Had the palaces at Nineveh been totally ruined in 612, the brick structures would have been quite eroded by the time those Achaemenid palaces were planned nearly a century later, and so would not have inspired imitation by successful and ambitious emperors. For royal-sponsored architects and designers to have viewed the palaces and gateways at Nineveh before embarking upon the design of Pasargadae, with its composite creatures dominating the main gateways, a certain degree of local security must have been relied upon. The designers and artists would have visited Sennacherib's palaces at Nineveh in order to copy and adapt marvels from the most famous palaces in the world.

As a major city of the Achaemenid period, Nineveh's size and importance is vehemently proclaimed by the biblical prophet Jonah, whose Hebrew book was probably composed at that time. But its testimony seems to be cancelled out by the *Anabasis* of Xenophon. He described how the battle of Cunaxa in Babylonia in 401 BC led to the death of Cyrus the Pretender and the consequent retreat northwards of his Greek soldiers. Those remnants of '10,000 men' marched through hostile territory that had once been the heartland of Assyria, passing ruined and abandoned cities with non-Assyrian names. He wrote the account more than thirty years later.

It is generally admitted that there are unsatisfactory aspects of the story as a description of true events.[59] Reacting to an earlier account now lost in which his involvement was described less creditably, Xenophon is thought to have remodelled events to exaggerate his own heroic role and to refute charges of bribery, corruption, of serving purely for personal enrichment.[60] Three months are not accounted for in his journal-like account, a 'Great Lacuna'.[61] Almost none of the places he named in Mesopotamia can be identified from contemporary texts, and some known cities that he might have mentioned are absent from his account. He did not even name the place where the vital battle took place—only elsewhere is it called Cunaxa. The Median Wall that he described cannot be located in the appropriate area.[62] Snow fell and disappeared with unreal rapidity in the highlands of Anatolia. He omitted to mention that his troops, working their way up the Tigris valley on its eastern side, had to cross the Lower Zab, a river of significant size.

On reaching the region where the three great royal cities of Assyria—Nineveh, Nimrud and Khorsabad—were located, he spoke of deserted cities named Larissa and Mespila. Larissa was a common

Greek word for any citadel but Mespila is found neither in Akkadian nor in Greek.[63] Most scholars assume that those are alternative names for Nimrud and Nineveh, but they are not so named in any other source. There is no reason why Xenophon should not have known, at the very least, the name of Nineveh, since it was used in a wide variety of literature both during his lifetime and later: as Ninus or Nineve to Ctesias, later to Strabo,[64] Diodorus Siculus and Tacitus,[65] and much later to Ammianus Marcellinus.[66] As Ninue it was known in the Aramaic stories of *Ahiqar* and *Ashurbanipal and Shamash-shum-ukin* which were popular in Ptolemaic Egypt; as Nineveh to the authors of the Book of Jonah; and as 'Ninus, the time-honoured capital of Assyria' to the biblical Greek story of Judith. The Assyrian name of Nimrud as Calah is also preserved in Strabo's mention of Calachene.[67] Those two city names are not the only ones to have survived through hard times and changes up to the present day; many others bear witness to continuous residence.[68] Elsewhere loss of a city's civic life leads to renaming when it is revived at a much later date.

Also at odds with the picture given by Xenophon is the evidence from a letter of Arshama, royally born satrap of Egypt in the late 5th century BC, referring to his emissary travelling through Assyria with written permission to claim rations from Arshama's estates. The regions are named, and they include several parts of the Assyrian heartland, one of them a district near Nineveh (see Figure 66).[69] Arshama's administrators would have repaired and maintained the sturdy infrastructure that delivered water to his farms and orchards, given the incentive of royal patronage. The Assyrian water channels would have been too valuable to neglect.

It would have added to the verisimilitude of his account, had Xenophon mentioned the Assyrian cities by their known names. Both Mespila and Larissa are said to have belonged to the Medes before they were conquered in circumstances which Xenophon attributes in legendary or novelistic fashion to a persistent cloud and to a thunderstorm respectively. The extant fragment B of the novel *Ninos and Semiramis*, preserved on a papyrus dating to the early 1st century AD,[70] echoes some of the motifs in the *Anabasis*, in particular about Armenians, crossing rivers, ice and snow in mountain passes, a similarity encouraging the view that the *Anabasis* shares with Xenophon's *Cyropaedia* some of the character of a novel.[71] At that time the novel was gaining popularity—a new form of prose literature— weakening the link between fiction and factual narrative. A growing

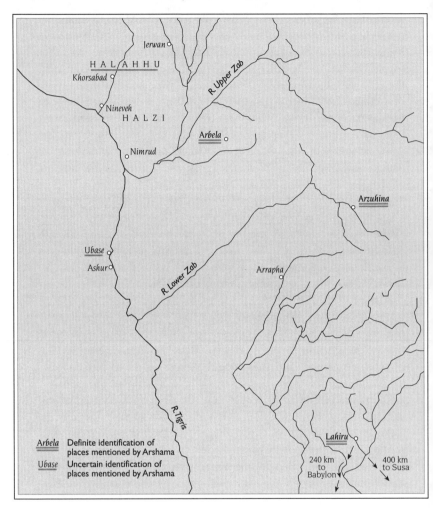

Fig. 66 Sketch map showing locations in which Arshama, satrap of Egypt under Darius II, owned estates, *c.*425 BC.

fashion for composing prose fiction, coloured with touches of genuine historical background, may explain why Ctesias' *Persica*, preserved only in fragments, seems to mix historical fact with legend.

Xenophon understood that part of Assyria belonged to Media, for which no other evidence can be found. His view belongs to a scheme for world history in terms of the rise and fall of great empires, which was popular at that time. Since the supposed Median empire had been the most recent to fall, there is a suspicion that a schematic literary-historical pattern has influenced his composition, presenting a picture of an almost empty land following the dramatic end of Assyrian imperial power. In presenting Assyria as a land lacking visible monuments, Xenophon implied that it was outside known history, in accordance with the general idea that public monuments serve as markers of historical time; their destruction abolishes it.[72] In fact the Assyrian heartland was certainly well within the Achaemenid Persian empire at the time, and had previous belonged to the Neo-Babylonian empire. The letter written by Arshama the satrap shows that literacy and careful accounting were still in force there; and those literate qualities belong to city life and centralized education.[73]

When we turn to the Seleucid and early Parthian periods, Greek inscriptions, Hellenistic sculpture, and coins found in and around the ancient Assyrian buildings at Nineveh give datable evidence, but there is no trace of Greek-style civic architecture such as stoa, theatre and hippodrome. One may compare a similar lack in Babylonian cities under Seleucid rule, apart from Babylon itself.[74]

Fortunately Layard found 'the remains of several dishes and vases in serpentine and marble', one fragment having an inscription of a priest of Amun from Ptolemaic Egypt,[75] contemporary with Seleucid rulers, which testifies to Nineveh's international ties. This evidence is augmented by a remarkable inscription, carved in well-formed Greek letters on a stone column, which was found in the temple of Nabu recording a dedication by Apollophanes son of Asklepiades on behalf of Apollonius, who is called '*stratēgos* and *epistatēs* of the city (polis)'. Its date is probably around 32 BC, so an earlier inscription on the stone column, which had been erased, presumably dates to the Seleucid period.[76] Two of the names contain the name Apollo, who was regarded as the Greek equivalent of the Mesopotamian god Nabu.[77] The rather vaguely recorded evidence for repairs to the temple of Nabu scarcely helps to reconstruct the use of the building after 612, but the date recorded on the column inscription, probably 32/31 BC, combined with the find-spot, allows the possibility that the temple of Nabu was still in use.

Further evidence that Nineveh was officially a Greek polis comes from a Greek dedication 'to the polis' by Apollonius son of Demetrius—a different man?—'the *archon*', a title used alongside *stratēgos* at Palmyra. The inscription, carved on a massive stone altar, had been added beside an Assyrian cuneiform dedication to the Sibitti-gods, 'The

Seven', which had been inscribed in the 9th century BC, and never erased.[78] The altar, 0.68 m high, 1.03 long and 0.74 wide, imitates a piece of wooden furniture with lion's paws for feet set into the stone block. The Assyrian inscription proclaims the power of the Seven Gods, the Pleiades, in Nineveh:

To the Seven, great gods, noble warriors, lovers of reed thickets, who patrol mountain tracks(?), surveyors of heaven and earth, who maintain shrines, heed prayers, accept pleas, receive entreaties, fulfil desires; who fell foes—compassionate gods to whom it is good to pray, who dwell in Nineveh, . . . I, Shalmaneser, appointee of the god Enlil, vice-regent of the god Ashur . . . dedicated this to the Seven, my lords, for my life, that my days might be long, my years many, for the prosperity of my seed and land, security of my vice-regal throne; for burning my foes, destroying all my opponents, to make the kings who oppose me kneel at my feet, I dedicated (this altar) to the Seven.

The Greek inscription has a simple dedication:

Apollonios son of Demetrios the *archon*. To the City (*polis*).

The addition was superficial here. In the temple of the Seven Gods at Khorsabad an *iwan* (a type of hall characteristic of the Parthian and Sassanian periods) was built on to the courtyard, implying continuity of use and perhaps of worship.[79] The presence of a *stratēgos/archon* at Nineveh perhaps implies that the city was refounded as a *polis* during the Seleucid period, whether around 300 BC under Seleucus I or under one of his successors.[80]

Under Seleucid rule, the *stratēgos* had a variety of responsibilities: the defence of his region, implying that troops were garrisoned in or near Nineveh under his command; the management of royal land; and the distribution of royal documents.[81] But not every holder of the title had the same remit, and Apollonius may not have served a Seleucid king, since the title continued in use as the Seleucid empire fragmented. Coins of Antiochus IV (175–164 BC) found at Nineveh give one possible reign when the *stratēgos* would have held office, but no better evidence has come to light for dating his tenure.

At very roughly the same time as Apollonius governed Nineveh, the poet Antipater of Thessalonica travelled to 'Asia' to visit his patron in Cilicia, 'O Phoebus, . . . grant me to go with fair sailing through the waves to the Asian land in the wake of Piso's long vessel', and claimed to have seen the Hanging Garden.[82] He probably went to Hierapolis—Castabala in Cilicia, a significant location because not far

away in Tarsus was a temple built by Sennacherib whose typically
Assyrian images of deities were still used on plaques of the Seleucid
period and on Roman imperial coins including those of Hadrian and
Gallienus—evidence that some kind of legacy from Sennacherib still
exercised a fascination in Cilicia, even if it had evolved into the stuff
of legend.[83]

Seven metres down below the surface in one of the palaces at
Nineveh Rassam found a fine statue of Heracles Epitrapezios '(sitting)
on a table', dated to the 1st or 2nd century AD, inscribed with the
name Sarapiodorus son of Artemidorus, and signed by one Deiogenes
(see Plate 17). It is just over half a metre high. This is excellent
evidence for elite occupation of that palace building in the Parthian
period. The name Deiogenes—the same man?—had been added in
Greek beside the mouth of a beardless man on a sculpture in the
North Palace of Ashurbanipal, dated roughly to the same period, and
there seems to have been an earlier, mainly erased inscription alongside it (see Figure 67).[84] In proximity to the donkey, the inscription
may be interpreted: 'Deiogenes is an ass!' [85]

A substantial piece of evidence for Graeco-Assyrian worship at
Nineveh comes from the second citadel mound of Nineveh, Nebi
Yunus, which faces Kouyunjik (the other citadel mound) across the
Khosr river. A shrine there contained a limestone statue 1.35 m tall, of

Fig. 67 Graffito with the name Deiogenes in Greek as if emerging from the
mouth of a beardless boy, on a stone wall panel found in place in a sloping
passage in Ashurbanipal's palace at Nineveh.

Fig. 68 Limestone statue of Hermes, painted in red, blue and orange; eyes inlaid with glass and mother-of-pearl, found at Nineveh. Ht. 135 cm.

a slender winged figure identified as Hermes (see Figure 68). It stood originally on a pedestal inside a small mud-brick shrine built to an Assyrian-style plan. This building proved to be a part of a much bigger complex containing several other shrines.[86] The statue had hair painted orange-red, wings red and blue, eyes inlaid with mother-of-pearl and blue glass, although it had no caduceus—the snake-entwined wand that he usually held as herald of the gods. It is dated to the late 2nd or early 3rd century AD.[87]

Alabaster was valuable, for it had to be imported from far away, so it was a material suitable only for the top of society. This is relevant for a finely carved alabaster base made for two or three statues, long broken away (see Figure 69). It bore a dedication in Greek, perhaps to be translated 'Be lucky!' as well as 'To Eutyche'—the goddess of good fortune.[88] If the latter, by analogy with sculpture panels dedicated to Tyche 'Fortune' found at Palmyra and Dura Europus, a reconstruction might show the city goddess centrally placed and seated, with the Tyche figure standing on her left holding a palm of victory. This would then be evidence for officially refounding the city.

Fig. 69 Alabaster base for three small statues, Greek inscription translated either 'for Eutyche', deity of good luck, or 'Good luck!'. Length 19.6 cm, ht. 8.0 cm.

Fine Parthian gold jewellery of the 2nd century AD came from tombs, of a richness to indicate 'that they are those of very important members of the settlement at Nineveh, or even perhaps its leaders'.[89] A coin of Tiberius (42 BC–AD 30) and impressions of a coin of Trajan (AD 98–117) on gold leaves, also found in the tombs, show that Roman objects were valued as grave goods. The discovery at Nineveh of a list of Macedonian month names dated to the 3rd century AD shows the persistence of Seleucid influence.[90]

A comparison for Nineveh's fate may be made with Khorsabad. Even today many scholars refer to the city as one abandoned at the death of Sargon in 705 BC, perpetuating the misleading certainty of the archaeologists who excavated there, both in the mid 19th and the mid 20th century. But dated cuneiform records, still unpublished,[91] show that it remained an administrative centre for a century after Sargon's death. Moreover, all its main buildings and rooms are now thought to have been used after 612 BC.[92] An inscription of Nebuchadnezzar II names it as one of the cities of Assyria,[93] and it was presumably the provincial capital of Halahhu district during the Achaemenid period when Arshama the satrap owned estates there.[94] The clean-living Persians left very little of their own debris behind, and did not clear away relics of Assyrian residence.

In all three of the great northern capitals, Nineveh, Nimrud and Khorsabad, it is significant that the conquerors and later occupiers apparently left many important vestiges of Assyrian power, especially clay tablets and objects of ivory and other precious materials, as if to pay homage to its greatness. In Fort Shalmaneser, a huge building at Nimrud, two rooms in the south-west area containing ivories of the 9th and 8th centuries were not cleared when that part of the building was in use after the fall of Assyria.[95] In Babylon too, administrative records from the reign of Nebuchadnezzar remained in his palace and were still not cleared out when the building was used by Hellenistic rulers who repaired the roof with Greek-style tiles.[96] It was simply wrong to deduce that dated texts, objects of metal, stone and ivory found in a damaged building gave the date of destruction.

During the Roman period a new kingdom named Adiabene sprang up and became a strong power based in its capital Arbela, and the description of Nineveh as 'a great city of Adiabene', given by Ammianus Marcellinus, cannot be doubted. The deity Issar-Bel/ Sharbel worshipped there in the 4th century AD has been identified as an Assyrian form of Ishtar with the honorific title Bel attached.[97]

Exactly how long the South-West Palace, or a part of it, remained accessible to visitors is uncertain. At Taq-i Bustan in north-western Iran a rock sculpture shows the Sassanian king Khusrau II (AD 591–628) hunting boar in marshes (see Figure 70).[98] It bears a very strong resemblance to Sennacherib's sculpture in the South-West Palace showing his campaign against Babylonians in the marshes of southern Babylonia: the background of reeds in which the boats of huntsmen make their attack, and the way that different episodes are shown alongside and above one another, are too similar to be dismissed as coincidental. They are markedly different from the normal heraldic arrangements in Sassanian art, of figures with lateral symmetry. Similarly a rock sculpture at Sar Mashhad in Fars province, dating to the late 3rd century AD, shows the Sassanian king Bahram II (AD 276–293) on foot stabbing a rearing lion while another lion dies at his feet, in a scene that resembles the lion hunts of Ashurbanipal on bas-relief panels from the North Palace at Nineveh.[99] If the comparison is valid, some of the bas-reliefs of Sennacherib and Ashurbanipal would still have been visible in the 6th century AD.

Scholars have counted on a variety of factors to 'explain', with hindsight, the collapse of an empire.[100] Theological and moral corruption of the Deuteronomic kind favoured by blood-and-thunder preachers, Ctesias and Sidney Smith, was once popular but is currently out of fashion; socio-economic explanations arising from pure theory often have no textual or archaeological support; climate change and tectonic events have recently become popular explanations for swift and total decline, but are still impossible to date with precision.

There is no doubt that Nineveh itself suffered a severe decline. Resources would have been diverted away from the old centres of power. The virtual civil war that divided the ruling powers just before

Fig. 70 Sassanian rock carving in the grotto at Taq-i Bustan in NW Iran, scene of hunting in marshes, reminiscent of Sennacherib's marshland scenes in the South-West Palace at Nineveh.

the final defeat would have made the efficient collection and use of taxes impossible. Enormous expense needed to support competing armies, diminishing returns from tribute-paying vassals, let alone the impossibility of new conquests, must have meant a swift degradation of buildings and the infrastructure of communications.[101] Agriculture would inevitably have declined, leading to shortages within the cities. Whether disease or climate change contributed to hardships is impossible to say for lack of reliable evidence.[102]

A huge city, such as Nineveh was in the late 7th century BC, does not become deserted overnight. Due to its position on a main road commanding the crossing over the Tigris, as a city maintained for thousands of years, its people would not have abandoned it. Nineveh's enormous palace walls would not be destroyed even by the fiercest conflagration.

For certain the powerful ideological values centred upon the national god Ashur and Assyrian kingship broke down, but that did not stop the cult continuing to be celebrated in a more modern building set on top of the Assyrian temple of Ashur, worship that lasted to the beginning of the Sassanian period. Even at that time people were still using the name of the god in their own names written in Aramaic script.[103] Worshippers of the Assyrian goddess Ishtar of Nineveh and Arbela, known to Herodotus as Mylitta, also perpetuated traditional beliefs through the medium of Aramaic. It is possible that Nineveh remained impoverished throughout the Neo-Babylonian period (612–539 BC) and through much or all of the Achaemenid period (539–333 BC)—lying more or less dormant for some two centuries until a revival eventually took place under Seleucid rule. But during that time the monumentally sturdy buildings—its walls, palaces and temples—remained standing, if damaged, and its water-channelling schemes too, for the admiration of visitors: for the inspiration that Achaemenid Persians derived from late Assyrian art and architecture, manifest at Pasargadae and at Persepolis, and for the amazement of scouts in Alexander's army encamped at Gaugamela.

Literary hyperbole must take some of the blame for misleading historians for so long. Whenever a city was captured, it was a catastrophe which could only be understood as abandonment by its gods. Deserted by the deities, it was compared to a city ruined by a devastating flood, its people scattered, a haunt for owls and jackals. Throughout Near Eastern history the theme recurs: Ur, Nippur, Babylon, Jerusalem—all great, ancient cities, all in turn abandoned by their gods, utterly ruined. Archaeology, and occasionally texts too, sometimes tell a different story.

In conclusion, the Hanging Garden itself was not necessarily still visible and visited as a marvel in Hellenistic and later times, but the palaces with some of their sculptured panels portraying the garden could still be visited, at least in part, and the great works at Bavian and Jerwan were still highly visible. The evidence collected in this chapter leaves open the possibility that people could still visit Nineveh in the centuries after 612, and see some evidence for the World Wonder built by Sennacherib.

Conclusion

But I shall let the little I have learnt go forth into the day in order that someone better than I may guess the truth, and in his work may prove and rebuke my error. At this I shall rejoice that I was yet a means whereby this truth has come to light.

Albrecht Dürer: quoted by Karl Popper,
Conjectures and Refutations

This book has shown that the Hanging Garden was built at Nineveh, not Babylon, by Sennacherib, not Nebuchadnezzar or Semiramis. At long last specific evidence has come to light to reveal the solution to a complex question. The correct decipherment of a 7th-century BC Assyrian inscription gives a match with the crucial elements in descriptions of later Greek authors. Sennacherib's palace garden fulfils the criteria for a World Wonder: the whole project is magnificent in conception, spectacular in engineering, and brilliant in artistry, from the start at Khinnis through the aqueduct at Jerwan, into the citadel at Nineveh, the garden itself, and the palace with wall sculptures showing scenes from the garden.

When in 1854 Hormuzd Rassam excavated at Nineveh in the North Palace, he uncovered a sculpture showing a garden with 'a bridge having three pointed arches', and noted, 'This has been identified by Assyrian scholars as a representation of the hanging gardens of Babylon.'[1] (See Figure 13) He thought that the Nineveh sculpture showing the garden was a picture of a scene in Babylon.[2] Despite its recognizable similarity to the Greek descriptions of the Hanging Garden, there were three main reasons why nobody pursued the possibility that it was connected directly with the World Wonder.

Josephus had expressly claimed that Nebuchadnezzar in Babylon was
the builder. Besides, there was no reason to think that Nineveh was
ever known as 'Babylon', nor that Sennacherib was called 'Nebuchadnezzar'. Nineveh was supposed to have been utterly destroyed in 612
BC; if that were the case, the palace garden of Sennacherib would have
been abandoned and neglected long before it had a chance to enter
into Greek tradition.

But the famous Hanging Garden was said by Q. Curtius Rufus to
have been so well built that it flourished for many centuries, and since
Babylon was continuously occupied into the Islamic period, scholars
could take his words at face value:

Although lapse of time gradually undermines and destroys not only works
made by the hand of man, but also those of Nature herself, this huge
structure, although worked upon by the roots of so many trees and loaded
with the weight of so great a forest, endures unchanged.

For those reasons many people supposed the match between the Assyrian
evidence and the Greek descriptions showed that Sennacherib's
garden was a forerunner to the real Hanging Garden built by Nebuchadnezzar in Babylon a century and a half later.

All the arguments to be found in this book stem from the better
understanding of an original Assyrian text. The sculptured stone
panel from the palace of Ashurbanipal at Nineveh, now in the British
Museum, displays other elements from those later descriptions. The
drawing made of another panel, now known as Original Drawing IV
77, displays yet another extraordinary feature in accord with the
Greek authors (see Figure 13).[3] With this core of evidence, other
apparent difficulties can be resolved, leaving no doubt that the Assyrian king Sennacherib built the garden, which he himself proclaimed
as a wonder for all peoples, in his capital city Nineveh. The concept of
building a World Wonder dates from this period, and continued into
the following rule of the great Babylonian king Nebuchadnezzar II.

In support of the new understanding comes some evidence for
survival at Nineveh, and the evidence that cities other than Babylon
proper could also be known as 'Babylon'. Above all, the whole
complex of palace, garden and watering system are self-evidently
brilliant enough to qualify as a marvel, as Sennacherib himself described
them.

Several scenarios could be called up to explain the survival of
knowledge and interest for eleven centuries, from around 700 BC

when Sennacherib built the garden and wrote his prism text, to *c.* AD 400 when Philo wrote his description.

Supposing the garden was wrecked completely in 612 BC, the bronze screws melted down and their emplacements smashed, one might posit that all the details of construction and appearance became known to Alexander's men in 331 BC by local knowledge at Jerwan and Gaugamela, but with legends already proliferating over whether an Assyrian king, or Semiramis, or Nebuchadnezzar, was the builder. Later, during the Seleucid and early Parthian periods when Nineveh was once again a great city and governed by a *stratēgos*, the appearance of the garden was still visible on the two bas-reliefs in the two partially ruined palaces to maintain public interest in a vanished marvel. In this case the supposed eye-witness accounts of Classical authors are not to be taken literally. However, it is still a problem that knowledgeable guides would have been needed to explain that water was raised invisibly by screws from the aqueduct to the top of the garden, since presumably they were not to be seen on the sculptured panels.

If several complete and more-or-less undamaged panels showing the garden, both in the South-West Palace and in the North Palace, were still visible in the time when Philo of Byzantium was writing, and if at that time the Hanging Garden was no longer tended, one might have expected some mention of the fact that it only survived in sculpture, and that one could see only ruined remains. Such a theme would have been welcome as a romantic topic for Greek and Latin poets, and a remarkable example of ecphrasis. When the Roman poet Sextus Propertius mused upon the transitory nature and deterioration of World Wonders, he did not include the Hanging Garden. When some of the older World Wonders had been superseded by younger marvels, as in the list of Gregory of Nazianz, the garden was still included.

Suppose, on the other hand, that the garden survived the sack of 612 BC, that Nabopolassar was able to prevent the robbing of the screws and damage to their emplacements, that the garden was maintained during the Achaemenid, Seleucid and early Parthian periods with intermittent renovation. The two bas-reliefs in the partially ruined palaces would also have been seen by visitors. However, by the time of Alexander, people in Assyria could no longer read cuneiform, so the name of the builder passed into legend. Visitors to Nineveh could have seen screws in operation, and the roof-top trees, still alive on the pillared walkway, would have remained a striking feature. In this case eye-witness accounts would have been available for Classical authors.

It remains uncertain whether the machinery that lifted water to the top of the garden could have been kept in working order, or whether it was restored under Seleucid government. If the cast bronze screws were looted in 612 BC or shortly afterwards, the top terraces of the garden would have dried up, leaving the colonnade with its heavy roofing carrying dead trees. Even if they were not looted, the screws might have corroded, though it is significant to note that the great bronze barrier of the 12th century BC found at Susa is still in good condition in the Louvre. If Nabopolassar managed to restrain major looting—'an abomination to Marduk'—before the vandals reached the garden, the screw might have persisted for centuries with minimal maintenance, until the civic pride of the first *stratēgos* put the garden once again under firm management.

Was the sturdy engineering that brought mountain water to the gardens, orchards and fields around Nineveh still functioning, centuries after 700 BC? The Shallalat dam which probably belongs to that system was still in use as recently as the 20th century, and the Jerwan aqueduct is recognizably in place today. Even if the enemy in 612 BC had cut down trees and damaged installations, the essential provision of abundant water was still there for the environs of the city. Depletion of income to the city through trade, and the tax evasion that inevitably accompanies a breakdown of law and order, would not have stopped the water flowing even if some of the channels were damaged or obstructed. Some temporary flooding might have resulted, but such well-drained land is most unlikely to have been degraded over more than a small part, and local labour could have made repairs as necessary.

Crucial was the state of the aqueduct. If it remained undamaged or was immediately repaired, it would have ensured that the citadel could still attract elite occupation. The lower part of the garden with its supply of water by aqueduct would have remained viable, even if knowledge of the screws was relegated to literary sources and to folk memory, available to Strabo and to Philo of Byzantium.

The solution offered in this book essentially began with the unearthing of that Assyrian sculpture at Nineveh in 1854, long before I was born. From detailed articles already published, the attribution of the Hanging Garden to Sennacherib at Nineveh has now been accepted by many scholars.[4] Three linked but individual parts to the ancient wonder have been identified. One is the garden itself, with its terraces and pavilions, conveniently set beside the palace, and its cunningly integrated, innovative water-raising system. Another is the complex network of watercourses—aqueducts, canals and sluices, tunnels and dams that brought water from the mountains to the garden on the citadel. The third is the sculptured grottoes, rock carvings and springs from which waters were drawn, so far distant from their destination.

That the Hanging Garden was built in Babylon by Nebuchadnezzar the Great is a fact learned at school and can be 'verified' in encyclopaedias and histories of ancient times. To challenge such a universally accepted truth might seem the height of arrogance, revisionist scholarship at its worst. But Assyriology is a relatively recent discipline, and a new understanding is necessary in this instance. Of course, the old, displaced facts cannot physically be removed from the encyclopaedias, but even in Assyriology and ancient history, some of the facts that once seemed secure become redundant. Compendia of knowledge serve a wonderful purpose in collecting together the received wisdom of one generation, but like archaeological strata, they are superseded by later levels as time and progress move ahead, to become relics of the past, preserving the misguided certainties and unacknowledged assumptions of their time.

Not every aspect of the matter has yielded to investigation. How the screw was rotated is still unknown. The location of the gardens, while plausible, rests upon an informed guess. Speculative is the part played by either of Sennacherib's two successive queens, Tashmetu-sharrat and Naqia. How much Sennacherib himself was the genius behind the project, whether he (and his father) inspired a genius engineer and architect, is unlikely ever to be revealed by any kind of ancient Mesopotamian source.

Research sometimes leads one along unexpected paths. Two serendipitous discoveries have been Milton's use of a Greek description of the garden for the Garden of Eden in book IV of *Paradise Lost*, and Ezekiel's description of Assyria, equating Assyria with the garden and its channels for watering, a garden so wonderful that it challenged God. Sennacherib's hubris in showing himself in the company of the great gods at Khinnis matches Ezekiel's accusation.

Another satisfying result has been to show how advanced Assyrian engineering was by the time Sennacherib came to the throne. We have come a long way since 1877—twenty-three years after the discovery of the panel in Ashurbanipal's palace—when Lewis Morgan attributed to Greek and Roman civilization the invention of 'fire-baked brick . . . the aqueduct and sewer . . . the arch, the balance scale . . . and alphabetic writing'.[5] All of those inventions are now generally accepted, mainly as a result of archaeological work, to have been common in the ancient Near East before the rise of Classical Greek civilization.

Sennacherib can now take his rightful place alongside the great emperors of later time: Nero with his Domus Aurea, the Sun-king Louis XIV of France with Versailles, Frederick the Great of Prussia with Sans Souci, and Henry VIII with Nonsuch ('unrivalled'), all great builders of palaces who created gardens as an integral part of their overall design.

Like the other six, this Wonder really existed, and can no longer be written off as a figment of the imagination, a legend without historical substance, nor was the garden at Nineveh merely a precursor of the real thing. To Sennacherib, king of Assyria, belongs the credit for creating one of the seven Wonders of the ancient world.

The Section of Prism Inscription Describing the Palace and Garden

Two versions are extant, one in Baghdad, the other in Chicago: A. Heidel, 'The octagonal Sennacherib Prism in the Iraq Museum', *Sumer* 9 (1953), 152–70, which dates to 694 BC, and D. D. Luckenbill, *The Annals of Sennacherib* (1924), dated 689 BC. The author's translation and notes here follow the Akkadian text of Heidel, col. v.53–viii.13, pp. 152–70, with updating.

The form of the record as a clay prism indicates that the text was hidden from view, intended for posterity. Heidel's prism was found in the west wall of the city of Nineveh.

The use of grammatical forms from the 'Hymnic-Epic dialect', and rare words, elsewhere best known from the *Epic of Creation*, indicate that this inscription was designed to endure as high literature.

1. Col. v lines 53–63 describes Nineveh in epic terms, as the city whose foundation was planned in heaven, as the residence of all gods and goddesses, echoing the creation of Babylon in the *Epic of Creation*. The description of Assyrians as 'Enlil's people' implies a claim to Nippur as the equivalent of Nineveh.[1] The word Lalgar is a rare literary one referring to the Apsu, fresh water beneath the earth; likewise rare are *duruššu* 'foundation' and *pelludê* 'rites'.

At that time Nineveh the exalted metropolis, the city beloved of Ishtar, in which all the ceremonies of gods and goddesses take place, the eternal base, the everlasting foundation whose plan was drawn in the writing of the firmament at the beginning of time, and whose structure was then made known; a clever place where hidden knowledge resides for every kind of skilful work. All sorts of rites, secrets from Lalgar are planned within it, whence the kings my predecessors and forefathers had exercised rule over Assyria from time immemorial before me, and had governed Enlil's people.

2. Col. v lines 64–76. Sennacherib emphasizes the inadequacy of predecessors in planning and building the city. The word *kummu* translated as 'dwelling' is normally used for the cella of deities.

Yet nobody among them had even thought to widen the residential area of the city, to rebuild city walls or straighten streets and dig canals, to plant new orchards, let alone taken the initiative. Nor had anyone considered or assessed the palace within it, a dwelling for a seat of government, in which the accommodation was too meagre, whose workmanship was not skilful enough.

3. Col. v lines 77–86. The king conceives his wise plan and musters conquered peoples for the labour of building. The passage contains two apocopated suffixes typical of the Hymnic-Epic dialect.

I myself planned it, and I took the initiative, I Sennacherib king of the world, king of Assyria, to carry out that work in accordance with the plan of the god. I uprooted peoples from Chaldaea, Aram, Mannay, Que, Cilicia, Philistia and Tyre, who had not submitted to my yoke, and made them carry the head-pad, and they made bricks.

4. Col. v line 87–col. vi line 14. He reiterates that he needed to replace an inadequate palace built by his forebears, who had mismanaged their operations, sinking boats and damaging the health of the workmen.

The previous palace was 360 cubits long and 95 cubits wide, and so its accommodation was too meagre—the one which the kings my predecessors and forefathers had built as a seat of government, but had not done the work on it cleverly enough. They had quarried (?) for guardian colossi (*aladlammû*) of white limestone in Tastiate on the far side of the Tigris to hold their gateways. To have ships constructed they caused a shortage of large trees in forests throughout their land, and then in the month of Ayyar, the time of the spring spate, they had difficulty bring them across to this bank; they sank some large ships at the quay crossing, and exhausted their labour force, they made them ill with exertion and effort, but eventually fetched them with difficulty and installed them in their gateways.

5. Col. vi lines 15–27. The chaotic and destructive power of river water is described, and the measures taken by the king to bring it under control.

The flood-prone river, a strong current which in former times had flowed close to the palace at its full flood, had let a marsh form around its base, loosening its foundation.[2] I pulled down that small palace in its entirety. I diverted the course of the flood-prone river from the city centre and directed its outflow into the land which surrounds the city at the back. For half an acre along the water course I bonded four (courses of?) great limestone slabs with bitumen and laid reeds from reed thickets and canes over them.

6. Col. vi lines 28–38. The king creates extra space from dredged soil to extend the area available for his palace.

A stretch of ground 340 cubits long and 289 cubits wide from the Khosr river and the outskirts of the city I took as extra land. I added it to the extent of the earlier city terrace, and I raised the top to a level of 190 courses of brick throughout. To prevent the foundation of the fill weakening as time went by, due to the strength of the current, I surrounded its substructure with large blocks of limestone and I strengthened its earthwork.

7. Col. vi lines 39–65. The king specifies the large size of the new palace, and adjacent pavilions, and the rare and costly materials used in its

construction and decoration. The king designates his feminine door-way figures of alabaster and ivory as a wonder, literally 'for gazing at', which may indicate that the public sometimes had access. Twice the narrative present tense is used, as also in epic; there are four examples of apocopated suffixes and two examples of the ŠD verb stem, another characteristic of the Hymnic-Epic dialect.

I increased the outline of the palace to 700 large cubits at the side, and 440 large cubits at the front, and enlarged its dwelling space. I built other palatial pavilions of gold, silver, bronze, carnelian breccia, alabaster, elephant tusk, ebony, boxwood, rosewood, cedar, cypress, pine, *elammaku*-wood, and Indian wood (sandalwood?) for my royal abodes, and I constructed a *hilāni*-building like a North Syrian palace, opposite the gates. I laid over it beams of cedar and cypress whose fragrance is sweet, grown on the mountains of Amanus and Sirara. I bound door-leaves of cedar, cypress, pine and Indian wood with bands of silver and copper, and fix(ed) them in the door-frames. In the upper rooms within the private apartments I open(ed) up latticed(?) windows. I placed feminine protective statues in their doors, fashioned from alabaster and ivory, carrying flowers and holding hands(?), they radiate poise and charm, they are so beautiful that I have made of them a wonder. As for the ceilings inside the main rooms (?), I lightened their darkness and made them as bright as day. I made silver and copper pegs with knobs encircle their interiors. I decorated with baked brick glazed with blue the arches(?), friezes, and all of their cornices(?), in order to make the work in my palace splendid, and to perfect the touch of my hands.

8. Col. vi line 66–col. vii line 6. The gods Ashur and Ishtar reveal to the king a new source of huge trees in the Sirara mountains, and a new source for big blocks of alabaster in the mountains of the West.

At that time Ashur and Ishtar, who approve my tenure of the priesthood and call me by my name, revealed to me the place where flourish gigantic cedars which have been growing since ancient times and have become quite massive, standing in secret within the mountains of Sirara; access also to alabaster, which was especially prized for dagger pommels in the days of the kings my forefathers, they opened up to me. And breccia for huge storage jars such as have never before been discovered, revealed itself in the village of Dargila in the region of Til Barsip. Next to Nineveh in the territory of Balaṭa, white limestone was revealed in large quantities in accordance with the will of the gods, and I created great bull-colossi and other limbed figures of alabaster which were made out of a single block of stone, perfectly proportioned, standing tall on their own bases; cow-colossi of alabaster with most attractive features, their bodies radiant like a bright day, and high threshold stones of breccia. I cut the blocks out from their matrix on two sides and had them hauled into Nineveh for the work on my palace. I gave birth to bull-colossi and cow-colossi of white limestone with the touch of Nin-kura,[3] and made their forms perfectly.

9. Col. vii lines 7–52. The king describes his new method of casting copper for pillars (with bases in the form of?) striding lions,[4] which

together with bull- and cow-colossi of alabaster, are designated a second wonder.

Whereas in former times the kings my forefathers had created copper statues imitating real forms, to put on display inside temples, and in their method of work they had exhausted all the craftsmen for lack of skill and failure to understand principles(?); they needed so much oil, wax and tallow for the work that they caused a shortage in their own lands—I, Sennacherib, leader of all princes, knowledgeable in all kinds of work, took much advice and deep thought over doing that work. Great pillars of copper, colossal striding lions, such as no previous king had ever constructed before me, with the technical skill that Ninshiku brought to perfection in me, and at the prompting of my intelligence and desire of my heart I invented a technique for copper and made it skilfully. I created clay moulds as if by divine intelligence for cylinders (*gišmahhu*—tall tree-trunks) and screws (*alamittu*—date palms), tree of riches; twelve fierce lion-colossi together with twelve mighty bull-colossi which were perfect castings; 22 cow-colossi invested with joyous allure, plentifully endowed with sexual attraction; and I poured copper into them over and over again; I made the castings of them as perfectly as if they had only weighed half a shekel each. Two of the copper bull-colossi were then coated with electrum. I installed alabaster bull-colossi alongside white limestone bull- and cow-colossi at the door-bolts of my royal pavilions. I bound tall pillars of copper alongside pillars of mighty cedar, the gift of the Amanus mountains, with bands of copper and tin, and stood them on lion bases, and then positioned door-leaves to crown their gateways. I positioned alabaster cow-colossi alongside cow-colossi cast in copper coated with electrum, and cow-colossi cast with tin, to make very shiny surfaces, also pillars of ebony, cypress, cedar, juniper, pine and Indian wood, inlaid with *pasallu*-gold and silver, on top of them, and positioned them in the dwelling-place, my seat of government, as door-posts for them. Threshold stones of brecchia and alabaster, and threshold stones that were large blocks of limestone, I put around their footings, and I have made a wonder of them.

10. Col. vii lines 53–63. He describes the new mechanism for watering the garden, the completion of the pavilions, the raising of ground around the palace, the naming of the palace, and the plantings.

In order to draw water up all day long I had ropes, bronze wires and bronze chains made, and instead of a shaduf I set up the great cylinders and *alamittu*-screws over cisterns. I made those royal pavilions look just right. I raised the height of the surroundings of the palace to be a wonder for all peoples. I gave it the name 'Incomparable Palace'. A park imitating the Amanus mountains I laid out next to it, with all kinds of aromatic plants, orchard fruit trees, trees that sustain the mountains and Chaldaea, as well as trees that bear wool, planted within it.

11. Col. vii lines 64–74. He extended the residential area of Nineveh and built huge outer and inner fortification walls. The section has asyndeton, which is a mark of literary style represented here by a dash.

Nineveh, whose settlement area had been 9,300 cubits from time immemorial, nor had any of the rulers who preceded me built an outer or inner fortification wall—I added 12,515 (cubits) from the outskirts that surrounded the city over and above the previous dimensions, and confirmed its size as 21,815 large cubits. For its great wall— the one called 'wall whose radiance casts down the enemy'—for it I made a foundation upon limestone and made it 40 bricks thick. I raised its height to 180 courses of brickwork.

12. Col. vii line 75–col. viii. line 13. The king names the 15 city gates which he built into his new wall. A narrative present tense is used for the first verb. By naming most of the gates after deities as well as the town towards which they faced, Sennacherib was making Nineveh into a 'gate of gods', which was the meaning of the name of Babylon. Other inscriptions name 14 or 18 gates. The use of *sekru* for *zikru* 'namings' is a literary usage.

I put 15 gates as openings through it to the four winds: front and back with a double track for those who come in and those who go out (to pass each other):

Gate of the god Ashur to the citadel: 'May the Steward of Ashur prevail'

Gate of Sennacherib to the district Halzi: 'Overthrows every foe'

Gate of the god Shamash to the land Gagal: 'Enlil confirms my rule'

Gate of the goddess Mullissu to the town Kar-Mullissi: 'The rule of Sennacherib is confirmed by the constellation of the Wagon'

Gate of the ramp: 'Gets rid of taboo flesh'

Gate to the town Shibaniba: 'Good fortune from the gods of grain and herd is dependable there'

Gate to the district Halahhu: 'Brings in the fruits of the mountains'

Total 7 city gates to the East that face South and East; I pronounced their names.

Gate of the god Adad of the hunting park:[5] 'Adad bestows abundance upon the country'

Gate of the god Nergal of the town Tarbiṣu: 'Erra, slaughterer of my enemies'

Gate of Sin: 'Divine Luminary who guards my regal crown'

Total 3 city gates that face North; I called them by their namings.

Gate of watering places: 'The god Ea who controls my spring'

Gate of the quay: 'Lets in the products of human habitations'

Gate of the desert: 'Gifts of the men of Sumu-El (Ishmael?) and of Tayma come in through it'

Gate of the Arsenal: 'Stocks everything'

Gate of the *handuri*:[6] 'The god Sharur, the divine weapon that fells the king's foes'

Total 5 city gates that face West: thus I proclaimed their names.

Notes

INTRODUCTION

1. M. Streck, 'Grosses Fach Altorientalistik: Der Umfang des keilschriftlichen Textkorpus', *Mitteilungen der Deutschen Orient-Gesellschaft zu Berlin* 142 (2010), 38.
2. 86 tons, if the heavy version of the weight was meant.
3. S. Dalley, 'Neo-Assyrian textual evidence for bronze-working centres', ed. J. E. Curtis, *Bronze-Working Centres of Western Asia c.1000–539 B.C.* (1988), 97–110.
4. It was not alphabetic, and was gradually replaced by the much simpler alphabetic, linear script used for the Aramaic language.
5. Laterculi Alexandrini: Pap Berolinensis 13044v, col. 8.22ff., as cited by K. Brodersen, *Die sieben Weltwunder: Legendäre Kunst- und Bauwerke der Antike* (1996, 6th edn. 2004), 9.
6. Diodorus Siculus, *The Library of History*, II.11.5.
7. See the invaluable Appendix in P. Clayton and M. Price, *The Seven Wonders of the Ancient World* (1988), 169–70.
8. See e.g. Brodersen, *Die Sieben Weltwunder* (1996), 92–117.
9. W. Burkert, *The Orientalizing Revolution: Near Eastern Influence on Greek Culture in the Early Archaic Age* (1992), 106–14.
10. See e.g. W. Horowitz, *Mesopotamian Cosmic Geography* (1998), 208; U. Koch-Westenholz, *Mesopotamian Astrology* (1995), 119.
11. See A. R. George, *Babylonian Topographical Texts* (1992), 18.
12. M. Streck, *Assurbanipal und die letzten assyrischen Könige* (1916), vol. 2, 236–9, Cylinder L6 lines 16–22.
13. E. Leichty, *The Royal Inscriptions of Esarhaddon, King of Assyria* (2011), 199 and 207.
14. F. N. H. al-Rawi, 'Nabopolassar's restoration on the wall Imgur-Enlil at Babylon', *Iraq* 47 (1985), 1–13.
15. C. B. F. Walker, *Cuneiform Brick Inscriptions* (1981), no. 96.
16. W. Abdul-Razak, 'Ishtar Gate and its inner wall', *Sumer* 35 (1979), 116–17.
17. H.-P. Schaudig, *Die Inschriften Nabonids von Babylon und Kyros' des Grossen* (2001), 554–6.

18. J. Harmatta, 'Les Modèles littéraires de l'édit babylonien de Cyrus', *Acta Iranica* 1 (1974), 29–44.
19. Schaudig, *Die Inschriften Nabonids von Babylon* (2001), 554.
20. R. Sack, *Images of Nebuchadnezzar* (2nd edn. 2004), 67.
21. H. Tadmor, *The Inscriptions of Tiglath-Pileser III King of Assyria* (1994), 174–5, Summary Inscription 7.
22. Prism Inscription VII.45 and VII.49–52; see Chapter 4.

CHAPTER 1

1. O. Pedersén, *Archive und Bibliotheken in Babylon: Die Tontafeln der Grabung Robert Koldeweys 1899–1917* (2005), 111–27.
2. W. Nagel, 'Wo lagen die "Hängende Gärten" in Babylon?', *Mitteilungen der Deutsch-Orient Gesellschaft* 110 (1978), 19–28; D. J. Wiseman 'Mesopotamian gardens', *Anatolian Studies* 33 (1983), 137–44.
3. See T. Boiy, *Late Achaemenid and Hellenistic Babylon* (2004), 78–9.
4. R. van der Spek, 'Berossus as Babylonian chronicler and Greek historian', eds. R. van der Spek *et al.*, *Studies in Ancient Near Eastern World View and Society, presented to Marten Stol on the Occasion of his 65th Birthday* (2008), 306 and n. 47. J. E. Reade, 'Alexander the Great and the Hanging Gardens', *Iraq* 62 (2000), 200, asserted without evidence that 'Cyrus evidently restored or maintained the Hanging Gardens, and may even have added to them'.
5. Reade, 'Alexander the Great and the Hanging Gardens', *Iraq* 62 (2000), 213 fig. 11, drawn by his son William Reade.
6. K. Polinger Foster, 'The Hanging Gardens of Nineveh', *Iraq* 66 (2004), 207–20.
7. See e.g. M. Sauvage, *La Brique et sa mise en œuvre en Mésopotamie des origines à l'époque achéménide* (1998), 69–70; 170.
8. C. L. Woolley, *Excavations at Ur* (1929), revised by P. R. S. Moorey as: *Ur 'of the Chaldees'* (1982), 145–6.
9. Three other examples are: BM 89769 (see D. Collon, *First Impressions*, no. 773); A. Moortgat, *Vorderasiatische Rollsiegel*, nos. 591 (from Ashur) and 592 (from Babylon).
10. See D. T. Potts, 'Some horned buildings in Iran, Mesopotamia and Arabia', *Revue d'Assyriologie* 84 (1990), 33–40, esp. n. 14.
11. Gilbert White, *Natural History and Antiquities of Selborne* (2nd edn. 1813).
12. Thomas Browne, *On the Garden of Cyrus*, written in the 1650s.
13. Most of the Classical sources refer to the World Wonder in the singular.
14. See Liddell and Scott, *Greek–English Lexicon* (9th edn. 1996), 993b for reference.
15. See R. Da Riva, *The Neo-Babylonian Royal Inscriptions: An Introduction* (2008), 14 n. 68 with references.

16. This was a genuine event, see H.-P. Schaudig, 'The restoration of temples in the Neo- and Late Babylonian periods', ed. M. Boda and J. Novotny, *From the Foundations to the Crenellations* (2010), 152–3.

17. The deduction that he ruled Egypt was based on a misunderstanding of a fragmentary text and his later legendary reputation as a world conqueror. See M. Streck, *Reallexikon der Assyriologie* Band 9 (1998–2001), s.v. Nebukadnezar II; and Schaudig, *Inschriften Nabonids von Babylon* (2001), 579–80.

18. R. Da Riva, 'The Nebuchadnezzar twin inscriptions of Brisa (Wadi esh-Sharbin, Lebanon): transliteration and translation', *Bulletin d'archéologie et d'architecture libanaises* 12 (2008), 229–333.

19. J. Börker-Klähn, *Altvorderasiatische Bildstelen und vergleichbare Felsreliefs*, Baghdader Forschungen 4 (1982), vol. 2, nos. 259 and 260.

20. See R. Da Riva, *The Neo-Babylonian Inscriptions: An Introduction* (2008), 13.

21. The suggestion that he had a museum of antiquities in Babylon has been overturned by E. Klengel-Brandt, 'Gab es ein Museum in der Hauptburg Nebukadnezars II. in Babylon?', *Forschungen und Berichte* 28 (1990), 41–7.

22. See S. Dalley, 'Why did Herodotus not mention the Hanging Gardens of Babylon?', eds. P. Derow and R. Parker, *Herodotus and his World* (2003), 171–89.

23. J. and E. Romer, *The Seven Wonders of the World: A History of the Modern Imagination* (1995), 107–28.

24. Implied e.g. by A. L. Oppenheim, *Ancient Mesopotamia: Portrait of a Dead Civilization* (1964), 153–4; by Seton Lloyd, *The Archaeology of Mesopotamia* (1978), 231, and by S. M. Burstein, *The Babyloniaca of Berossus* (1978), 5.

25. See now Boiy, *Late Achaemenid and Hellenistic Babylon* (2004), 137–65.

26. W. Allinger-Csollich *et al.*, 'Babylon. Past, present, future. The project "Comparative Studies Babylon–Borsippa": a synopsis', ed. P. Matthiae, *6th ICAANE 2008* (2010), 29–38.

27. See e.g. W. Horowitz, 'Antiochus I, Esagil and a celebration of the ritual for the renovation of temples', *Revue d'Assyriologie* 85 (1991), 75–7; R. J. van der Spek, 'The size and significance of the Babylonian temples under the Successors', eds. P. Briant and F. Joannès, *La Transition entre l'empire achéménide et les royaumes hellénistiques*, Persika 9 (2006), 261–307.

28. O. Pedersén, *Archives and Libraries* (1998), 256; F. Rochberg, 'Scribes and scholars: the tupšar Enūma Anu Enlil', eds. J. Marzahn and H. Neumann, *Assyriologica et Semitica: Festschrift für Joachim Oelsner* (2000), 366–9.

29. H. Hunger, *Babylonische und assyrische Kolophone* (1968), no. 148; A. R. George, *The Epic of Gilgamesh* (2003), 740.

30. See T. Boiy, 'Assyriology and the history of the hellenistic period', *Topoi* 15 (2007), 7–20.

CHAPTER 2

1. See e.g. A. S. Becker, *The Shield of Achilles and the Poetics of Ekphrasis* (1995), 42–3.
2. See Brodersen, *Die Sieben Weltwunder* (1996), 51; I. Finkel, 'The Hanging Gardens of Babylon', eds. Clayton and Price, *The Seven Wonders of the Ancient World* (1988), 44. But R. Koldewey, *Das wiedererstehende Babylon* (1914), 95 and Boiy, *Late Achaemenid and Hellenistic Babylon* (2004), 71–2, assign to Ctesias the passage on the Hanging Garden given in Diodorus II.10; certainty is not possible. For an evaluation of Ctesias' work according to which he switched characters and events deliberately, see Chapter 6 with n. 5.
3. K. Clarke, 'Universal perspectives in historiography', ed. C. S. Kraus, *The Limits of Historiography: Genre and Narrative in Ancient Historical Texts* (1999), 253.
4. The Greek text has *syringges* 'pipes'. The image may be that the arches in the long walls looked like a row of finger holes in a music pipe.
5. Diodorus Siculus, *Library of History* II.10. Translation of C. H. Oldfather, Loeb edition (1933).
6. Water wheels are known no earlier than the 3rd century BC, see A. Wilson, 'Machines in Greek and Roman technology', ed. J. P. Oleson, *Oxford Handbook of Engineering and Technology in the Classical World* (2008), 351–2.
7. At Cineköy near Adana in SE Turkey. The languages are Luwian (written in Hittite hieroglyphic script) and Phoenician (written in linear alphabetic script). See R. Rollinger, 'The terms "Assyria" and "Syria" Again', *Journal of Near Eastern Studies* 65 (2006), 283–7.
8. That 'Syria' could also include Babylonia is unlikely.
9. Conversion to modern measures according to M. J. T. Lewis, *Surveying Instruments of Greece and Rome* (2001): 1 stade = *c*.185 m, 1 plethron = one-sixth of a stade, i.e. *c*.30.8 m, 1 cubit = 1™ ft. = *c*.31 cm.
10. This implies human, not animal exertions.
11. Strabo, *Geography* XVI.1.5, translation adapted from H. L. Jones, Loeb edn. (1961).
12. A. Gow and D. L. Page, *The Greek Anthology: The Garland of Philip* (1968) vol. 1, 68–9. no. xci.
13. Gow and Page, *Greek Anthology*, vol. 2, 18. There is a possible confusion with the earlier poet Antipater of Sidon; Brodersen, *Die Sieben Weltwunder* (1996), 10, opts for the earlier man.
14. He was based perhaps at Hierapolis–Castabala in Cilicia, where an inscription naming him has been found. See R. Syme, 'Galatia and Pamphylia under Augustus: the governorships of Piso, Quirinus and Silvanus', *Klio* 27 (1934), 127–31.

15. Gow and Page, *Greek Anthology*, vol. 1, 37 no. xl.
16. The duplication by Josephus was not realized by Finkel, eds. Clayton and Price, *Seven Wonders* (1988), in which translations of the two works are given from two different scholars, making it appear as if there were two different Greek texts.
17. Finkel, 'The Hanging Gardens of Babylon', eds. Clayton and Price, *Seven Wonders* (1988), 41, and Reade, 'Alexander the Great and the Hanging Gardens of Babylon', *Iraq* 62 (2000), 199.
18. Finkel, eds. Clayton and Price (1988).
19. Burstein, *Babyloniaca of Berossus* (1978), 27.
20. Van der Spek, 'Berossus as Babylonian chronicler and Greek historian', eds. Van der Spek *et al.*, *Studies in Ancient Near Eastern World View and Society* (2008), 300–2.
21. Genesis 11: 1–9.
22. Josephus, *Jewish Antiquities* I.113–19.
23. T. Hägg, *The Novel in Antiquity* (1983), 5–6; G. P. Goold, *Chariton, Callirhoe* (1995), 1–3.
24. Translation of Goold, *Chariton* (1995).
25. Van der Spek, 'Berossus as Babylonian chronicler and Greek historian' (2008), 280–3. Comparisons with the *Istanbul Stela* of Nabonidus show that Berossus used that text too, see W. Gallagher, 'The Istanbul stela of Nabonidus', *Wiener Zeitschrift für die Kunde des Morgenlandes* 86, Festschrift for H. Hirsch (1996), 119–26.
26. Van der Spek, 'The size and significance', ed. Briant, *La Transition* (2006), 275; 'Berossus as a Babylonian chronicler and Greek historian', ed. Van der Spek (2008), 296–302.
27. Burstein, *The Babyloniaca of Berossus* (1978), 5.
28. See e.g. Boiy, *Late Achaemenid and Hellenistic Babylon* (2004), 137–65; P. van Nuffelen, 'Le Culte royal de l'empire des Séleucides: une réinterprétation', *Historia* 53 (2004), 278–301.
29. A. Annus, 'The survivals of the ancient Syrian and Mesopotamian intellectual traditions in the writings of Ephrem Syrus', *Ugarit Forschungen* 38 (2006, published 2007), 17–23.
30. See P.-A. Beaulieu, 'The historical background of the Uruk prophecy', eds. M. E. Cohen, D. Snell and D. Weisberg, *The Tablet and the Scroll*, Festschrift for W. Hallo (1993), 41–52.
31. Reade, 'Alexander the Great and the Hanging Gardens of Babylon', *Iraq* 62 (2000), 200, maintained that Berossus' own words were conveyed by Josephus, and that Berossus was especially offended by a 'failure to recognize the contribution of Nebuchadnezzar'. What he meant is obscure.

32. See *The Oxford Classical Dictionary* (3rd edn. 1996), s.v. Curtius Rufus; and E. Baynham, *Alexander the Great: The Unique History of Quintus Curtius* (1998).
33. He uses a plural term, *pensiles horti*, in contrast to the singular term *kremastos kēpos* used in all the Greek sources with the exception of Antipater.
34. Q. Curtius Rufus, *History of Alexander* V.1.10–45. Loeb edn., translation of J. C. Rolfe (1946).
35. See e.g. R. Thomas, *Herodotus in Context: Ethnography, Science and the Art of Persuasion* (2000), 200–10.
36. The wrong one, with the wrong date, is given by Finkel, 'The Hanging Gardens of Babylon', eds. Clayton and Price, *Seven Wonders* (1988), 45–6; by R. Bichler and R. Rollinger, 'Die Hängenden Gärten zu Ninive: Die Lösung eines Rätsels?', ed. R. Rollinger, *Von Sumer bis Homer, Festschrift für Manfred Schretter* (2005), 172–98, and by Reade, 'Alexander the Great and the Hanging Gardens of Babylon', *Iraq* 62 (2000), 199; corrected by I. Finkel and M. Seymour, *Babylon Myth and Reality*, British Museum Exhibition catalogue 2008, 185 n. 162.
37. *The Oxford Classical Dictionary* (3rd edn. 1996) does not include an entry for the later of the two.
38. K. Gutzwiller, *A Guide to Hellenistic Literature* (2009), 166.
39. See D. Haynes, *The Technique of Greek Bronze Statuary* (1992), 121–8.
40. R. Hercher, *Aeliani de natura animalium, . . . Porphyrii philosophi . . . Philonis Byzantii* (1858), 101–2.
41. K. Brodersen, *Reiseführer zu den Sieben Weltwundern: Philon von Byzanz und andere antike Texte* (1992).
42. The translation of D. Oates given by Finkel, eds. Clayton and Price, *Seven Wonders* (1988), 45–6, was made largely from Hercher's Latin translation which is partly a paraphrase; a few of Oates's phrases are given here in the following notes, to indicate differences. The translation made by Hugh Johnstone in J. and E. Romer, *The Seven Wonders of the World* (2000), appendix 230–1, contains some good insights; but on p. ix he gives the wrong dating to Philo, so presumably made his translation without the benefit of Brodersen's 1999 edition.
43. Oates's 'This is the technique of its construction' is in Hercher's Latin text, but not in the Greek original.
44. Oates: 'grafting and propagation'. It is uncertain whether grafting was practised in the 7th century BC.
45. The normal word for an aqueduct is used. Oates's 'elevated sources' avoids translating as 'aqueduct' which is the translation given by Johnstone, and in dictionaries.
46. Oates: 'bends and spirals', Johnstone 'in a screw'.
47. Oates: 'the twists of these devices', Johnstone 'round and round in a spiral'.

CHAPTER 3

1. H. Rassam, *Asshur and the Land of Nimrod* (1897), 365.
2. Bull inscription lines 41–2, see A. Fuchs, *Die Inschriften Sargons II aus Khorsabad* (1994), 66–7.
3. Rassam, *Asshur and the Land of Nimrod* (1897), 352–5.
4. Bellino cylinder, see D. D. Luckenbill, *The Annals of Sennacherib* (1924), 99; E. Frahm, *Einleitung in die Sanherib-Inschriften* (1997), 46–7.
5. See M. T. Larsen, *The Conquest of Assyria: Excavations in an Antique Land* (1994), 190, and 346–9.
6. R. D. Barnett, E. Bleibtreu and G. Turner, *The Sculptures from the Southwest Palace of Sennacherib* (1998), 16.
7. J. E. Reade, 'Nineteenth-century Nimrud: motivation, orientation, conservation', eds. J. E. Curtis, H. McCall, D. Collon and L. Al-Gailani Werr, *New Light on Nimrud* (2008), 6. For the instrument see M. Kemp, *The Science of Art: Optical Themes in Western Art from Brunelleschi to Seurat* (1992), 200–1, and plates 396 and 397.
8. J. E. Reade, 'Assyrian illustrations of Nineveh', *Iranica Antiqua* 33 (1998), 81–94; Barnett *et al.*, *Sculptures from the Southwest Palace of Sennacherib*, vol. 1 (1998), 84–5.
9. A. H. Layard, *Discoveries in the Ruins of Nineveh and Babylon* (1853), 232.
10. Barnett *et al.*, *Sculptures from the Southwest Palace of Sennacherib* (1998), plates 223–5.
11. BM 124939. See R. D. Barnett, *Sculptures from the North Palace of Assurbanipal at Nineveh* (1976), plate 23.
12. Some modern drawings of the scene on this panel do not show the terraces above the aqueduct, and so give a misleading impression.
13. This is the convention known as rabattement. See *Lexikon der Aegyptologie* s.v. Architekturdarstellung.
14. See Chapter 7 for more detail.
15. Some drawings of the panel are too sketchy to show this adequately.
16. M. I. Finley, 'Technical innovation and economic progress in the ancient world', *Economic History Review* 18 (1965), 29–45, with K. Greene, 'Technical innovation and economic progress in the ancient world: M. I. Finley re-considered', *Economic History Review* 53 (2000), 29–59.
17. See e.g. D. Charpin, 'Archivage et classification: un récapitulatif de créances à Mari sous Zimri-Lim', *Proceedings of the 51st Rencontre Assyriologique Internationale 2005* (2008), 3–15, and bibliography in note on p. 3.
18. See especially the inscription quoted in Chapter 4.
19. Plutarch, *Life of Marcellus* XVII.3–4.

20. Diodorus Siculus, *Library of History* I.34.2 and (quoting Posidonius of Apamea) V.37.3.

21. Gutzwiller, *A Guide to Hellenistic Literature* (2007), 157–8.

22. E. J. Dijksterhuis, *Archimedes* (1956), 22–3.

23. See e.g. D. L. Simms, 'Archimedes the engineer', *History of Technology* 17 (1995), 45–111.

24. Dijksterhuis, *Archimedes* (1956), 21–2; B. Gille, 'Machines', eds. C. Singer, E. J. Holmyard, A. R. Hall and T. I. Williams, *A History of Technology*, vol. ii (1956), 631; R. J. Forbes, *Studies in Ancient Technology*, 2 (2nd edn. 1965), 40; B. Cotterell and J. Kamminga, *Mechanics of Pre-industrial Technology* (1990), 94.

25. A. Kleingünther, *Protos Heuretes* (1933).

26. George, *Babylonian Epic of Gilgamesh* (2003), vol. i, 708–9, tablet XI, line 86.

27. E. Robson, 'Three Old Babylonian methods for dealing with "Pythagorean" Triangles', *Journal of Cuneiform Studies* 49 (1997), 51–2.

28. Genesis 4.

29. See J. Barr, 'Philo of Byblos and his "Phoenician History"', *Bulletin of the John Rylands University Library of Manchester* 57 (1974), 17–68.

30. e.g. in India around 2500 BC at Rahman Dehri, in Egypt on the 19th-century BC site of El-Lahun, and in north-western Iran on the 7th-century BC citadel at Bastam. See A. Sagona and P. Zimansky, *Ancient Turkey* (2009), 328–31 for the latter.

31. A. Mazar and N. Panitz-Cohen, 'It is the land of honey: bee-keeping in Iron Age IIA Tel Rehov—culture, cult and economy', *Near Eastern Archaeology* 70 (2007), 202–19.

32. G. Frame, *Rulers of Babylonia from the Second Dynasty of Isin to the End of Assyrian Domination (1157–612 BC)*, Royal Inscriptions of Mesopotamia Babylonian Periods, vol. 2 (1995), 281–2. See also E. Crane, *The World History of Bee-Keeping and Honey-Hunting* (1999), 170–2.

CHAPTER 4

1. Here, as elsewhere, the text sometimes uses the word for copper, perhaps as a deliberate archaism imitating epics of earlier times.

2. Date of the inscriptions: Iraq Museum prism, dated 694 BC published by A. Heidel, 'The octagonal Sennacherib Prism in the Iraq Museum', *Sumer* 9 (1953), 117–88; Chicago Prism dated 689 BC published by D. D. Luckenbill, *The Annals of Sennacherib* (1924), 28–47.

3. Strabo, *Geography* XVII.1.10.

4. The dots indicate that other details of building works in the text have been omitted here to gather up passages relevant to the waterworks; castings were also used for metal column bases, and special alloys for

shining surfaces, as shown elsewhere in this chapter. The complete text is given in translation in the Appendix.

5. Perhaps for rotation. The cog may not yet have been invented; but see the 'Bronze Gears' of the Early Iron Age found at Marlik, described later in this chapter.

6. This intrusive line probably marks an imperfect arrangement of extracts taken from more detailed texts. See pp. 142–44.

7. The modern equivalent to half a shekel is about 4 grams.

8. J. Laessøe, 'Reflexions on modern and ancient oriental water works', *Journal of Cuneiform Studies* 7 (1953), 5–26.

9. The word 'copper', omitted in Laessøe's translation, was damaged on the prism available to Luckenbill, but well-preserved on the prism edited by Heidel, just too late for Laessøe to take into account.

10. J. Laessøe, 'The meaning of the word *alamittu*', *Compte rendu de la Rencontre Assyriologique Internationale 1952* (1954), 150–6, and 'Reflexions on modern and ancient oriental water works', *Journal of Cuneiform Studies* 7 (1953), 16.

11. *saqia*: a wheel with bucket-like compartments fixed to its rim, rotated either by men treading the rim or by animals yoked to a capstan with right-angled gearing. The *cerd* is a mechanism mainly for drawing well water with rope, pulley and self-dumping bucket, pulled by a draft animal that walks away from the well, then back again.

12. I. Löw, *Die Flora der Juden*, vol. 2 (1924), 302–3.

13. See F. N. H. al-Rawi and M. Roaf, 'Ten Old Babylonian mathematical problems', *Sumer* 43 (1984), 184.

14. S. Dalley, 'Nineveh, Babylon and the Hanging Gardens: cuneiform and classical sources reconciled', *Iraq* 56 (1994), 52.

15. *The Concise Dictionary of Akkadian* (revised edn. 2000) gives the meaning '(a wild species of date palm)'.

16. See e.g. M. Giovino, *The Assyrian Sacred Tree: A History of Interpretations* (2007), 31–7.

17. A fairly common word thought to mean a crossbar is *tallu* or *gištallu*. *Tallu* is used in mathematical texts, see O. Neugebauer and A. Sachs, *Mathematical Cuneiform Texts*, American Oriental Society 29 (1945), 98.

18. C. L. Woolley, *Excavations at Ur* (revised by P. R. S. Moorey 1982, as *Ur 'of the Chaldees'*), 155.

19. See B. as-Soof, 'Mounds in the Rania plain and excavations at Tell Basmusian 1956', *Sumer* 26 (1970), 65–104, and J. Eidem, *The Shemshara Archives*, vol. 2 (1992), 54 and map 2.

20. Vitruvius, *De Architectura* book IV, c. 1, 6–7.

21. T. Howard-Carter, 'An interpretation of the sculptural decoration of the second millennium temple at Tell Al-Rimah', *Iraq* 45 (1983), 64–8.

22. D. Collon, *First Impressions Cylinder Seals in the Ancient Near East* (1987), nos. 765 and 773.

23. A. Livingstone, *Court Poetry and Literary Miscellanea*, State Archives of Assyria vol. 3 (1989), no. 7.

24. In other instances the 'male' tree with spiral patterned trunk may be a conifer. P. Collins, 'Trees and gender in Assyrian art', *Iraq* 68 (2006), 100–1. Conifers, of course, are not dioecious, so the gender in this case is presumably symbolic only.

25. N. Franklin, 'From Megiddo to Tamassos and back: putting the "Proto-Ionic capital" in its place', eds. I. Finkelstein and N. Na'aman, *The Fire Signals of Lachish*, Festschrift for David Ussishkin (2011), 129–40.

26. The technique is well described by P. Meyers, 'Characteristics of casting revealed by the study of ancient Chinese bronzes', ed. R. Maddin, *The Beginning of the Use of Metals and Alloys* (1988), 284.

27. F. W. König, *Die elamische Königsinschriften* (1965), 169, text no. 78, and description, p. 22.

28. See H. Maryon and H. J. Plenderleith, 'Fine metal-work', eds. C. Singer *et al.*, *A History of Technology*, vol. 1 (1954), 632.

29. For comparison of dimensions and angle with Roman screws used for mining, 'typically a screw would be about 3 m long and set at an angle of between 30–40 degrees and could raise water about a metre . . . . (and in Japan) 3.5 m long, set at 40 degrees, raised water through about 2 m.' See P. T. Craddock, *Early Metal Mining and Production* (1995), 78.

30. Diodorus Siculus, *Library of History*, II.10.

31. Strabo, *Geography*, XVI.1.

32. See P. R. S. Moorey, *Ancient Mesopotamian Materials and Industries: The Archaeological Evidence* (1999), 269–73.

33. See e.g. J. Rawson, 'Carnelian beads, animal figures and exotic vessels: traces of contact between the Chinese states and Inner Asia, ca.1000–650 BC', *Archaeology in China*, 1: *Bridging Eurasia* (2010), 1–42.

34. It is uncertain whether the light talent or the heavy one was used in the relevant inscriptions. For the heavy one, the weight is doubled.

35. e.g. E. Lipiński, *The Aramaeans: Their Ancient History, Culture, Religion* (2000), 548. See E. Frahm, 'Wer den Halbschekel nicht ehrt—nochmals zu Sanheribs angeblichen Münzen', *Nouvelles assyriologiques brèves et utilitaires* 45 (2005).

36. See A. Kose, 'Die Wendelrampe der Ziqqurrat von Dūr Šarrukīn—keine Phantasie vom Zeichentisch', *Baghdader Mitteilungen* 30 (1999), 115–37.

37. K 1356, see B. Pongratz-Leisten, *Ina šulmi erub*, Baghdader Forschungen 16 (1994), 207–9; and Frahm, *Einleitung in die Sanherib-Inschriften* (1997), T 184.

38. F. Millar, *The Roman Near East 31 BC–AD 337* (1993), 82–3.

39. J. P. Oleson, *Greek and Roman Mechanical Water-Lifting Devices: The History of a Technology* (1984), figs. 71, 86 and 101.

40. Many Old Testament scholars date a first version to the reign of Josiah, late 7th century; and a final redaction during the Achaemenid period which ended *c*.331 BC.

41. Philo Judaeus, *On the Confusion of Tongues*, 38, quoted by J. P. Oleson, eds. J. W. Humphrey, J. P. Oleson and A. N. Sherwood, *Greek and Roman Technology: A Sourcebook* (1998), 318.

42. E. O. Negahban, *Marlik: The Complete Excavation Report* (1996), 303 and plate 134, nos. 931 and 932. Average inside diameter 2.5 cm, outside diameter 6.5 cm, cast bronze, found with 'small bronze tools and equipment'.

43. A. Wilson, 'Machines in Greek and Roman technology', ed. J. P. Oleson, *Oxford Handbook of Greek and Roman Technology* (2008), 341; O. Wikander, 'Gadgets and scientific instruments', same vol., 791–3.

44. R. Hannah, 'Timekeeping', ed. Oleson, *Oxford Handbook of Engineering and Technology* (2008), 740–58; T. Freeth, A. Jones, J. M. Steele and Y. Bitsakis, 'Calendars with Olympiad display and eclipse prediction on the Antikythera mechanism', *Nature* 454 (July 2008), 614–17.

45. In the BBC television Channel 4 series *Secrets of the Ancients* (1999).

46. Suggested e.g. by F. R. Stephenson, 'A proposal for the irrigation of the Hanging Gardens of Babylon', *Iraq* 54 (1992), 35–46.

47. J. P. Oleson, 'Irrigation', ed. O. Wikander, *Handbook of Ancient Water Technology* (2000), 222–5. See also n. 5 in this chapter.

48. Dated probably to the reign of Tiglath-pileser III, grandfather of Sennacherib, although a few of the panels in that group date from the time of Assurnasirpal II, in the 9th century; see J. N. Postgate and J. E. Reade, *Reallexikon der Assyriologie* 5 (1976–80), s.v. Kalhu.

49. A. Bagg, *Assyrische Wasserbauten*, Baghdader Forschungen 24 (2007), 18 and 21, BM 118906; M. E. L. Mallowan, *Nimrud and its Remains* (1966), vol. 1, 124.

50. The lexical list HAR-ra = hubullu, tablet VI, ed. B. Landsberger, *Materialien zum sumerischen Lexikon* vol. 6 (1958), 64–5.

51. Sometimes under an alternative form *hulamētu*.

52. However, in an intriguing entry the logogram bu.bu.i has Akkadian equivalents that include not only *alamittu* but also *šuqqû* which can mean 'raising, lifting to a higher level', information from the lexical list ALAM=Lanu A lines 189 ff. according to the *Chicago Assyrian Dictionary* s.v. alamittu and šaqû A. Reasons for grouping such items are often obscure. An irrigation device of uncertain identity in a list within a section dealing with ropes used for various purposes is GIŠ GÚ *zi-rí-kum* which may refer to a pulley or to a part of a shaduf. See forerunner of HAR-ra = *hubullu* tablet 6, 148, ll. 73–5, ed. B. Landsberger, *Materials for the Sumerian Lexicon* 6 (1958), also Nabnitu IV 378, ed. I. Finkel, *The Series SIG7 = ALAN = Nabnītu, Materials for the Sumerian Lexicon* 16 (1982),

and lexical series *ana ittišu* 4.ii.33–5, ed. B. Landsberger, *ana ittišu, Materials for the Sumerian Lexicon* 1 (1937).

53. D. Frayne, *Ur III Period (2112–2004 BC)*, Royal Inscriptions of Mesopotamia Early Periods 3/2 (1997), 27, no. 5.

54. See J.-G. Glassner, *Mesopotamian Chronicles* (2004), 156–9.

55. V. Place, *Ninive et l'Assyrie*, vol. 2 (1867), especially 275–9, with plates 38 and 39. See Rassam, *Asshur and the Land of Nimrod* (1897), 219–20, and S. Dalley, 'Water supply for cities in the late eighth and seventh centuries BC: Assyria and Urartu', eds. A. Çilingiroglu and G. Darbyshire, *Anatolian Iron Ages 5*, British Institute at Ankara Monograph 31 (2005), 39–43.

56. Luckenbill, *Annals of Sennacherib* (1924), 129, vi.57.

57. The *qanat* is explained and discussed in Chapter 5.

58. See e.g. M. Huxley, 'Sennacherib's addition to the Temple of Assur', *Iraq* 62 (2000), 107–37.

59. G. Turner, 'The state apartments of late Assyrian palaces', *Iraq* 32 (1970), 177–213.

60. See S. Blaylock, *Tille Höyük 3.1 The Iron Age: Introduction, Stratification and Architecture* (2009), 129–34 and 158–62.

61. A. R. George, 'The bricks of E-sagil', *Iraq* 57 (1995), 173–97; and see Chapter 8.

CHAPTER 5

1. Translation made using M. Greenberg, *Ezekiel 21–37* (1997), 635–9, and P. M. Joyce, *Ezekiel: A Commentary* (2007), 185.

2. A. K. Grayson, *Assyrian Rulers of the Early First Millennium BC*, vol. 1, Royal Inscriptions of Mesopotamia, Assyrian Periods 2 (1991), 55.

3. M. Birot, *Lettres de Yaqqim-Addu*, Archives Royales de Mari XIV (1974).

4. For a variant on it, known from his reign in Assyria, as tunnels with inscriptions, see in this chapter the description of the Negoub tunnel.

5. See A. Fuchs in R. Borger, *Beiträge zum Inschriftenwerk Assurbanipals* (1996), 283, §132.

6. See D. T. Potts, *The Arabian Gulf in Antiquity* (1990), 390; R. Boucharlat, 'Archaeology and artifacts of the Arabian peninsula', ed. J. M. Sasson, *Civilizations of the Ancient Near East*, vol. 2 (1995), 1345–6; and W. Y. al-Tikriti, 'The origin of the falaj: further evidence from the United Arab Emirates', eds. L. Al-Gailani-Werr, J. E. Curtis, H. Martin, A. McMahon, J. Oates and J. E. Reade, *Of Pots and Plans* (2002), 339–55. For the persisting incorrect attribution to the Persians see e.g. T. Hodge, 'Qanats', ed. O. Wikander, *Handbook of Ancient Water Technology* (2000), 35–8; J. P. Oleson, 'Irrigation', in the same volume, 196; M. J. T. Lewis, *Surveying Instruments of Greece and Rome* (2001), 18.

7. See e.g. H. Goblot, *Les Qanats: Une technique d'acquisition de l'eau* (1979), 67–9; D. Parry, *Engineering in the Ancient World* (2005), 32.

8. R. Ghirshman, *Tchoga Zanbil: Mémoires de la délégation en Perse*, 40, vol. 2 (1968), 98–100. The name of the king Untash-Napiriša was previously read Untash-GAL. See e.g. D. T. Potts, *The Archaeology of Elam* (1999), 222–30.

9. See S. Dalley, 'Water management in Assyria from the ninth to the seventh centuries BC', *ARAM* 13–14 (2001–2), 443–60; D. Oates and J. Oates, *Nimrud: An Assyrian Imperial City Revealed* (2001), 33–5; J. N. Postgate, *Reallexikon der Assyriologie*, vol. 9 (1998–2001), s.v. Negub.

10. F. Safar, 'Sennacherib's project for supplying Erbil with water', *Sumer* 3 (1947), 23–5; J. Laessøe, 'The irrigation system at Ulhu, 8th century BC', *Journal of Cuneiform Studies* 5 (1951), 29–30; A. Bagg, *Assyrische Wasserbauten* (2000), 225–6.

11. M. O. Korfmann, *Troia/Wilusa Guidebook* (revised edn. 2005), 123–5.

12. V. Aravantinos, E. Kountouri and I. Fappas, 'To mykēnaiko apostraggistiko systēma tēs Kopaidas', *Proceedings of the 2nd International Conference on Ancient Greek Technology, Athens* (2006), 557–64.

13. Details are given by Lewis, *Surveying Instruments* (2001), chapter 10.

14. According to J. Ur, 'Sennacherib's northern Assyrian canals', *Iraq* 67 (2005), 340.

15. G. Loud and C. B. Altman, *Khorsabad Part II: The Citadel and the Town* (1938), 56.

16. R. Hope-Simpson, 'The Mycenaean highways', *Classical Views, Échos du monde classique* 42 (1998), 244–51.

17. T. Jacobsen and S. Lloyd, *Sennacherib's Aqueduct at Jerwan* (1935), 6.

18. Some of them are extensively discussed by Bagg, *Assyrische Wasserbauten* (2000), 147–54.

19. Bull inscription 36–42, see A. Fuchs, *Die Inschriften Sargons II aus Khorsabad* (1994), 66, lines 36–42.

20. Cylinder inscription 34–7, see Fuchs, *Die Inschriften Sargons II* (1994), 292.

21. V. Place, *Ninive et l'Assyrie*, vol. 2 (1867), 275–9, plates 38 and 39.

22. Author's translation based on Fuchs, *Die Inschriften Sargons II* (1994), 280. The change from a first to a third person narrative—'I' to 'he'—suggests that two earlier inscriptions have been combined.

23. M. S. Drower, 'Water supply, irrigation, and agriculture', eds. C. Singer *et al.*, *A History of Technology*, vol. 1 (1954), 528–32 also described the aqueduct.

24. See Bagg, *Assyrische Wasserbauten* (2000), 207–24.

25. J. E. Reade, 'Studies in Assyrian geography Part 1: Sennacherib and the waters of Nineveh', *Revue d'Assyriologie* 73 (1978), 47–72, and *Reallexikon der Assyriologie*, vol. 9 (1998–2001), 404–7 s.v. 'Ninive', with fig. 9.

26. The sketch-map of Nineveh (Fig. 26) shows two lines labelled 'conduit of Sennacherib' located alongside a projected part of the South-West Palace. See R. Campbell Thompson and R. Hutchinson, 'The excavations on the temple of Nabu at Nineveh', *Archaeologia* 79 (1929), pl. LXII. They might indicate how and where the water reached the palace.

27. Jacobsen and Lloyd, *Sennacherib's Aqueduct*; Reade, 'Studies in Assyrian geography', *Revue d'Assyriologie* 72 (1978), 47–72 (note that fig. 13b there is upside down); J. Ur, 'Sennacherib's northern Assyrian canals', *Iraq* 67 (2005), 317–45.

28. Bavian and Khinnis are the names of an adjacent hamlet and village; the rock inscription and the rock sculptures are known by both names.

29. For a colour photograph of the dam in recent times see J. Reade, *Assyrian Sculpture* (1983), fig. 104.

30. Frahm, *Einleitung* (1997), 151–4, updated the edition on which T. Jacobsen, in *Sennacherib's Aqueduct at Jerwan* (1935), 36–40, based his translation.

31. Jacobsen and Lloyd, *Sennacherib's Aqueduct* (1935), 28–30.

32. The word for 'aqueduct' and 'causeway' is the same as the word for 'bridge'.

33. Jacobsen and Lloyd, *Sennacherib's Aqueduct* (1935), 19–27, author's modified translation.

34. See S. Parpola and M. Porter, *The Helsinki Atlas of the Near East in the Neo-Assyrian Period* (2001), 28.

35. For details see L. Pearson, *The Lost Histories of Alexander the Great* (1960), 162 and 234–5.

36. Layard, *Nineveh and Babylon* (1853), 207–8. See also Jacobsen and Lloyd, *Sennacherib's Aqueduct* (1935), 4 and 32 fig. 9; J. E. Reade, 'Greco-Parthian Nineveh', *Iraq* 60 (1998), 66; R. Lane Fox, *Alexander the Great* (1973), 228–31.

37. C. L. Woolley, *The Sumerians* (1928), 191; A. W. Lawrence, *Greek Architecture* (3rd edn. 1973), 228–9, and (4th edn. 1983), 295 for a pointed arch in a Lycian heroon of the early 4th century BC at Trysa.

38. L. Lancaster, 'Roman engineering and construction', ed. Oleson, *Oxford Handbook of Engineering and Technology* (2008), 260.

39. Jacobsen and Lloyd, *Sennacherib's Aqueduct* (1935), 15–16. Compare for a similar surprise E. C. Stone, D. H. Linsley, V. Pigott, G. Harbottle and M. T. Ford, 'From shifting silt to solid stone: the manufacture of synthetic basalt in ancient Mesopotamia', *Science* 280 (1998), 2091–3.

40. Herodotus, *History*, book 1, 185, translation by A. de Sélincourt, Penguin Classics (1954), 87.

41. Bagg, *Assyrische Wasserbauten* (2000), 337, lines 209–16.

42. Bavian Inscription lines 27–34. Author's translation based on Jacobsen in *Sennacherib's Aqueduct* (1935), 38, with improved readings of Frahm, *Einleitung* (1997), 152–4.

43. Burstein, *Babyloniaca of Berossus* (1978), 27: a quotation attributed to Abydenus in the Chronicle of Eusebius.

44. Apsu refers to the fresh water beneath the earth in which the god Ea lived, and which he controlled.

45. Luckenbill, *Annals of Sennacherib* (1924), 74–5, lines 74–81.

46. Xenophon, *Oeconomicus*, ed. S. Pomeroy (1994), extracts from 123–7.

47. See C. Ambos, 'Building rituals from the first millennium BC: the evidence from the ritual texts', eds. M. J. Boda and J. Novotny, *From the Foundations to the Crenellations* (2010), 227–8; and J. Novotny, 'Temple building in Assyria: evidence from royal inscriptions', same vol., 119–20.

48. BM 90864 and 90865.

49. Cotton was grown in Egypt in the reign of Ramesses II, see L. Manniche, *An Ancient Egyptian Herbal* (1989), 19–20, and has been found in Assyria in the time of Sennacherib, see J. Alvarez-Mon, *The Arjan Tomb: At the Crossroads of the Elamite and Persian Empires* (2010), 35.

50. Prism inscription V.53–63.

51. See Chapter 9.

52. T. Ornan, 'The god-like semblance of a king: the case of Sennacherib's rock reliefs', eds. J. Cheng and M. Feldman, *Ancient Near Eastern Art in Context: Studies in Honor of Irene J. Winter* (2007), 169.

CHAPTER 6

1. See G. Farber, *Reallexikon der Assyriologie*, vol. 7 (1987–90), s.v. 'me', 610–13.

2. For a translation see G. Farber, 'Inanna and Enki', ed. W. Hallo, *The Context of Scripture*, vol. 1 (1997), 522–6.

3. R. Khoury, 'Babylon in der ältesten Version über die Geschichte der Propheten im Islam', ed. G. Mauer, *Ad bene et fideliter seminandum, Festschrift for K.-H. Deller* (1988), 129.

4. Xenophon, *Cyropaedia* books II and VI.

5. J. Macginnis, 'Ctesias and the fall of Nineveh', *Illinois Classical Studies* 13/1 (1988), 37–41, to be understood as a deliberate transposition according to the work of R. Bichler, 'Ktesias "korrigiert" Herodot: Zur literarischen Einschätzung der Persika', eds. H. Heftner and K. Tomaschitz, *Ad Fontes!, Festschrift für Gerhard Dobesch* (2004), 105–16.

6. Diodorus Siculus II.8.6.

7. See A. R. George, *Babylonian Topographical Texts* (1992), 18–29.

8. Pongratz-Leisten, *Ina šulmi erub* (1994), 210.

9. For an edition of lists giving fifteen of them with variants, see Pongratz-Leisten, *Ina šulmi erub* (1994), 211–15.

10. Ibbi-Su'en of Ur used the motif in a year-name, and Lipit-Ishtar of Isin in a hymn.

11. M. Rivaroli, 'Nineveh from ideology to topography', *Iraq* 66 (2004), 199–205; M. van de Mieroop, 'A tale of two cities: Nineveh and Babylon', *Iraq* 66 (2004), 1–5.

12. See 'Enki's Journey to Nibru', eds. J. Black, G. Cunnungham, E. Robson and G. Zolyomi, *The Literature of Ancient Sumer* (2004), 330–3.

13. 'Song of the Pickaxe', see R. J. Clifford, *Creation Accounts in the Ancient Near East* (1994), 30–2.

14. See e.g. A. R. George, 'Marduk and the cult of the gods of Nippur at Babylon', *Orientalia* 66 (1997), 65–70.

15. See M. Krebernik, *Reallexikon der Assyriologie*, vol. 9 (1998–2001), s.v. 'Ninlil (Mulliltu, Mulissu)', 453.

16. A. Fuchs, 'Die Inschrift vom Ištar-Tempel', chapter VII in R. Borger, *Beiträge zu Inschriftenwerk Assurbanipals* (1996), 258–96.

17. P.-A. Beaulieu, 'The cult of AN.ŠÁR/Aššur in Babylonia after the fall of the Assyrian empire', *State Archives of Assyria Bulletin* 11 (1997), 55–74.

18. A. Livingstone, *Court Poetry and Literary Miscellanea*, State Archives of Assyria 3 (1989), 18, no. 7, line 6.

19. T. Abusch, 'The form and meaning of a Babylonian prayer to Marduk', *Journal of the American Oriental Society* 103 (1983), 3–15, notes alterations that Sargon II made to a much earlier hymn to show a close association between Calah (Nimrud) and Babylon, suggesting that Calah too may have been another 'Babylon'.

20. A. K. Grayson, *Assyrian and Babylonian Chronicles*, Texts from Assyrian and Babylonian Sources 5 (1970), no. 16, lines 1–4.

21. E. Frahm, 'Counter-texts, commentaries, and adaptations: politically motivated responses to the Babylonian Epic of Creation in Mesopotamia, the biblical world, and elsewhere', ed. A. Tsukimoto, *Conflict, Peace and Religion in the Ancient Near East*, Orient 45 (2010), 3–33.

22. E. Frahm, 'Die *akītu*-Häuser von Ninive', *Nouvelles assyriologiques brèves et utilitaires* 66 (2000).

23. E. Frahm, *Babylonian and Assyrian Commentaries: Origins of Interpretation* (2011), 349–55.

24. For details see S. Dalley, 'Babylon as a name for other cities including Nineveh', eds. R. D. Biggs, J. Myers and M. T. Roth, *Proceedings of the 51st Rencontre Assyriologique Internationale 2005* (2008), 25–33.

25. V. Angenot, 'A Horizon of Aten in Memphis?', *Journal of the Society for the Study of Egyptian Antiquities* 35 (2008), 7–26.

26. Also known as Ibn al-Zarqallu.

27. See A. Becker and U. Becker, '"Altes" und "Neues" Babylon', *Baghdader Mitteilungen* 22 (1991), 508.

28. Herodotus, *History*, I.185.

29. Diodorus Siculus, *Library of History*, II.3, 2–4. An overview of this confusion, with references, is given in Dalley, 'Babylon as a name for other cities' (2008), 25–33, where detailed references can be found.

30. Grayson, *Assyrian Rulers of the Early First Millennium BC II (858–745 BC)* (1996), 204–5.

31. Ṣalmu means a statue or stela that represents a person, not necessarily with a physical likeness. See e.g. Z. Bahrani, *The Graven Image* (2003), 123.

32. Grayson, *Assyrian Rulers of the Early First Millennium BC II* (1996), 226.

33. Grayson, *Assyrian Rulers of the Early First Millennium BC II* (1996), 226–7.

34. M. Mallowan, *Nimrud and its Remains*, vol. 1 (1966), 260. The statues are in the British Museum, BM 118888 (Ht.1.78) and 118889. See Reade, *Assyrian Sculpture* (1983), fig. 43 for a photograph.

35. See Mallowan, *Nimrud and its Remains*, vol. 2 (1966), 443–50, esp. plate on p. 447.

36. Mallowan, *Nimrud and its Remains*, vol. 1, 284–5.

37. See S. Dalley, 'The Greek Novel Ninus and Semiramis', ed. T. Whitmarsh, *The Romance between Greece and the East*, forthcoming.

38. K. Clarke, 'Universal perspectives in historiography', ed. C. S. Kraus, *The Limits of Historiography: Genre and Narrative in Ancient Historical Texts* (1999), 253, re the universal history of Pompeius Trogus.

39. See R. Lane Fox, *Alexander the Great* (1973), 387.

40. J. C. Yardley, *Justin: Epitome of the Philippic History of Pompeius Trogus, Books 11–12* (1997), 268, quoting Nearchus apud Arrian 6.24.2–3, and Strabo, 15.1.5. C 686.

41. S. Dalley, 'Semiramis in history and legend', ed. E. Gruen, *Cultural Borrowings and Ethnic Appropriations in Antiquity* (2005), 11–22. See also S. C. Melville, *The Role of Naqia/Zakutu in Sargonid Politics* (1999), and Dalley, 'The Greek Novel Ninus and Semiramis', ed. T. Whitmarsh, *The Romance between Greece and the East*, forthcoming.

42. R. Borger, *Die Inschriften Asarhaddons Königs von Assyrien* (1956), §86—a five-sided foundation prism, extant in three separate copies.

43. S. Cole and P. Machinist, *Letters from Priests*, State Archives of Assyria XIII (1998), nos. 61, 76, 77; and see Melville, *The Role of Naqi'a-Zakutu* (1999), 44–7.

44. S. Parpola, *Letters from Assyrian and Babylonian Scholars*, State Archives of Assyria X (1993), no. 348.

45. Melville, *The Role of Naqia/Zakutu* (1999), appendix A, lists the sources.

46. Diodorus Siculus, *Library of History*, II.8.8. See Melville, *The Role of Naqia/Zakutu* (1999), figs. 1 and 2.
47. E. Leichty, *The Royal Inscriptions of Esarhaddon, King of Assyria*, Royal Inscriptions of the Neo-Assyrian period vol. 4 (2011), 323, no. 2010.
48. Borger, *Inschriften Asarhaddons* (1956), §86.
49. A. Kuhrt and S. Sherwin-White, 'Aspects of Seleucid royal ideology', *Journal of Hellenic Studies* 111 (1991), 71–86.
50. J. Lightfoot, *Lucian, On the Syrian Goddess* (2003), 351–2.
51. B. Yildirim, 'Identities and empire: local mythology and the self-representation of Aphrodisias', ed. B. E. Borg, *Paideia: The World of the Second Sophistic* (2004), 23–52.

CHAPTER 7

1. Translated by John Evelyn, 1673.
2. Sargon uses the word bronze perhaps meaning copper. See J. A. Brinkman, 'Textual evidence for bronze in Babylonia in the Early Iron Age, 1000–539 B.C.', ed. J. E. Curtis, *Bronze-Working Centres of Western Asia c.1000–539 B.C.* (1988), 135–68.
3. This is Classical Mt. Cassius, named here after the great god Ba'al-of-the-North; the other named mountains have not been identified. See A. M. Bagg, *Die Orts- und Gewässernamen der neuassyrischen Zeit, Teil 1: Die Levante* (2007), s.v. Ba'al-Ṣapuna.
4. A. Fuchs, *Inschriften Sargons II aus Khorsabad* (1994), 128–30, Annals §222.
5. The *hilāni* palaces are discussed below.
6. S. Parpola, *The Correspondence of Sargon II Part 1: Letters from Assyria and the West* (1987), no. 66. See the description later in this chapter, and Fig. 46.
7. See P. Albenda, *The Palace of Sargon* (1986).
8. L. Kataja and R. Whiting, *Grants, Decrees and Gifts of the Neo-Assyrian Period* (1995), 20–2.
9. Fuchs, *Inschriften Sargons II* (1994), 78 and 309.
10. Muṣaṣir, now located in north-western Iran, cult centre of the great Urartian god Haldi.
11. Sadly damaged, see Barnett, *Sculptures from the North Palace of Ashurbanipal* (1976), pl. 23, BM 124939.
12. The dimensions are comparable to those of Windsor Castle in England.
13. References and updating are given by Frahm, *Einleitung in die Sanherib-Inschriften* (1997), 267–8, nos. 6–11.
14. Frahm, *Einleitung* (1997), 268, no. 26; Luckenbill, *Annals of Sennacherib* (1924), 120–1, col. vi lines 47–53; A. Heidel, 'The octagonal Sennacherib Prism in the Iraq Museum', *Sumer* 9 (1953), 160, col. vi, lines 66–84.

15. See J. M. Russell, *Sennacherib's Palace Without Rival at Nineveh* (1991), 6.

16. E. Frahm, 'Die Bilder in Sanheribs Thronsaal', *Nouvelles assyriologiques brèves et utilitaires* 55 (1994).

17. Mallowan, *Nimrud and its Remains*, vol. 2 (1966), 480; J. E. Curtis, 'Glass inlays and Nimrud ivories', *Iraq* 61 (1999), 59–69; J. E. Reade, 'Assyrian architectural decoration: techniques and subject-matter', *Baghdader Mitteilungen* 10 (1979), 25.

18. Rock crystal, which Assyrian craftsmen were adept at carving; they made effective lenses from it too. See Layard, *Nineveh and Babylon* (1853), 197–8.

19. G. Smith, *Assyrian Discoveries* (1875), 98.

20. S. Dalley, 'Ancient Assyrian textiles and the origins of carpet design', *Iran* 29 (1991), 117–35.

21. S. Dalley, 'Hebrew TAHAŠ, Akkadian DUHŠU, faience and beadwork', *Journal of Semitic Studies* 45 (2000), 1–19.

22. J. J. Orchard, 'Some miniature painted glass plaques from Fort Shalmaneser, Nimrud', part I, *Iraq* 40 (1978), 1–22. Their function was not established.

23. J. M. Russell, 'Sennacherib's Palace Without Rival Revisited', eds. S. Parpola and R. Whiting, *Assyria 1995* (1997), 300.

24. J. Macginnis, 'Some inscribed horse troughs of Sennacherib', *Iraq* 51 (1989), 187–92.

25. Esther 1: 6.

26. Suggestions that an upper storey and windows were also features of a *bīt hilāni* are based on a mistaken analysis of *hilāni* and *appāti*, the former word probably Hittite and Luwian referring to a room with pillars, the latter a Hurrian word for a portico. See M. Novak, 'Hilani und Lustgarten', eds. M. Novak *et al.*, *Die Aussenwirkung des späthethitischen Kulturraumes* (2009), 299–305.

27. An Egyptian type of villa may have been one influence on the design. See e.g. L. Manniche, *An Ancient Egyptian Herbal* (1989), 9.

28. Or double, 35 tons, if the heavy version of the talent is meant.

29. E. Fugmann, *Hama*, vol. 2/1, *L'Architecture des périodes pré-Hellenistiques* (1958), 204, fig. 257; K. Kohlmeyer, 'The Temple of the Storm God in Aleppo during the Late Bronze and Early Iron Ages', *Near Eastern Archaeology* 72 (2009), 190–202.

30. D. Oates and J. Oates, *Nimrud: An Assyrian Imperial City Revealed* (2003), plate 12c.

31. See J. M. Russell, *The Writing on the Wall: Studies in the Architectural Context of Late Assyrian Palace Inscriptions* (1999), 107.

32. e.g. M. Cogan, 'Ashurbanipal Prism F: notes on scribal techniques and editorial procedures', *Journal of Cuneiform Studies* 29 (1977), 97–107;

A. K. Grayson, 'The Walters Art Gallery inscription', *Archiv für Orient-forschung* 20 (1963), 84 n. 7. Another example is the Nimrud Monolith inscription of Ashurnasirpal II (883–859 BC), in which the king as subject in the first person 'I' changes briefly in lines 74–5 to third person 'he'. See Grayson, *Assyrian Rulers of the Early First Millennium BC*, 1: *1114–859 BC* (1991), 241.

33. I. Ephal and H. Tadmor, 'Observations on two inscriptions of Esarhaddon', eds. Y. Amit and N. Na'aman, *Essays on Ancient Israel in its Near Eastern Context* (2006), 155–70.

34. Russell, *The Writing on the Wall* (1999), 180.

35. Pointed out by J. A. Black, 'Babylonian textual evidence', *Northern Akkad Project Reports* 1 (1987), 21.

36. I am grateful to Martin Worthington for discussion and for allowing me to quote this example from his Cambridge Ph.D. thesis.

37. Barnett *et al.*, *Sculptures from the Southwest Palace*, vol. 2 (1998), plates 223–6, and note in vol. 1, p. 86 suggesting that some features may represent the landscape of Khinnis and Bavian. See also J. E. Reade, 'Assyrian illustrations of Nineveh', *Iranica Antiqua* 33 (1998), 81–94.

38. R. Borger, 'König Sanheribs Eheglück', *Annual Review of the Royal Inscription of Mesopotamia Project* 6 (1988), 5–11, with a different interpretation in S. Dalley, 'More about the Hanging Gardens', ed. L. Al-Gailani-Werr *et al.*, *Of Pots and Plans* (2002), 68.

39. J. D. Hawkins, *Corpus of Hieroglyphic Luwian Inscriptions*, vol. 1 part 1 (1999–2000), 96–104.

40. F. W. König, *Handbuch der chaldischen Inschriften* (1955–7), no. 40a.

41. It has been suggested that Naqia is a Hebrew name, which would imply that she was related to Hezekiah in Jerusalem. See Melville, *The Role of Naqia/Zakutu* (1999), 14 n. 10, quoting M. Weinfeld.

42. K.-H. Deller, 'SAG.DU UR.MAH, Löwenkopfsitula, Löwenkopfbecher', *Baghdader Mitteilungen* 16 (1985), 327–46.

43. Grayson, *Assyrian Rulers of the Early First Millennium BC*, 1: *114–859 BC* (1991), 27.

44. Terry was influenced in this by the design for watering the garden at Château de Marly, built for Louis XIV, with pumps set alongside steps.

45. See H. Frankfort, *The Art and Architecture of the Ancient Orient* (1954), 58.

CHAPTER 8

1. From *Bacon's Essays*, ed. A. S. West (1931).

2. R. van Leeuwen, 'Cosmos, temple, house: building and wisdom in Mesopotamia and Israel', ed. R. J. Clifford, *Wisdom Literature in Mesopotamia and Israel* (2007), 67–90.

3. W. Andrae, *Das wiedererstandene Assur* (1938), 64, fig. 42.

4. See J. Renger and J. S. Cooper, *Reallexikon der Assyriologie*, vol. 4 (1975), s.v. 'Heilige Hochzeit', 251–69, for qualifications and uncertainties.

5. W. Mayer, 'Ein Mythos von der Erschaffung des Menschen', *Orientalia* 56 (1987), 55–68; also J. van Seters, 'The creation of man and the creation of the king', *Zeitschrift für Alttestamentliche Wissenschaft* 101 (1989), 333–42.

6. See J. Dixon Hunt and P. Willis, eds., *The Genius of the Place: The English Landscape Garden 1620–1820* (1988), 58.

7. George, *The Babylonian Gilgamesh Epic* (2003), e.g. 265 line 38, and 268 line 17 (abode of the Enunnaki), 576 line 54 (Something Evil), 602 lines 6–7 (Cedar Mountain as dwelling of gods).

8. Translation adapted from D. Katz, 'Enki and Ninhursaga, part one: the story of Dilmun', *Bibliotheca Orientalis* 64 (2007), 568–89.

9. Promoted by S. N. Kramer, 'Enki and Ninhursag: a paradise myth', ed. J. B. Pritchard, *Ancient Near Eastern Texts relating to the Old Testament* (1950), 36–41, and still followed, e.g. by J. Day, *Yahweh and the Gods and Goddesses of Canaan* (2000), 29. The correct understanding dates from at least 1983; see B. Alster, 'Dilmun, Bahrain and the alleged paradise in Sumerian myth and literature', ed. D. Potts, *Dilmun* (1983), 39–74, and R. J. Clifford, *Creation Accounts in the Ancient Near East and the Bible* (1994), 35–8.

10. Genesis 4: 4b–5.

11. It was used in the 9th century BC according to a recently discovered bilingual text. See e.g. A. Millard, 'The etymology of Eden', *Vetus Testamentum* 34 (1984), 103–5.

12. See J. Bremmer, 'Paradise: from Persia, via Greece, into the Septuagint', ed. G. Luttikhuizen, *Paradise Interpreted* (1999), 18–19.

13. See B. Childs, in *The Interpreter's Dictionary of the Bible* (1962), s.v. 'Eden, Garden Of'.

14. L. Valentine, ed., introductory memoir, in *The Poetical Works of John Milton* (1896), 17.

15. John Milton, *Paradise Lost* IV.137–42, quoted from Milton's own edition of 1669.

16. See A. van der Kooij, 'The story of paradise in the light of Mesopotamian culture and literature', eds. K. Dell, G. Davies and Y. Koh, *Genesis, Isaiah and Psalms*, Vetus Testamentum supplement 135 (2010), 16–21.

17. J. Asmussen, *Manichaean Literature* (1975), 117.

18. References in *Chicago Assyrian Dictionary*, vol. Š, s.v. šāru.

19. A. Wilkinson, *The Garden in Ancient Egypt* (1998), 132–3.

20. J. E. Reade, 'Ideology and propaganda in Assyrian art', ed. M. T. Larsen, *Power and Propaganda* (1979), 330 and 340.

21. See e.g. D. Stronach, 'The garden as a political statement: some case studies from the Near East in the first millennium B.C.', *Bulletin of the Asia Institute* 4 (1990), 171–80.

22. M. Stol, *Reallexikon der Assyriologie*, vol. 10 (2003–5), 505, s.v. 'Pflanzenkunde A'.

23. Alvarez-Mon, *The Arjan Tomb*, Acta Iranica 49 (2010), 35. For recent discussion of the word *kutānum* see C. Michel and K. Veenhof, 'Textiles traded by the Assyrians in Anatolia', eds. C. Michel and M.-L. Nosch, *Textile Terminologies* (2010), 212 and 234.

24. K. R. Maxwell-Hyslop, 'Dalbergia sissoo Roxburgh', *Anatolian Studies* 33 (1983), 67–72; D. Potts, 'GIŠ.mes-magan-na (Dalbergia sissoo Roxb.) at Tell Abraq', *Arabian Archaeology and Epigraphy* 10 (1999), 129–33. Tell Abraq is in modern Sharjah, near Oman. Sennacherib's grandson Ashurbanipal is known to have accepted tribute from Izki in Oman where a town still bears that name.

25. Frahm, *Einleitung* (1997), 277.

26. Livingstone, *Court Poetry* (1989), no. 7 line 1.

27. B. Lion, 'Vignes au royaume de Mari', ed. J.-M. Durand, *Florilegium marianum, Recueil d'études en l'honneur de Michel Fleury* (1992), 107–13.

28. S. Parpola, *The Correspondence of Sargon II part 1* (1987), no. 226.

29. Parpola, *Correspondence* (1987), no. 227.

30. The text is quoted verbatim in Chapter 1.

31. M. De Odorico, *The Use of Numbers and Quantifications in the Assyrian Royal Inscriptions*, State Archives of Assyria Studies III (1995), 141–2.

32. Grayson, *Assyrian Rulers of the Early First Millennium BC I (1114–859 BC)* (1991), 290.

33. See M. Giovino, *The Assyrian Sacred Tree* (2007), esp. 103–13.

34. Manniche, *An Ancient Egyptian Herbal* (1989), 13; Wilkinson, *The Garden in Ancient Egypt* (1998), 137–9; N. Beaux, *Le Cabinet de curiosités de Thoutmosis III* (1990).

35. J. V. Kinnier Wilson, *The Nimrud Wine Lists*, Cuneiform Texts from Nimrud I (1972), no. 4: rev. 14'(?), no. 9: rev. 19; and M. Feldman, 'Nineveh to Thebes and back: art and politics between Assyria and Egypt in the seventh century BCE', *Iraq* 66 (2004), 141–50.

36. See P. M. Fraser, 'The world of Theophrastus', ed. S. Hornblower, *Greek Historiography* (1994), 167–92.

37. E. W. Budge, *Assyrian Sculptures in the British Museum: Reign of Assurnasirpal, 885–860 BC* (1914), plate XXI with caption: 'Assyrian soldiers crossing a river on inflated skins'.

38. Nabu, Ninurta and Bel are all attested; see e.g. *Chicago Assyrian Dictionary* s.v. 'lismu', many in texts edited by Livingstone, *Court Poetry* (1989).

39. Livingstone, *Court Poetry* (1989), no. 10, rev. 8.

40. Livingstone, *Court Poetry* (1989), no. 34, line 57.

41. W. Decker, *Sports and Games of Ancient Egypt* (1992).

42. Decker, *Sports* (1992), 64, calculated 100 km in 9 hours. The stela has no picture of the event.
43. See C. Morgan, *Athletes and Oracles* (1989), 220; more generally, M. Finley and H. Pleket, *The Olympic Games: The First Thousand Years* (1976).
44. Livingstone, *Court Poetry* (1989), no. 14, p. 37; see also M. Nissinen, 'Love lyrics of Nabu and Tašmetu: an Assyrian Song of Songs?' eds. M. Dietrich and I. Kottsieper, *Und Mose schrieb dieses Lied auf* (1998), 587–91.
45. Information from J. Kinnier Wilson, *Nimrud Wine Lists* (1972), with collations given by S. Dalley and J. N. Postgate, *Tablets from Fort Shalmaneser* (1984); also Luckenbill, *Annals of Sennacherib*, third campaign, lines 46–7.
46. See P. Mitsis, 'The institutions of Hellenistic philosophy', ed. A. Erskine, *A Companion to the Hellenistic World* (2003), 471.
47. Wilkinson, *The Garden in Ancient Egypt* (1998), 150.
48. See for example T. Ornan, 'The transition from figured to non-figured representations in first-millennium glyptic', ed. J. Goodnick Westenholz, *Seals and Sealings in the Ancient Near East* (1995), 39–56; and 'Idols and symbols: divine representation in first millennium Mesopotamian art and its bearing on the second commandment', *Tel Aviv* 31 (2004), 90–121.
49. See Reade, *Assyrian Sculpture* (1983), 36.
50. Barnett *et al.*, *Sculptures from the Southwest Palace* vol 2 (1998), nos. 152–3.
51. E. Cook, 'Near Eastern prototypes of the palace of Alkinoos', *American Journal of Archaeology* 108 (2004), 43–77; see also N. Luraghi, 'Traders, pirates, warriors: the proto-history of Greek mercenary soldiers in the eastern Mediterranean', *Phoenix* 60 (2006), 1–47.
52. See Brodersen, *Die Sieben Weltwunder* (1996), 93 and 50.
53. Homer, *Odyssey* book VII, translation of E. V. Rieu (1946), 115.
54. A. Kuttner, ' "Do you look like you belong here?" Asianism at Pergamon and the Makedonian diaspora', ed. E. S. Gruen, *Cultural Borrowings and Ethnic Appropriations in Antiquity* (2005), 137–206.
55. E. Netzer *et al.*, *Hasmonean and Herodian Winter Palaces at Jericho: Final Report* (2001), esp. ch. 13, 'Planning and reconstruction of Herod's third palace'. I. Nielsen, *Hellenistic Palaces: Tradition and Renewal* (1994), does not include Assyrian palaces as models, presumably supposing they were no longer visible.
56. Josephus, *Antiquities of the Jews* XVI. 9.
57. E. Segala, *Domus Aurea* (1999).

CHAPTER 9

1. See S. Kessler-Mesguich, 'Les Grammaires occidentales de l'hébreu', ed. S. Auroux, *Histoire des idées linguistiques* (1992), 251–70.

2. Nahum ch. 3, supported by Ezekiel 31: 3–18. See e.g. P. Joyce, *Ezekiel: A Commentary* (2007), 185–6.

3. Diodorus Siculus, *Library of History*, II.23.4.

4. R. Bichler, 'Ktesias "korrigiert" Herodot: Zur literarischen Einschätzung der Persika', eds. H. Heftner and K. Tomaschitz, *Ad Fontes!* (2004), 105–16.

5. J. MacGinnis, 'Ctesias and the fall of Nineveh', *Illinois Classical Studies* 13/1 (1988), 37–41. See also R. C. Steiner, 'The Aramaic text in demotic script', ed. W. Hallo, *The Context of Scripture* (1997), 309–27.

6. *Cambridge Ancient History*, 3: *The Assyrian Empire*, eds. J. B. Bury, S. A. Cook and F. E. Adcock (1st edn. 1925), 130–1.

7. Layard, *Nineveh and its Remains*, vol. 1 (1850), 31. See also B. Trigger, *A History of Archaeological Thought* (1989), 38–40.

8. P. R. S. Moorey, *A Century of Biblical Archaeology* (1991), 36, dated this halting change to early in the 20th century.

9. Xenophon, *Anabasis* III. 4.

10. Layard, *Nineveh and its Remains*, vol. 2 (1850), 159 and 309.

11. For lack of well-dated comparative pottery, dating of archaeological levels relied on texts, coins and supposed artistic styles. Lack of inscriptions or coins allowed the inference of abandonment. It is now known that coinage was very seldom used in Mesopotamia until well into Seleucid times.

12. J.-J. Glassner, *Mesopotamian Chronicles* (2004), 222, line 45.

13. Campbell-Thompson and Hutchinson, 'The excavations on the temple of Nabu', *Archaeologia* 79 (1929), 138.

14. R. Campbell-Thompson and R. Hutchinson, 'The British Museum excavations on the temple of Ishtar at Nineveh 1930–1931', *Liverpool Annals of Art and Archaeology* 19 (1932), 73–4, recognized that there was a problem in dating the main ash layer to 612 BC.

15. D. Stronach, 'The fall of Nineveh', ed. S. Parpola and R. Whiting, *Assyria 1995* (1997), 315–18; D. Pickworth, 'Excavations at Nineveh: the Halzi gate', *Iraq* 67 (2005), 295–316.

16. Diodorus Siculus, *Library of History*, II.28.7.

17. Lucian, *Charon,* 23.

18. For the survival of the lamentation into the Hellenistic period, see T. Boiy, *Late Achaemenid and Hellenistic Babylon* (2004), 100, and C. Ambos, *Mesopotamische Baurituale aus dem 1. Jahrtausend v. Chr.* (2004), 55 and 61.

19. The Book of Jonah is currently dated no later than the late 5th or early 4th century BC. See e.g. J. A. Soggin, *Introduction to the Old Testament* (1976), 358–9.

20. S. Dalley, 'The transition from Neo-Assyrians to Neo-Babylonians: break or continuity?', *Eretz-Israel* 27 (2003), 25–8.

21. A. Kuhrt, 'The Assyrian heartland in the Achaemenid period', ed. P. Briant, *Dans les pas des dix-mille*, Pallas 43 (1995), 239–54; J. Curtis, 'The Assyrian heartland in the period 612–539 BC', ed. R. Rollinger, *Continuity of Empire* (2003), 157–67.

22. Kouyunjik and Nebi Yunus are the names of the two citadel mounds at Nineveh.

23. Athenaeus, *Deipnosophistae,* XII. 529.

24. Strabo, *Geography*, XVI. 1.1.

25. Tacitus, *Annals*, XII. 12.

26. Ammianus Marcellinus, *History*, XVIII. 7.1.

27. Layard, *Nineveh and Babylon* (1853), 590–5, and note there.

28. Rassam, *Asshur and the Land of Nimrod* (1897), 35.

29. Rassam, *Asshur and the Land of Nimrod* (1897), 223. See also S. Simpson, 'Christians at Nineveh in late antiquity', *Iraq* 67 (2005), 285 with references.

30. T. Madhloum, 'Nineveh: the 1967–1968 campaign', *Sumer* 24 (1968), English section, 50.

31. Discrepancy and contradictory indications between text and archaeology are well discussed by A. Frendo, *Pre-exilic Israel, the Hebrew Bible, and Archaeology* (2011), e.g. 30–1.

32. BM 124773.

33. Reade, *Assyrian Sculpture* (1983), 40–1, plate 58 with caption, 'about 630–620 BC', to fit them in before the fall of Nineveh, which is of course quite likely.

34. Campbell Thompson and Hutchinson, 'The excavations on the temple of Nabu', *Archaeologia* 79 (1929), 107–8.

35. Campbell Thompson and Hutchinson, 'The site of the palace of Ashurnasirpal at Nineveh', *Liverpool Annals of Archaeology and Anthropology* 18 (1931), 90–2.

36. See J. Reade, *Reallexikon der Assyriologie*, vol. 9 (1998–2001), s.v. 'Ninive', 428b for references.

37. J. Reade, 'The Ishtar temple at Nineveh', *Iraq* 67 (2005), 385–6.

38. S. James, 'Evidence from Dura Europus for the origin of late Roman helmets', *Syria* 63 (1986), 117–19.

39. Glassner, *Mesopotamian Chronicles* (2004), 223.

40. Schaudig, *Die Inschriften Nabonids* (2001), Babylon Stela col. ii. 32'–41'.

41. Modern Sheh Hamad.

42. H. Kühne, 'Thoughts about Assyria after 612 BC', ed. L. Al-Gailani *et al.*, *Of Pots and Plans* (2002), 171–5. Subsequent field-work around other towns has found other examples, and a few more examples have now been recognized from the palace of Nebuchadnezzar in Babylon, found nearly a century ago. See O. Pedersén, 'Neo-Assyrian texts from Nebuchadnezzar's Babylon: a preliminary report', eds. M. Luukko *et al.*, *Of God(s), Trees, Kings and Scholars* (2009), 193–9.

43. P. de Miroschedji, 'Glyptique de la fin d'Élam', *Revue d'Assyriologie* 76 (1982), 51–63.

44. See Reade, *Reallexikon der Assyriologie*, vol. 9 (1998–2001), s.v. 'Ninive', 425b, and Potts, *The Archaeology of Elam* (1999), 301.

45. J. Alvarez-Mon, *The Arjan Tomb*, Acta Iranica 49 (2010), 166–7 and 177 n. 17.

46. R. Rollinger, 'Der Stammbaum des achaimenidischen Königshauses', *Archaeologische Mitteilungen aus Iran* 30 (1998), 155–209; M. Waters, 'Cyrus and the Achaemenids', *Iran* 42 (2004), 155–209; D. T. Potts, 'Cyrus the Great and the kingdom of Anshan', eds. V. Curtis and S. Stewart, *Birth of the Persian Empire: The Idea of Iran* (2005), 1–22.

47. J. Reade, 'Restructuring the Assyrian sculptures', ed. R. Dittmann *et al.*, *Variatio delectat: Gedenkschrift für Peter Calmeyer* (2000), 613.

48. A definite overlap between Media and Elam around 600 BC is pointed out by Potts, *Archaeology of Elam* (1999), 306. Lindsay Allen has suggested that 'Medes' changed its meaning to something like 'barbarian horsemen' in Greek sources (forthcoming).

49. Mallowan, *Nimrud and its Remains*, vol. 1 (1966), 286 'derelict city'; 299–300; vol. 2, 602.

50. Mallowan, *Nimrud and its Remains*, 1, 298.

51. Mallowan, *Nimrud and its Remains*, 1, 287 and 310.

52. See Canali di Rossi, *Iscrizioni dello estremo oriente greco: un repertorio* (2004), 45, no. 72 with a photograph of the amphora stamp. The volume gives information with photographs for all the Greek inscriptions mentioned in this chapter.

53. D. Barag, *Catalogue of Western Asiatic Glass in the British Museum*, vol. 1 (1985), no. 107.

54. D. Oates, *Studies in the History of Northern Iraq* (1968), 58.

55. P. Fiorina, 'Italian excavations at Nimrud-Kalhu: chronological and stratigraphical problems', eds. J. Curtis *et al.*, *New Light on Nimrud* (2008), 53–6; P. Fiorina, 'Nimrud–Fort Shalmaneser: entrepôts et ateliers de la zone SW', eds. S. M. Cecchini, S. Mazzoni and E. Scigliuzzo, *Syrian and Phoenician Ivories* (2009), 37.

56. W. Vogelsang, *The Rise and Organisation of the Achaemenid Empire* (1992), 309–10.

57. D. Stronach, 'Anshan and Parsa: early Achaemenid history, art and architecture on the Iranian plateau', ed. J. Curtis, *Mesopotamia and Iran in the Persian Period* (1997), 35–53.

58. T. Kawami, 'A possible source for the sculptures of the audience hall, Pasargadae', *Iran* 10 (1972), 146–8; M. Roaf, *Reallexikon der Assyriologie*, vol. 10 (2004), s.v. 'Persepolis'; see also Layard, *Nineveh and its Remains*, vol. 2 (1850), 288–91.

59. G. Cawkwell, *Xenophon: The Persian Expedition* (1972), introduction.

60. See V. Azoulay, 'Exchange as entrapment: mercenary Xenophon?', ed. R. Lane Fox, *The Great March* (2004), 289–304.

61. Lane Fox, *The Great March* (2004), introduction, 44–5.

62. H. Gasche, 'Habl aṣ-Ṣahr, nouvelles fouilles: l'ouvrage défensif de Nabuchodonosor au nord de Sippar', *Northern Akkad Project Reports* 2 (1989), 23–70.

63. The Akkadian noun *mušpalu* 'depression, lowland' has been suggested as the early form of the name Mosul on the other side of the Tigris, opposite Nineveh (Meissner and Lehmann, followed by Reade), but the word is nowhere else attested as a place-name.

64. Strabo, *Geography*, XI. 14.

65. Tacitus, *Annals*, XII. 12.

66. Ammianus Marcellinus, *History*, XVIII. 7.1.

67. Strabo XVI. 1.1.

68. e.g. Arba'il as Erbil, Kar-Mullissi as Keremleis, Shusharra as Shemshara, Balad as Balaṭa, Melid as Malatya, Harran as Harran, Isana as Isān köy, Nampigu as Membidj, Naṣibina as Nisibin, Raṣappa as Reṣep, Sarugu as Saruj.

69. B. Porten and A. Yardeni, *Textbook of Aramaic Documents from Ancient Egypt*, 1: *Letters* (1986), 114, but reading as Halahhu, a district NE of Nineveh, rather than Halṣu—the third consonant is damaged—Halzi has the correct sibilant. Cf. Oates, *Studies in the History of Northern Iraq* (1968), 59–60; B. Porten, *Archives from Elephantine* (1968), 54 and 71; P. Briant, *Histoire de l'empire Perse* (1996), 377. See Dalley, forthcoming, eds. J. Ma and C. Tuplin.

70. S. A. Stephens and J. J. Winkler, *Ancient Greek Novels: The Fragments* (1995), 23.

71. J. R. Morgan, 'Fiction and history: historiography and the novel', ed. J. Marincola, *A Companion to Greek and Roman Historiography*, vol. 2 (2007), 554.

72. See D. Feeney, *Caesar's Calendar* (2007), 102.

73. Porten and Yardeni, *Textbook of Aramaic Documents, 1: Letters* (1986), A6.9, and see Kuhrt, 'The Assyrian heartland in the Achaemenid period', ed. P. Briant, *Dans les pas des deux-mille*, Pallas 43 (1995), 345.

74. See Boiy, *Late Achaemenid and Hellenistic Babylon* (2004), 288.

75. Layard, *Nineveh and Babylon* (1853), 594–5. See J. Malek, *Topographical Bibliography*, vol. 7, s.v. 'Nineveh', a fragmentary stone vase of Kha'ip, second prophet of Amun.

76. '... about four feet above the floor of the central court.' See now Canali di Rossi, *Iscrizioni*, 40, no. 64, using Reade, 'Greco-Parthian Nineveh', *Iraq* 60 (1998), 69. The titles *stratēgos* 'general' and *epistatēs* 'governor' were also used at Babylon and Dura Europus. See L. Capdetrey, *Le Pouvoir séleucide: territoire, administration, finances d'un royaume hellénistique* (2007), 288–9.

77. The Greek name may have been adopted by a non-Greek, as happened in Babylonia. See e.g. Boiy, *Late Achaemenid and Hellenistic Babylon* (2004), 289.

78. Grayson, *Assyrian Rulers of the Early First Millennium BC II (858–745 BC)* (1996), 153–4, gives an edition of the cuneiform. Possibly the Greek inscription added to the altar, and the text on the stone column, refer to the same man Apollonios as is named on the column. For the Greek inscription see Canali di Rossi, *Iscrizioni* (2004), 41, no. 65.

79. F. Safar, 'The temple of Sibitti at Khorsabad', *Sumer* 13 (1957), 219–21.

80. Reade, 'Greco-Parthian Nineveh', *Iraq* 60 (1998), 68.

81. Capdetrey, *Le Pouvoir séleucide* (2007), 288–9.

82. For the debate over the veracity of such claims, see R. Thomas, *Herodotus in Context: Ethnography, Science and the Art of Persuasion* (2000), 200 with n. 73.

83. R. Syme, 'Galatia and Pamphylia under Augustus: the governorships of Piso, Quirinus and Silvanus', *Klio* 27 (1934), 127–31. See also S. Dalley, 'Sennacherib and Tarsus', *Anatolian Studies* 49 (1999), 73–80, for evidence that Assyrians were still remembered in Tarsus in the Roman period.

84. I owe this observation to Joyce Reynolds, who kindly checked the panel with an expert eye.

85. Canali di Rossi, *Iscrizioni* (2004), 43, no. 67. J. Reade, 'More about Adiabene', *Iraq* 63 (2001), 191–2, assumes a literate Greek drain digger whose cutting in fact missed the panel by several feet.

86. M. Scott and J. McGinnis, 'Notes on Nineveh', *Iraq* 52 (1990), 69.

87. M. Colledge, 'Sculptors' stone-carving techniques', *East and West* 29 (1979), 232.

88. BM 115642. See Reade, 'Greco-Parthian Nineveh', *Iraq* 60 (1998), 71 and fig. 5. Its provenance as Nineveh has no further detail. The name might be a calque on Assyrian *šēdu damqu*, 'favourable protecting deity'; but cf. Canali di Rossi, *Iscrizioni* (2004), no. 69, for the other interpretation.

89. J. Curtis, 'Parthian gold from Nineveh', *The Classical Tradition*, British Museum Yearbook I (1976), 47–66.

90. *Corpus Inscriptionum Graecorum* 4672. For the discovery see Campbell Thompson and Hutchinson, 'The excavations on the temple of Nabu at

Nineveh', *Archaeologia* 79 (1929), 142; Reade, *Reallexikon* (1998–2001), s.v. 'Nineveh', writes 'perhaps anachronistically' without explanation; Canali di Rossi, *Iscrizioni* (2004), 44 questions the find-spot without justification.

91. See J. A. Brinkman, *Prelude to Empire* (1984), 54 n. 254.
92. Curtis, 'The Assyrian heartland', eds. G. Lanfranchi, M. Roaf and R. Rollinger, *Continuity of Empire?* (2003), 157–67.
93. R. Da Riva, *The Neo-Babylonian Royal Inscriptions: An Introduction* (2008), 22, Eurmeiminanki cylinder ii.10'.
94. Whether Dur-šarrukki in late Babylonian texts may be identified with Khorsabad is currently disputed.
95. Fiorina, 'Nimrud–Fort Shalmaneser', ed. S. M. Cecchini *et al.*, *Syrian and Phoenician Ivories* (2009), 45–6.
96. See Boiy, *Late Achaemenid and Hellenistic Babylon* (2004), 290.
97. Ishtar of Nineveh was already referred to as Bel in the late Assyrian period. See Livingstone, *Court Poetry* (1989), no. 39, line 21.
98. See G. Herrmann, *The Iranian Revival* (1977), 17.
99. See L. Vanden Berghe, *Reliefs rupestres de l'Iran Ancien* (1984), cat. no. 94 with plate 38; and cat. no. 68 with plate 29; also S. Matheson, *Persia: An Archaeological Guide* (1976), 256.
100. M. Liverani, 'The fall of the Assyrian empire: ancient and modern interpretations', eds. S. Alcock *et al.*, *Empires* (2001), 374–91.
101. N. Yoffee, 'The collapse of ancient Mesopotamian states and civilization', eds. N. Yoffee and G. Cowgill, *The Collapse of Ancient States and Civilizations* (1988), 57; N. Yoffee, 'Notes on regeneration', eds. G. Schwartz and J. L. Nichols, *After Collapse: The Regeneration of Complex Societies* (2006), 222–7.
102. See Giovino, *The Assyrian Sacred Tree* (2007), chapter 9.
103. A. Livingstone, 'Remembrance at Assur: the case of dated Aramaic memorials', eds. M. Luukko *et al.*, *Of God(s), Trees, Kings and Scholars* (2009), 151–6.

CONCLUSION

1. Rassam, *Asshur and the Land of Nimrod* (1897), 33.
2. Rassam, *Asshur and the Land of Nimrod* (1897), 355.
3. Layard, *Nineveh and Babylon* (1853), 232, also reproduced in Barnett *et al.*, *The Sculptures of Sennacherib* (1998), plates 223–5.
4. R. M. Czichon, *Reallexikon der Assyriologie*, vol. 9 (1998–2001), 202, s.v. 'Nebukadnezar'; in *The Garden Book* (Phaidon 2000) s.v. 'Sennacherib'; Boiy, *Late Achaemenid and Hellenistic Babylon* (2004), 64; mentioned as perhaps correct on the British Museum website as updated in 2007; Van der Spek, 'Berossus as a Babylonian chronicler and Greek historian', ed.

Van der Spek, *Studies in Ancient Near Eastern World View and Society* (2008), 302–4.

5. L. Morgan, *Ancient Society* (1877); see K. Greene, ed. Oleson, *Oxford Handbook of Engineering* (2008), 62–3.

APPENDIX

1. See also the reasons inferred for choosing the word *kirimāhu* for the palace garden, Ch. 4.
2. In a similar passage in the Bellino cylinder the erosion of royal tombs by the uncontrolled river water is mentioned, which indicates that there were extended versions of parts of this inscription.
3. Patron god of craftsmen, especially stone-cutters and sculptors.
4. These are to be seen on the sculpture panel of Ashurbanipal from the North Palace, see Reade, *Assyrian Sculpture* (1983), 40 fig. 56 with caption.
5. The word used is *ambassu*. The name shows that there was a hunting park outside the city, distinct from the *kirimāhu*.
6. *handuri* may mean a projecting spur of a wall.

Bibliography

Restricted to works quoted in footnotes, and a very few other works that were consulted with profit.

Abdul-Razak, W. 1979. 'Ishtar Gate and its inner wall', *Sumer* 35, 116–17.

Albenda, P. 1986. *The Palace of Sargon, King of Assyria*. Paris: Éditions recherche sur les civilisations.

Allinger-Csollich, W., Heinisch, S. and Kuntner, W. 2010. 'Babylon. Past, present, future: the project "Comparative Studies Babylon–Borsippa": a synopsis', eds. P. Matthiae and L. Romano, *Rome, 6th International Congress for the Archaeology of the Ancient Near East*. Wiesbaden: Harrassowitz, 29–38.

al-Rawi, F. N. H. 1985. 'Nabopolassar's restoration on the wall Imgur-Enlil at Babylon', *Iraq* 47, 1–13.

——and Roaf, M. 1984. 'Ten Old Babylonian mathematical problems from Tell Haddad', *Sumer* 43, 175–218.

Alster, B. 1983. 'Dilmun, Bahrain and the alleged paradise in Sumerian myth and literature', ed. D. T. Potts, *Dilmun: New Studies in the Archaeology and Early History of Bahrain*. Berlin: Reimer, 39–74.

al-Tikriti, W. Y. 2002. 'The origin of the Falaj: further evidence from the United Arab Emirates', eds. L. Al-Gailani-Werr, J. E. Curtis, H. Martin, A. McMahon, J. Oates and J. E. Reade, *Of Pots and Plans: Papers on the Archaeology and History of Mesopotamia and Syria presented to David Oates*. London: NABU Publications, 339–55.

Alvarez-Mon, J. 2010. *The Arjan Tomb: At the Crossroads of the Elamite and Persian Empires*. Acta Iranica 49. Leuven: Peeters.

Ambos, C. 2004. *Mesopotamische Baurituale aus dem 1. Jahrtausend v. Chr: Mit einem Beitrag von A. Schmitt*. Dresden: Islet.

——2010. 'Building rituals from the first millennium BC: the evidence from the ritual texts', eds. M. J. Boda and J. Novotny, *From the Foundations to the Crenellations*, Alter Orient und Altes Testament 366. Münster: Ugarit-Verlag, 221–38.

Ammianus Marcellinus. *History*.

Andrae, W. 1938. *Das wiedererstandene Assur*. Munich: C. H. Beck.

Angenot, V. 2008. 'A Horizon of Aten in Memphis?', *Journal of the Society for the Study of Egyptian Antiquities* 35, 7–26.

Annus, A. 2006. 'The survivals of the ancient Syrian and Mesopotamian intellectual traditions in the writings of Ephrem Syrus', *Ugarit-Forschungen* 38 (published 2007), 1–25.

Antipater, see Gow and Page, *Greek Anthology* IX.

Aravantinos, V. L., Kountouri, E. and Fappas, I. 2006. 'To mykēnaiko apostraggistiko systēma tēs Kopaidas', *Proceedings of the 2nd International Conference on Ancient Greek Technology*. Athens, 557–64.

Asmussen, J. P. 1975. *Manichaean Literature: Representative Texts chiefly from Middle Persian and Parthian Writings*. New York: Delmar.

As-Soof, B. 1970. 'Mounds in the Rania plain and excavations at Tell Basmusian 1956', *Sumer* 26, 65–104.

Athenaeus, *Deipnosophistae*, Loeb edn. transl. C. B. Gulick. London: Heinemann, 1941, rev. edn. 1969.

Azoulay, V. 2004. 'Exchange as entrapment: mercenary Xenophon?', ed. R. Lane Fox, *The Long March*. New Haven and London: Yale University Press, 289–304.

Bacon, Francis. 1597. *Essay, Of Gardens*, ed. A. S. West. Cambridge: Cambridge University Press, 1931.

Bagg, A. M. 2000. *Assyrische Wasserbauten*, Baghdader Forschungen 24. Mainz-am-Rhein: Philipp von Zabern.

——2007. *Die Orts- und Gewässernamen der neuassyrischen Zeit, Teil 1: Die Levante*. Répertoire géographique des textes cunéiformes, vol. 7/1. Wiesbaden: Harrassowitz.

Bahrani, Z. 2003. *The Graven Image*. Philadelphia: University of Pennsylvania Press.

Barag, D. 1985. *Catalogue of Western Asiatic Glass in the British Museum*, vol. 1. London: British Museum Press.

Barnett, R. D. 1976. *Sculptures from the North Palace of Assurbanipal at Nineveh (668–627)*. London: British Museum Publications.

——Bleibtreu, E. and Turner, G. 1998. *The Sculptures from the Southwest Palace of Sennacherib*. London: British Museum Press.

Barr, J. 1974. 'Philo of Byblos and his Phoenician History', *Bulletin of the John Rylands University Library of Manchester* 57, 17–68.

Basmachi, F. 1976. *Treasures of the Iraq Museum 1975–76*. Baghdad.

Battini, L. 1999. 'Réflexions sur les noms des portes urbaines en Mesopotamie', *Isimu* 2, 31–46.

Baynham, E. 1998. *Alexander the Great: The Unique History of Quintus Curtius*. Ann Arbor: University of Michigan.

Beaulieu, P.-A. 1993. 'The historical background of the Uruk Prophecy', eds. M. E. Cohen, D. Snell and D. Weisberg, *The Tablet and the Scroll*. Festschrift for W. W. Hallo. Potomac, Md.: CDL, 41–52.

——1997. 'The cult of AN.ŠÁR/Aššur in Babylonia after the fall of the Assyrian empire', *State Archives of Assyria Bulletin* 11, 55–74.

——1998. 'Ba'u-asītu and Kaššaya, daughters of Nebuchadnezzar II', *Orientalia* New Series 67, 173–201.

Beaux, N. 1990. *Le Cabinet de curiosités de Thoutmosis III: Plantes et animaux du 'jardin botanique' de Karnak*. Leuven: Peeters.

Becker, A. and Becker, U. 1991. '"Altes" und "Neues" Babylon', *Baghdader Mitteilungen* 22, 501–11.

Becker, A. S. 1995. *The Shield of Achilles and the Poetics of Ekphrasis.* Baltimore: Rowman and Littlefield.

Beddome, R. H. 1869. *The Flora Sylvatica for Southern India*, vol. 1.

Besnier, M.-F. 1999. 'La Conception du jardin en Syro-Mésopotamie à partir des textes', *Ktema* 24, 195–212.

Beyer, D. 1996. 'Jardins sacrés d'Émar au Bronze Récent', ed. G. Siebert, *Nature et paysage dans la pensée et l'environnement des civilisations antiques.* Paris: de Boccard, 11–19.

Bianchi, R. S. 1990. 'Egyptian metal statuary of the Third Intermediate Period (c.1070–656 BC) from its Egyptian antecedents to its Samian examples', *Small Bronze Sculpture of the Ancient World.* Malibu: Paul Getty Museum, 61–84.

Bichler, R. 2004. 'Ktesias "korrigiert" Herodot: Zur literarischen Einschätzung der Persika', eds. H. Heftner and K. Tomaschitz, *Ad Fontes!*, Festschrift für Gerhard Dobesch. Vienna: im Eigenverlag der Herausgeber, 105–16.

——and Rollinger, R. 2005. 'Die Hängenden Gärten zu Ninive—Die Lösung eines Rätsels?', ed. R. Rollinger, *Von Sumer bis Homer*, Festschrift für Manfred Schretter, Alter Orient und Altes Testament 325. Münster, Ugarit-Verlag, 153–218.

Biddle, M. 1999. 'The gardens of Nonsuch: sources and dating', *Garden History* 27, 145–83.

Birot, M. 1974. *Lettres de Yaqqim-Addu, gouverneur de Sagaratum.* Archives Royales de Mari XIV. Paris: Paul Geuthner.

Black, J. 1987. 'Nebuchadnessar II's cross-country wall north of Sippar: Babylonian textual evidence'. *Northern Akkad Project Reports* 1, 15–20.

——Cunningham, G., Robson, E. and Zolyomi, G. 2004. *The Literature of Ancient Sumer.* Oxford: Oxford University Press.

Blaylock, S. 2009. *Tille Höyük 3.1 The Iron Age: Introduction, Stratification and Architecture.* London: British Institute at Ankara, Monograph 41.

Boiy, T. 2004. *Late Achaemenid and Hellenistic Babylon.* Leuven: Peeters.

——2007. 'Assyriology and the history of the hellenistic period', *Topoi* 15, 7–20.

Borger, R. 1956. *Inschriften Asarhaddons Königs von Assyrien.* Archiv für Orientforschung, Beiheft 9, reprint Osnabrück: Biblio-Verlag 1967.

——1988. 'König Sanheribs Eheglück', *Annual Review of the Royal Inscription of Mesopotamia Project* 6, 5–11.

——1996. *Beiträge zum Inschriftenwerk Assurbanipals.* Wiesbaden: Harrassowitz.

Börker-Klähn, J. 1982. *Altvorderasiatische Bildstelen und vergleichbare Felsreliefs.* Baghdader Forschungen 4. Mainz: Deutsches Archäologisches Institut Abteilung Baghdad.

Botta, P.-E. and Flandin, E. 1846–50. *Monument de Ninive*. 5 vols. Paris.

Boucharlat, R. 1995. 'Archaeology and artifacts of the Arabian peninsula', ed. J. M. Sasson, *Civilizations of the Ancient Near East*, vol. 2, 1335–53.

Bremmer, J. N. 1999. 'Paradise: from Persia, via Greece, into the Septuagint', ed. G. P. Luttikhuizen, *Paradise Interpreted*. Leiden and Boston: Brill, 1–20.

Briant, P. 1996. *Histoire de l'empire Perse*. Paris: Fayard.

Brinkman, J. A. 1984. *Prelude to Empire: Babylonian Society and Politics 747–626 BC*. Philadelphia: Occasional Publications of the Babylonian Fund 7.

———1988. 'Textual evidence for bronze in Babylonia in the Early Iron Age, 1000–539 BC', ed. J. E. Curtis, *Bronze-Working Centres of Western Asia c.1000–539 B.C.* London and New York: Kegan Paul International, 135–68.

Brodersen, K. 1992. *Reiseführer zu den Sieben Weltwundern: Philon von Byzanz und andere antike Texte*. Frankfurt am Main and Leipzig: Insel Verlag.

———1996. *Die Sieben Weltwunder: Legendäre Kunst- und Bauwerke der Antike*. Munich: C. H. Beck.

Browne, Thomas. *The Garden of Cyrus*.

Budge, E. A. W. 1914. *Assyrian Sculptures in the British Museum, Reign of Assurnasirpal, 885–860 BC*. London: British Museum.

Burkert, W. 1992. *The Orientalizing Revolution: Near Eastern Influence on Greek Culture in the Early Archaic Age*. Cambridge, Mass.: Harvard University Press.

Burstein, S. M. 1978. *The Babyloniaca of Berossus*. Malibu: Undena Publications.

Callatay, F. de, 1996. 'Abdissarès l'Adiabénien', *Iraq* 58, 135–45.

Calmeyer, P. 1994. 'Babylonische und assyrische Elemente in der achaimenidischen Kunst', ed. H. Sancisi-Weerdenburg, *Continuity and Change*, Achaemenid History 8. Ann Arbor, 131–47.

Campbell Thompson, R. and Hutchinson, R. W. 1929. 'The excavations on the temple of Nabu at Nineveh', *Archaeologia* 79, 103–48.

———1931. 'The site of the palace of Ashurnasirpal at Nineveh, excavated in 1929–30 on behalf of the British Museum', *Liverpool Annals of Archaeology and Anthropology* 18, 79–112.

——— and Hamilton, R. W. 1932. 'The British Museum excavations on the temple of Ishtar at Nineveh 1930–1931', *Liverpool Annals of Art and Archaeology* 19, 55–116.

Canali di Rossi, F. 2004. *Iscrizioni dello estremo oriente greco. Un repertorio: Inschriften griechischer Städte aus Kleinasien*, vol. 64. Bonn: Dr. Rudolf Habelt GMBH.

Capdetrey, L. 2007. *Le Pouvoir séleucide: territoire, administration, finances d'un royaume hellénistique*. Rennes: Presses Universitaires.

Cawkwell, G. 1972. *Xenophon. The Persian Expedition*. Harmondsworth: Penguin Classics.

Chapot, V. 1902. 'Antiquités de la Syria du Nord', *Bulletin de correspondance hellénique* 26, 205–6.

Charpin, D. 2008. 'Archivage et classification: un récapitulatif de créances à Mari sous Zimri-Lim', *Proceedings of the 51st Rencontre Assyriologique Internationale*. Chicago: Oriental Institute, 3–15.

Childe, V. Gordon. 1932. *New Light on the Most Ancient East: The Oriental Prelude to European Prehistory*. London: Routledge, 1952.

Childs, B. S. 1962. 'Eden, Garden of'. *The Interpreter's Dictionary of the Bible*. Nashville and New York: Abingdon Press.

Clarke, K. 1999. 'Universal perspectives in historiography', ed. C. S. Kraus, *The Limits of Historiography: Genre and Narrative in Ancient Historical Texts*. Leiden: Brill, 249–79.

Clayton, P. and Price, M. J., eds. 1988. *The Seven Wonders of the Ancient World*. London: Routledge.

Clifford, R. J. 1994. *Creation Accounts in the Ancient Near East and the Bible*. The Catholic Biblical Quarterly Monograph Series 26. Washington DC, 35–8.

Cogan, M. 1977. 'Ashurbanipal Prism F: notes on scribal techniques and editorial procedures', *Journal of Cuneiform Studies* 29, 97–107.

Cole, S. W. and Machinist, P. 1998. *Letters from Priests to the Kings Esarhaddon and Assurbanipal*, State Archives of Assyria XIII. Helsinki: Helsinki University Press.

Coleman, K. M. 2006. *Martial: Liber Spectaculorum*. Edited with introduction, translation and commentary. Oxford: Oxford University Press.

Colledge, M. 1979. 'Sculptors' stone-carving techniques in Seleucid and Parthian Iran, and their place in the "Parthian" cultural milieu: some preliminary observations', *East and West* 29, 221–40.

Collins, P. 2006. 'Trees and gender in Assyrian art', *Iraq* 68, 99–107.

Collon, D. 1987. *First Impressions: Cylinder Seals in the Ancient Near East*. London: British Museum Publications.

Cook, E. 2004. 'Near Eastern prototypes of the Palace of Alkinoos', *American Journal of Archaeology* 108, 43–77.

Cotterell, B. and Kamminga, J. 1990. *Mechanics of Pre-industrial Technology*. Cambridge: Cambridge University Press.

Craddock, P. T. 1995. *Early Metal Mining and Production*. Edinburgh: Edinburgh University Press.

Crane, E. 1999. *The World History of Bee-keeping and Honey-hunting*. London: Duckworth.

Curtis, J. E. 1976. 'Parthian gold from Nineveh', *The Classical Tradition*, British Museum Yearbook I, 47–66.

——1988. *Bronzeworking Centres of Western Asia c.1000–539 B.C.* London and New York: Kegan Paul International.

——1999. 'Glass inlays and Nimrud ivories', *Iraq* 61, 59–69.

Curtis, J. E. 2003. 'The Assyrian heartland in the period 612–539 BC', ed. R. Rollinger, *Continuity of Empire*, Padua: S.a.r.g.o.n. Editrice e Libreria, 157–67.

——2005. 'The Achaemenid period in northern Iraq', ed. P. Briant, *L'Archéologie de l'Empire achéménide: nouvelles recherches*. Persika 6, Paris: De Boccard, 342–7.

——McCall, H., Collon, D. and Al-Gailani Werr, L. eds. 2008. *New Light on Nimrud*. London: British Institute for the Study of Iraq.

Czichon, R. M. 1998–2001. *Reallexikon der Assyriologie*, vol. 9 s.v. 'Nebukadnezar', 202.

Dalley, S. M. 1988. 'Neo-Assyrian textual evidence for bronze-working centres', ed. J. E. Curtis, *Bronzeworking Centres of Western Asia c.1000–539 B.C.* London and New York: Kegan Paul International, 97–110.

——1991. 'Ancient Assyrian textiles and the origins of carpet design', *Iran* 29, 117–35.

——1993. 'Nineveh after 612 BC', *Altorientalische Forschungen* 20, 134–47.

——1994. 'Nineveh, Babylon and the Hanging Gardens: cuneiform and Classical sources reconciled', *Iraq* 56, 45–58.

——1997. 'The Hanging Gardens of Babylon at Nineveh', eds. H. Waetzoldt and H. Hauptmann, *Proceedings of the 39th Rencontre Assyriologique International, Heidelberg 1992*. Heidelberger Studien zum Alten Orient Band 6, 19–24.

——1999. 'Sennacherib and Tarsus', *Anatolian Studies* 49, 73–80.

——2000. 'Hebrew TAHAŠ, Akkadian DUHŠU, faience and beadwork', *Journal of Semitic Studies* 45, 1–19.

——2001–2. 'Water management in Assyria from the ninth to the seventh centuries BC', *ARAM* 13–14, 443–60.

——2002. 'More about the Hanging Gardens', eds. L. Al-Gailani-Werr, J. E. Curtis, A. McMahon and J. E. Reade, *Of Pots and Plans: Studies presented to David Oates*. Cambridge: Macdonald Institute, 67–73.

——2003. 'Why did Herodotus not mention the Hanging Gardens?', eds. P. Derow and R. Parker, *Herodotus and his World*. Oxford: Oxford University Press, 171–89.

——'The transition from Neo-Assyrians to Neo-Babylonians: break or continuity?', in *Eretz-Israel: Archaeological, Historical and Geographical Studies* 27, Hayim and Miriam Tadmor Volume. Jerusalem: Israel Exploration Society, 25–8.

——2005. 'Water supply for cities in the late eighth and seventh centuries BC: Assyria and Urartu', eds. A. Çilingiroglu and G. Darbyshire, *Anatolian Iron Ages* 5, British Institute at Ankara Monograph 31. London, 39–43.

——2005. 'The language of destruction and its interpretation', *Baghdader Mitteilungen* 36, 275–85.

——2005. 'Semiramis in History and Legend', ed. E. Gruen, *Cultural Borrowings and Ethnic Appropriations in Antiquity*. Stuttgart: F. Steiner Verlag, 11–22.

——2008. 'Babylon as a name for other cities including Nineveh', *Proceedings of the 51st Rencontre Assyriologique Internationale 2005* = *Studies in Ancient Oriental Civilization*, no. 62, eds. R. D. Biggs, J. Myers and M. T. Roth. Chicago: Oriental Institute, 25–33.

——and Oleson, J. P. 2003. 'Sennacherib, Archimedes and the water screw: the context of invention in the ancient world', *Technology and Culture* 44, 1–26.

——and Postgate, J. N. 1984. *Tablets from Fort Shalmaneser*. Cuneiform Texts from Nimrud III. London: British School of Archaeology in Iraq.

—— 'The Greek novel *Ninus and Semiramis*: its background in Assyrian and Seleucid history and monuments', ed. T. Whitmarsh, *The Romance between Greece and the East*, Cambridge University Press, forthcoming.

Dandamaev, M. 1997. 'Assyrian traditions during Achaemenid times', eds. S. Parpola and R. Whiting, *Assyria 1995*. Helsinki: Helsinki University Press, 41–8.

Da Riva, R. 2008. 'The Nebuchadnezzar twin inscriptions of Brisa (Wadi esh-Sharbin, Lebanon): transliteration, and translation', *Bulletin d'archéologie et d'architecture libanaises* 12, 229–333.

——2008. *The Neo-Babylonian Royal Inscriptions: An Introduction*. Münster: Ugarit-Verlag.

Day, J. 2000. *Yahweh and the Gods and Goddesses of Canaan*. Journal of the Society for the Study of the Old Testament, Supplement Series 265. Sheffield: Sheffield Academic Press.

Decker, W. 1992. *Sports and Games of Ancient Egypt*. New Haven and London: Yale University Press.

Deller, K.-H. 1985. 'SAG.DU UR.MAH, Löwenkopfsitula, Löwenkopfbecher', *Baghdader Mitteilungen* 16, 327–46.

De Odorico, M. 1995. *The Use of Numbers and Quantifications in the Assyrian Royal Inscriptions*. State Archives of Assyria Studies III. Helsinki: Helsinki University Press.

Dijksterhuis, E. J. 1956. *Archimedes*. Copenhagen: Munksgaard.

Diodorus Siculus. *Library of History* book II, transl. C. H. Oldfather, Loeb edn. Cambridge, Mass.: Harvard University Press, 1933.

Dixon Hunt, J. and Willis, P. eds. 1988. *The Genius of the Place: The English Landscape Garden 1620–1820*. Cambridge, Mass., and London: Massachusetts Institute of Technology Press.

Drower, M. S. 1956. 'Water supply, irrigation, and agriculture', eds. C. Singer, E. J. Holmyard, A. R. Hall and T. I. Williams, *A History of Technology* II, Oxford: Clarendon Press, 528–32.

Eidem, J. 1992. *The Shemshara Archives, 2: The Administrative Texts.* Copenhagen: Munksgaard.

Ekschmitt, W. 1984. *Die sieben Weltwunder: Ihre Erbauung, Zerstörung und Wiederentdeckung.* Mainz am Rhein: P. von Zabern.

Ephal, I. and Tadmor, H. 2006. 'Observations of two inscriptions of Esarhaddon', eds. Y. Amit *et al.*, *Essays on Ancient Israel in its Near Eastern Context. A Tribute to Nadav Na'aman.* Winona Lake, Ind.: Eisenbrauns, 155–70.

Farber, G. 1997. 'Inanna and Enki', eds. W. Hallo and K. Lawson Younger, *The Context of Scripture*, vol. 1. Leiden: Brill, 522–6.

——1987–90. *Reallexikon der Assyriologie*, vol. 7, s.v. 'me', 610–13.

Feeney, D. 2007. *Caesar's Calendar.* Berkeley and Los Angeles: University of California Press.

Feldman, M. 2004. 'Nineveh to Thebes and back: art and politics between Assyria and Egypt in the seventh century BCE', *Iraq* 66, 141–50.

Finkel, I. 1982. *The Series SIG7 = ALAN = Nabnītu*, Materials for the Sumerian Lexicon XVI. Rome: Pontifical Biblical Institute.

——1988. 'The Hanging Gardens of Babylon', eds. P. Clayton and M. J. Price, *The Seven Wonders of the Ancient World.* London: Routledge.

——and Seymour, M. 2008. *Babylon Myth and Reality.* Exhibition catalogue, London: British Museum.

Finley, M. I. 1965. 'Technical innovation and economic progress in the ancient world', *Economic History Review* 18, 29–45.

——1975. *The Use and Abuse of History.* London: Chatto and Windus.

——and Pleket, H. W. 1976. *The Olympic Games: The First Thousand Years.* London: Chatto and Windus.

Fiorina, P. 2008. 'Italian excavations at Nimrud-Kalhu: chronological and stratigraphical problems', eds. J. Curtis, H. McCall, D. Collon and L. Al-Gailani Werr, *New Light on Nimrud*, Proceedings of the Nimrud Conference 2002. London: British Institute for the Study of Iraq, 53–6.

——2009. 'Nimrud–Fort Shalmaneser: entrepôts et ateliers de la zone SW', eds. S. M. Cecchini, S. Mazzoni and E. Scigliuzzo, *Syrian and Phoenician Ivories.* Pisa: Edizioni ETS, 27–46.

Fleming, D. 1989. 'Eggshell Ware Pottery in Achaemenid Mesopotamia', *Iraq* 51, 165–85.

Forbes, R. J. 1965. *Cosmetics and Perfumes.* Studies in Ancient Technology II. 2nd edn. Leiden: Brill.

——1972. *Copper; Tin and Bronze; Antimony and Arsenic; Iron.* Studies in Ancient Technology IX, 2nd edn. Leiden: Brill.

Frahm, E. 1994. 'Die Bilder in Sanheribs Thronsaal', *Nouvelles assyriologiques brèves et utilitaires* 55 (1994).

——1997. *Einleitung in die Sanherib-Inschriften.* Archiv für Orientforschung Beiheft 26.

———2000. 'Die *akītu*-Häuser von Ninive', *Nouvelles assyriologiques brèves et utilitaires* 66 (2000).

———2005. 'Wer den Halbschekel nicht ehrt—nochmals zu Sanheribs angeblichen Münzen', *Nouvelles assyriologiques brèves et utilitaires* 45 (2005).

———2010. 'Counter-texts, commentaries, and adaptations: politically motivated responses to the Babylonian Epic of Creation in Mesopotamia, the biblical world, and elsewhere', ed. A. Tsukimoto, *Conflict, Peace and Religion in the Ancient Near East*. Orient 45, 3–33.

———2011. *Babylonian and Assyrian Text Commentaries: Origins of Interpretation*. Guides to the Mesopotamian Textual Record vol. 5. Münster: Ugarit-Verlag.

Frame, G. 1995. *Rulers of Babylonia from the Second Dynasty of Isin to the End of Assyrian Domination (1157–612 BC)*. Royal Inscriptions of Mesopotamia Babylonian Periods Volume 2. Toronto: Toronto University Press.

Franklin, N. 2011. 'From Megiddo to Tamassos and back: putting the "proto-Ionic capital" in its place!', eds. I. Finkelstein and N. Na'aman, *Fire Signals of Lachish*, Festschrift for David Ussishkin. Winona Lake, Ind.: Eisenbrauns, 129–40.

Fraser, P. M. 1994. 'The world of Theophrastus', ed. S. Hornblower, *Greek Historiography*. Oxford: Clarendon Press, 167–92.

Frayne, D. 1997. *Ur III Period (2112–2004 BC)*. Royal Inscriptions of Mesopotamia Early Periods 3/2. Toronto: Toronto University Press.

Freeth, T., Jones, A., Steele, J. M. and Bitsakis, Y. 2008. 'Calendars with olympiad display and eclipse prediction on the Antikythera mechanism', *Nature* 454, 614–17.

Frendo, A. 2011. *Pre-exilic Israel, the Hebrew Bible, and Archaeology*. New York and London: T & T Clark.

Fuchs, A. 1994. *Die Inschriften Sargons II aus Khorsabad*. Göttingen: Cuvillier Verlag.

———1996. 'Die Inschrift vom Ištar-Tempel', chapter VII in R. Borger, *Beiträge zu Inschriftenwerk Assurbanipals*. Wiesbaden: Harrassowitz, 258–96.

Fugmann, E. 1958. *Hama: Fouilles et recherches 1931–1938*, vol. 2/1, *L'Architecture des périodes pré-hellénistiques*. Copenhagen: National Museum.

Gallagher, W. 1996. 'The Istanbul stela of Nabonidus', *Wiener Zeitschrift für die Kunde des Morgenlandes* 86, Festschrift for H. Hirsch, 119–26.

Gasche, H. 1989. 'Habl aṣ-Ṣahr, nouvelles fouilles: l'ouvrage défensif de Nabuchodonosor au nord de Sippar', *Northern Akkad Project Reports* 2, 23–70.

George, A. R. 1992. *Babylonian Topographical Texts*. Orientalia Lovaniensia Analecta 40. Leuven: Peeters.

———1995. 'The bricks of E-sagil', *Iraq* 57, 173–97.

———1997. 'Marduk and the cult of the gods of Nippur at Babylon', *Orientalia* 66, 65–70.

——2003. *The Babylonian Gilgamesh Epic: Introduction, Critical Edition and Cuneiform Texts*. Oxford: Oxford University Press.

Ghirshman, R. 1968. *Tchoga Zanbil: Temenos, temples, palais, tombes*. Mémoires de la délégation en Perse 40 vol. 2. Paris: Geuthner.

Gille, B. 1956. 'Machines', eds. C. Singer, E. J. Holmyard, A. R. Hall and T. I. Williams, *A History of Technology* II. Oxford: Clarendon Press.

Giovino, M. 2007. *The Assyrian Sacred Tree: A History of Interpretations*. Orbis Biblicus et Orientalis 230. Göttingen: Academic Press Fribourg, Vandenhoeck and Ruprecht.

Glassner, J.-J. 2004. *Mesopotamian Chronicles*. Atlanta: Society of Biblical Literature.

Goblot, H. 1979. *Les Qanats: Une technique d'acquisition de l'eau*. Industrie et artisanat 9, École des hautes études en sciences sociales. Paris and New York: Éditions Mouton.

Goode, P. and Lancaster, M., eds. 1986. *Oxford Companion to Gardens*. Oxford: Oxford University Press.

Goold, G. P. 1995. *Chariton, Callirhoe*. Loeb edn. Cambridge, Mass.: Harvard University Press.

Gow, A. and Page, D. L. 1968. *The Greek Anthology: The Garland of Philip*. Cambridge: Cambridge University Press.

Grayson, A. K. 1963. 'The Walters Art Gallery inscription of Sennacherib', *Archiv für Orientforschung* 20, 83–96.

——1970. *Assyrian and Babylonian Chronicles*. Texts from Assyrian and Babylonian Sources 5. New York: J. J. Augustin.

——1991. *Assyrian Rulers of the Early First Millennium BC I (1114–859 BC)*. Royal Inscriptions of Mesopotamia, Assyrian Periods 2. Toronto: Toronto University Press.

——1996. *Assyrian Rulers of the Early First Millennium BC II (858–745 BC)*. Royal Inscriptions of Mesopotamia, Assyrian Periods 3. Toronto: Toronto University Press.

Greenberg, M. 1997. *Ezekiel 21–37*. Anchor Bible commentary. New York etc.: Doubleday.

Greene, K. 2000. 'Technical innovation and economic progress in the ancient world: M. I. Finley reconsidered', *Economic History Review* 53, 29–59.

Groeber, K. 1925. *Palästina, Arabien und Syrien: Baukunst, Landschaft, Volksleben*. Berlin: Verlag von Ernst Wasmuth A.G.

Gutzwiller, K. 2009. *A Guide to Hellenistic Literature*. Oxford: Blackwell.

Hägg, T. 1983. *The Novel in Antiquity*. Oxford: Blackwell.

Haller, A. 1953. *Die Gräber und Grüfte von Assur*, Wissenschaftliche Veröffentlichungen der Deutschen Orient-Gesellschaft 65.

Hallo, W. W. and Lawson Younger, K. eds. 1997. *The Context of Scripture*. Leiden: Brill.

Hannah, R. 2008. 'Timekeeping', ed. J. P. Oleson, *Oxford Handbook of Engineering and Technology in the Classical World*. New York: Oxford University Press, 740–58.

Harmatta, J. 1974. 'Les Modèles littéraires de l'édit babylonien de Cyrus', *Acta Iranica* 1, 29–44.

Haupt, P. 1907. 'Xenophon's account of the fall of Nineveh', *Journal of the American Oriental Society* 28, 99–107.

Hawkins, J. D. 1999. *Corpus of Hieroglyphic Luwian Inscriptions*. Berlin: Walter de Gruyter.

Haynes, D. 1992. *The Technique of Greek Bronze Statuary*. Mainz am Rhein: Philipp von Zabern.

Heidel, A. 1953. 'The octagonal Sennacherib prism in the Iraq Museum', *Sumer* 9, 117–88.

Helck, W. *et al.* 1972–92. *Lexikon der Aegyptologie*. Wiesbaden: Harrassowitz.

Hendel, R. 2009. 'Other Edens', ed. J. D. Schloen, *Exploring the Longue durée*. Essays in Honor of Lawrence E. Stager. Winona Lake, Ind.: Eisenbrauns, 185–9.

Hercher, R. 1858. *Aeliani de natura animalium, . . . Porphyrii philosophi . . . Philonis Byzantii*. Paris.

Herodotus. *The Histories*. Transl. A. de Sélincourt. Harmondsworth: Penguin, 1954.

Herrmann, G. 1977. *The Iranian Revival*. Oxford: Elsevier-Phaidon.

——1992. *Ivories from Nimrud V: The Small Collections from Fort Shalmaneser*. London: British School of Archaeology in Iraq.

Hodge, T. 2000. 'Qanats', ed. O. Wikander, *Handbook of Ancient Water Technology*. Leiden: Brill, 35–8.

Homer. *Iliad*.

——*Odyssey*.

Hope-Simpson, R. 1998. 'The Mycenaean highways', *Classical Views. Échos du monde classique* 42, 239–60.

Hornblower, S. and Spawforth, A. 1996. *Oxford Classical Dictionary*. 3rd edn. Oxford: Oxford University Press.

Horowitz, W. 1991. 'Antiochus I, Esagil and a celebration of the ritual for the renovation of temples', *Revue d'Assyriologie* 85, 75–7.

——1998. *Mesopotamian Cosmic Geography*. Winona Lake, Ind.: Eisenbrauns.

Howard-Carter, T. 1983. 'An interpretation of the sculptural decoration of the second millennium temple at Tell Al-Rimah', *Iraq* 45, 64–72.

Humphrey, J. W., Oleson, J. P. and Sherwood, A. N. eds. 1998. *Greek and Roman Technology: A Sourcebook*. London: Routledge.

Hunger, H. 1968. *Babylonische und assyrische Kolophone*. Alter Orient und Altes Testament 2. Kevelaer and Neukirchen-Vluyn.

Huxley, M. 2000. 'Sennacherib's addition to the temple of Assur', *Iraq* 62, 107–37.

Invernizzi, A. 1989. 'L'Heracles Epitrapezios de Ninive', eds. L. de Meyer and E. Haerinck, *Archaeologia Iranica et Orientalis: Miscellanea in honorem Louis Vanden Berghe*, vol. 2. Gent: Peeters.

Jacobsen, T. and Lloyd, S. 1935. *Sennacherib's Aqueduct at Jerwan*. Oriental Institute Publications 24. Chicago: Chicago University Press.

James, S. 1986. 'Evidence from Dura Europus for the origins of the late Roman helmets', *Syria* 63, 107–34.

Jewish Encyclopaedia 1938 s.v. 'Adiabene'. London: Shapiro, Vallentine.

Josephus. *Jewish Antiquities*.

Joyce, P. M. 2007. *Ezekiel: A Commentary*. Edinburgh: T & T Clark.

Kataja, L. and Whiting, R. 1995. *Grants, Decrees and Gifts of the Neo-Assyrian Period*, State Archives of Assyria XII. Helsinki: Helsinki University Press.

Katz, D. 2007. 'Enki and Ninhursaga, part one: the story of Dilmun', *Bibliotheca Orientalis* 64, 568–89.

Kawami, T. 1972. 'A possible source for the sculptures of the audience hall, Pasargadae', *Iran* 10, 146–8.

Kemp, M. 1992. *The Science of Art: Optical Themes in Western Art from Brunelleschi to Seurat*. New Haven and London: Yale University Press.

Kessler-Mesguich, S. 1992. 'Les Grammaires occidentales de l'hébreu', ed. S. Auroux, *Histoire des idées linguistiques*. Liège: P. Mardaga, 251–70.

Khoury, R. 1988. 'Babylon in der ältesten Version über die Geschichte der Propheten im Islam', eds. G. Mauer and U. Magen, *Ad bene et fideliter seminandum: Festgabe für K.-H. Deller*, Alter Orient und Altes Testament 220. Münster: Ugarit-Verlag, 123–44.

King, L. W. 1902. *Cuneiform Texts in the British Museum*, vol. 15, London: British Museum.

Kinnier Wilson, J. V. 1972. *Nimrud Wine Lists*. Cuneiform Texts from Nimrud I. London: British School of Archaeology in Iraq.

Kleingünther, A. 1933. *Protos Heuretēs*. Leipzig: Dieterisch'sche Verlagsbuchhandlung.

Klengel-Brandt, E. 1990. 'Gab es ein Museum in der Hauptburg Nebukadnezars II. in Babylon?', *Forschungen und Berichte* 28, 41–7.

Koch, E. 2001. *Mughal Art and Imperial Ideology: Collected Studies*. New Delhi and Oxford: Oxford University Press.

Koch-Westenholz, U. 1995. *Mesopotamian Astrology: An Introduction to Babylonian and Assyrian Celestial Divination*. Copenhagen: Museum Tusculanum Press.

Kohlmeyer, K. 2009. 'The Temple of the Storm God in Aleppo during the Late Bronze and Early Iron Ages', *Near Eastern Archaeology* 72, 190–202.

Koldewey, R. 1914. *Das wiedererstehende Babylon*. Leipzig: J. C. Hinrichs.

——1931. *Die Königsburgen von Babylon I*. Leipzig: J. C. Hinrichs.

König, F. W. 1955-7. *Handbuch der chaldischen Inschriften*. Graz: E. Weidner.

——1965. *Die elamische Königsinschriften*. Archiv für Orientforschung, Beiheft 16. Graz: E. Weidner.

Korenjak, M. and Rollinger, R. 2001. '"Phokylides" und der Fall Ninives', *Philologus, Zeitschrift für antike Literatur und ihre Rezeption*, 145/2, 195–202.

Korfmann, M. O. 2005. *Troia/Wilusa: Guidebook*, revised edn. Tübingen: Çanakkale-Tübingen Troia Vakfı.

Kose, A. 1999. 'Die Wendelrampe der Ziqqurrat von Dūr Šarrukīn—keine Phantasie vom Zeichentisch', *Baghdader Mitteilungen* 30, 115–37.

Kosmin, P. forthcoming. 'Monarchic ideology and cultural interaction in the Borsippa cylinder'.

Kramer, S. N. 1955. 'Enki and Ninhursag: a paradise myth', ed. J. B. Pritchard, *Ancient Near Eastern Texts related to the Old Testament*. 2nd edn. Princeton: Princeton University Press, 36–41.

Kraus, C. S. 1999. *The Limits of Historiography: Genre and Narrative in Ancient Historical Texts*. Leiden: Brill.

Krebernik, M. 1998–2001. *Reallexikon der Assyriologie*, vol. 9, s.v. 'Ninlil (Mulliltu, Mulissu)', 452–61.

Kühne, H. 2002. 'Thoughts about Assyria after 612 BC', eds. L. Al-Gailani-Werr, J. Curtis, H. Martin, A. McMahon, J. Oates and J. E. Reade, *Of Pots and Plans: Studies presented to David Oates*. Cambridge: Macdonald Institute and London: NABU Publications.

Kuhrt, A. 1995. 'The Assyrian heartland in the Achaemenid period', ed. P. Briant, *Dans les pas des dix-mille*, Pallas 43, 239–54.

——and Sherwin-White, S. 1987. *Hellenism in the East*. London: Duckworth.

——1991. 'Aspects of Seleucid royal ideology: the cylinder of Antiochus I from Borsippa', *Journal of Hellenic Studies* 111, 71–86.

Kuttner, A. 2005. '"Do you look like you belong here?" Asianism at Pergamon and the Makedonian diaspora', ed. E. S. Gruen, *Cultural Borrowings and Ethnic Appropriations in Antiquity*, Oriens et Occidens 8. Wiesbaden: Franz Steiner Verlag, 137–206.

Laessøe, J. 1951. 'The irrigation system at Ulhu, 8th century BC', *Journal of Cuneiform Studies* 5, 21–32.

——1953. 'Reflexions on modern and ancient Oriental water works', *Journal of Cuneiform Studies* 7, 5–26.

——1954. 'The meaning of the word *alamittu*', *Compte rendu de la Rencontre Assyriologique Internationale 1952*, Paris, 150–6.

Lancaster, L. 2008. 'Roman engineering and construction', ed. J. P. Oleson, *The Oxford Handbook of Engineering and Technology in the Classical World*, chapter 10. Oxford: Oxford University Press.

Landsberger, B. 1937. *ana ittišu*, Materials for the Sumerian Lexicon 1. Rome: Pontifical Biblical Institute.

——1958. *HAR-ra = hubullu V–VII*, Materialien zum sumerischen Lexikon, vol. 6. Rome: Pontifical Biblical Institute.

Lane Fox, R. 1973. *Alexander the Great*. London: Allen Lane.

——ed. 2004. *The Great March: Xenophon and the Ten Thousand*. New Haven: Yale University Press.

Langdon, S. 1912. *Die neubabylonischen Königsinschriften*. Vorderasiatische Bibliothek 4. Leipzig: J. C. Hinrich'sche Buchhandlung.

Larsen, M. T. 1994. *The Conquest of Assyria: Excavations in an Antique Land*. London and New York: Routledge.

Lawrence, A. W. 1973 (3rd edn.) and 1983 (4th edn.). *Greek Architecture*. Harmondsworth: Penguin.

Layard, A. H. 1850. *Nineveh and its Remains*. London: John Murray.

——1853. *Discoveries in the Ruins of Nineveh and Babylon*. London: John Murray.

Leichty, E. 2011. *The Royal Inscriptions of Esarhaddon, King of Assyria (680–669 BC)*. Royal Inscriptions of the neo-Assyrian period vol. 4. Winona Lake, Ind.: Eisenbrauns.

Lewis, M. J. T. 2001. *Surveying Instruments of Greece and Rome*. Cambridge: Cambridge University Press.

Liddell, H. G. and Scott, R. 1996. *Greek–English Lexicon*, 9th edn. Oxford: Clarendon Press.

Lightfoot, J. 2003. *Lucian, On the Syrian Goddess*. Oxford: Oxford University Press.

Lion, B. 1992. 'Vignes au royaume de Mari', ed. J.-M. Durand, *Florilegium marianum: Recueil d'études en l'honneur de Michel Fleury*, Mémoires de N.A.B.U.1. Paris: SEPOA, 107–13.

Lipinski, E. 2000. *The Aramaeans: Their Ancient History, Culture, Religion*. Leuven: Peeters.

Liverani, M. 2001. 'The fall of the Assyrian empire: ancient and modern interpretations', eds. S. Alcock, T. d'Altroy, K. Morrison and C. Sinopoli, *Empires: Perspectives from Archaeology and History*. Cambridge: Cambridge University Press, 374–91.

Livingstone, A. 1989. *Court Poetry and Literary Miscellanea*, State Archives of Assyria vol. III. Helsinki: Helsinki University Press.

——2009. 'Remembrance at Assur: the case of dated Aramaic memorials', eds. M. Luukko, S. Svärd and R. Mattila, *Of God(s), Trees, Kings and Scholars*. Studies in Honour of Simo Parpola. Helsinki: Finnish Oriental Society, 151–6.

Lloyd, S. 1978. *The Archaeology of Mesopotamia*. London: Thames and Hudson.

Loud, G. and Altman, C. B. 1938. *Khorsabad Part II: The Citadel and the Town*. Chicago: Chicago University Press.

Löw, I. 1924. *Die Flora der Juden*, vol 2. Vienna and Leipzig: R. Löwit.

Luckenbill, D. D. 1924. *The Annals of Sennacherib*. Oriental Institute Publications 2. Chicago: Chicago University Press.

Luraghi, N. 2006. 'Traders, pirates, warriors: the proto-history of Greek mercenary soldiers in the eastern Mediterranean', *Phoenix* 60, 1–47.

Luttikhuizen, G. P., ed. 1999. *Paradise Interpreted: Representations of Biblical Paradise in Judaism and Christianity*. Leiden: Brill.

Macginnis, J. 1988. 'Ctesias and the fall of Nineveh', *Illinois Classical Studies* 13/1, 37–41.

——1989. 'Some inscribed horse troughs of Sennacherib', *Iraq* 51, 187–92.

Madhloum, T. 1968. 'Nineveh: the 1967–1968 campaign', *Sumer* 24, 45–51.

Malbran-Labat, F. 1995. *Les Inscriptions royales de Suse*. Paris: Louvre.

Malek, J. *et al.* 2000. *Topographical Bibliography of Ancient Egyptian Hiero-glyphic Texts, Reliefs, and Paintings, 7: Nubia, the Deserts, and Outside Egypt*. Oxford: Griffith Institute, Ashmolean Museum, s.v. 'Nineveh'.

Mallowan, M. E. L. 1966. *Nimrud and its Remains*. London: Collins.

Manniche, L. 1989. *An Ancient Egyptian Herbal*. London: British Museum Press.

Maryon, H. and Plenderleith, H. J., 1954. 'Fine metalwork', eds. C. Singer, E. J. Holmyard, A. R. Hall and T. I. Williams, *A History of Technology*, vol. 1. Oxford: Clarendon Press, 623–62.

Matheson, S. A. 1976. *Persia: An Archaeological Guide*. London: Faber and Faber, revised version.

Maxwell-Hyslop, K. R. 1983. 'Dalbergia sissoo Roxburgh', *Anatolian Studies* 33, 67–72.

Mayer, W. R. 1987. 'Ein Mythos von der Erschaffung des Menschen', *Orientalia* 56, 55–68.

Mazar, A. and Panitz-Cohen, N. 2007. 'It is the land of honey: bee-keeping in Iron Age IIA Tel Rehov—culture, cult and economy', *Near Eastern Archaeology* 70, 202–19.

Melville, S. 1999. *The role of Naqia/Zakutu in Sargonid Politics*. State Archives of Assyria Studies IX. Helsinki: Helsinki University Press.

Merrilees, P. H. 2005. *Catalogue of the Western Asiatic Seals in the British Museum, Cylinder Seals, 6: Pre-Achaemenid and Achaemenid Periods*. London: British Museum Press.

Meyers, P. 1988. 'Characteristics of casting revealed by the study of ancient Chinese bronzes', ed. R. Maddin, *The Beginning of the Use of Metals and Alloys*. Cambridge, Mass.: The MIT Press, 283–95.

Michel, C. and Veenhof, K. R. 2010. 'Textiles traded by the Assyrians in Anatolia', eds. C. Michel and M.-L. Nosch, *Textile Terminologies in the Ancient Near East and Mediterranean from the Third to the First Millennia BC*. Oxford: Oxbow, 210–71.

Millar, F. 1993. *The Roman Near East 31 BC–AD 337*. Cambridge, Mass.: Harvard University Press.

Millard, A. R. 1984. 'The Etymology of Eden', *Vetus Testamentum* 34, 103–5.

Milton, John. *Paradise Lost. The Poetical Works of John Milton*, see Valentine, *The Poetical Works of John Milton* (1896).

Mitsis, P. 2003. 'The institutions of Hellenistic philosophy', ed. A. Erskine, *A Companion to the Hellenistic World*. Oxford: Blackwell, 464–76.

Moorey, P. R. S. 1982. *Ur 'of the Chaldees'*. London: Book Club Associates; see also Woolley, *Excavations at Ur: A Record of Twelve Years' Work* (1954).

——1991. *A Century of Biblical Archaeology*. Cambridge: Lutterworth Press.

——1999. *Ancient Mesopotamian Materials and Industries: The Archaeological Evidence*. Winona Lake, Ind.: Eisenbrauns.

Moortgat, A. 1940. *Vorderasiatische Rollsiegel*. Berlin: Gebr. Mann Verlag.

Morgan, C. 1989. *Athletes and Oracles*. Cambridge: Cambridge University Press.

Morgan, J. R. 2007. 'Fiction and history: historiography and the novel', ed. J. Marincola, *A Companion to Greek and Roman Historiography*, vol. 2. Oxford: Wiley-Blackwell, 553–64.

Morgan, L. 1877. *Ancient Society: or, Researches in the Lines of Human Progress from Savagery through Barbarism to Civilization*. Chicago: Charles H. Kerr.

Nagel, W. 1978. 'Wo lagen die "Hängende Gärten" in Babylon?', *Mitteilungen der Deutschen Orient-Gesellschaft* 110, 19–28.

Negahban, E. O. 1996. *Marlik: The Complete Excavation Report*. Philadelphia: University Museum, Pennsylvania.

Nesselrath, H.-G. 1999. 'Herodot und Babylon', ed. J. Renger, *Babylon: Focus mesopotamischer Geschichte*. Saarbrücker Druckerei und Verlag.

Netzer, E. 2001. *Hasmonean and Herodian Winter Palaces at Jericho*. Final report, chapter 13, 'Planning and reconstruction of Herod's third palace'. Jerusalem: Israel Exploration Society.

Neugebauer, O. and Sachs, A. 1945. *Mathematical Cuneiform Texts*. New Haven: American Oriental Society and American Schools of Oriental Research.

Nielsen, I. 1994. *Hellenistic Palaces: Tradition and Renewal*. Aarhus: Aarhus University Press.

Nissinen, M. 1998. 'Love lyrics of Nabu and Tašmetu: an Assyrian Song of Songs?', eds. M. Dietrich and I. Kottsieper, *Und Mose schrieb dieses Lied auf*, Festschrift for O. Loretz. Alter Orient und Altes Testament 250. Münster: Ugarit-Verlag, 587–91.

Novak, M. 2004. 'Hilani und Lustgarten', ed. M. Novak, F. Prayon and A.-M. Wittke, *Die Aussenwirkung des späthethitischen Kulturraumes*, Alter Orient und Altes Testament 323. Münster: Ugarit-Verlag, 299–305.

Novotny, J. 2010. 'Temple building in Assyria: evidence from royal inscriptions', eds. M. J. Boda and J. Novotny, *From the Foundations to the Crenellations*. Alter Orient und Altes Testament 366. Münster: Ugarit-Verlag, 109–40.

Oates, D. 1968. *Studies in the Ancient History of Northern Iraq*. London: British Academy.

——and Oates, J. 2001. *Nimrud: An Assyrian Imperial City Revealed*. London: British School of Archaeology in Iraq.

Oleson, J. P. 1984. *Greek and Roman Mechanical Water-Lifting Devices: The History of a Technology*. Toronto: Toronto University Press.

——2000. 'Irrigation', ed. O. Wikander, *Handbook of Ancient Water Technology*. Leiden: Brill, 183–215.

——2008. *Oxford Handbook of Engineering and Technology in the Classical World*. Oxford: Oxford University Press.

Oppenheim, A. L. 1965. 'On royal gardens in Mesopotamia', *Journal of Near Eastern Studies* 24, 328–33.

——1964. *Ancient Mesopotamia: Portrait of a Dead Civilization*. Chicago: Chicago University Press.

Orchard, J. J. 1978. 'Some miniature painted glass plaques from Fort Shalmaneser, Nimrud, part I', *Iraq* 40, 1–22.

Ornan, T. 1995. 'The transition from figured to non-figured representations in First-Millennium glyptic', ed. J. Goodnick Westenholz, *Seals and Sealings in the Ancient Near East*. Jerusalem: Bible Lands Museum, 39–56.

——2004. 'Idols and symbols: divine representation in First Millennium Mesopotamian art and its bearing on the second commandment', *Tel Aviv* 31, 90–121.

——2007. 'The god-like semblance of a king: the case of Sennacherib's rock reliefs', eds. J. Cheng and M. Feldman, *Ancient Near Eastern Art in Context: Studies in Honor of Irene J. Winter*. Leiden and New York: Brill, 161–78.

Parpola, S. 1987. *The Correspondence of Sargon II part 1*. State Archives of Assyria, vol. 1. Helsinki: Helsinki University Press.

——1993. *Letters from Assyrian and Babylonian Scholars*, State Archives of Assyria, vol. 10. Helsinki: Helsinki University Press.

——and Porter, M. 2001. *The Helsinki Atlas of the Near East in the Neo-Assyrian Period*. The Casco Bay Assyriological Institute and the Neo-Assyrian Text Corpus Project. Helsinki: Helsinki University Press.

Parry, D. 2005. *Engineering in the Ancient World*. Stroud: Sutton Publishing.

Paterson, A. 1915. *Assyrian Sculptures: Palace of Sinacherib*.

Pearson, L. 1960. *The Lost Histories of Alexander*. New York: American Philological Association.

Pedersén, O. 1998. *Archives and Libraries in the Ancient Near East 1500–300 BC*. Bethesda, Md.: CDL Press.

——2005. *Archive und Bibliotheken in Babylon: Die Tontafeln der Grabung Robert Koldeweys 1899–1917*. Saarbrücken: In Kommission bei SDV.

——2009. 'Neo-Assyrian texts from Nebuchadnezzar's Babylon: a preliminary report', eds. M. Luukko, S. Svärd and R. Mattila, *Of God(s), Trees,*

Kings and Scholars. Neo-Assyrian and Related Studies in Honour of Simo Parpola. Helsinki: Finnish Oriental Society, 193–9.

Peeters, P. 1925. 'Le "Passionaire d'Adiabène"', *Analecta Bollandiana* 43, 261–304.

Philo Judaeus, 'On the confusion of tongues'.

Pickworth, D. 2005. 'Excavations at Nineveh: the Halzi gate', *Iraq* 67, 295–316.

Pinker, A. 2006. 'Nahum and the Greek tradition on Nineveh's fall', *Journal of Hebrew Scriptures* 6 (online journal).

Place, V. 1867. *Ninive et l'Assyrie*, vol. 2. Paris.

Plutarch. *Life of Marcellus*.

Polinger Foster, K. 2004. 'The Hanging Gardens of Nineveh', *Iraq* 66, 207–20.

Pomeroy, S. 1994. *Xenophon, Oeconomicus: A Social and Historical Commentary*. Oxford: Clarendon Press.

Pongratz-Leisten, B. 1994. *Ina šulmi erub: Die kulttopographische und ideologische Programmatik der akitu-Prozession in Babylonien und Assyrien im 1. Jahrtausend v. Chr.* Baghdad Forschungen 16.

Porten, B. 1968. *Archives from Elephantine: The Life of an Ancient Jewish Military Colony*. Berkeley and Los Angeles: University of California Press.

——and Yardeni, A. 1986. *Textbook of Aramaic Documents from Ancient Egypt I Letters*. Winona Lake, Ind.: Eisenbrauns.

Porter, B. and Moss, R. see Malek, J.

Postgate, C., Oates, D. and Oates, J. 1997. *The Excavations at Tell Al-Rimah: The Pottery*. London: British School of Archaeology in Iraq.

Postgate, J. N. 1970. 'An Assyrian altar from Nineveh', *Sumer* 26, 133–6.

——1998–2001. *Reallexikon der Assyriologie*, vol. 9, s.v. 'Negub'.

——and Reade, J. E. 1976–80. *Reallexikon der Assyriologie*, vol. 5, s.v. 'Kalhu'.

Potts, D. T. 1990. 'Some horned buildings in Iran, Mesopotamia and Arabia', *Revue d'Assyriologie* 84, 33–40.

——1999. 'GIŠ.mes.magan.na (Dalbergia sissoo Roxb.) at Tell Abraq', *Arabian Archaeology and Epigraphy* 10, 129–33.

——1999. *The Archaeology of Elam*. Cambridge: Cambridge University Press.

——2005. 'Cyrus the Great and the Kingdom of Anshan', eds. V. Curtis and S. Stewart, *Birth of the Persian Empire: The Idea of Iran*. London: I. B. Tauris, 1–22.

Pritchard, J. B. 1950. *Ancient Near Eastern Texts relating to the Old Testament*. Princeton: Princeton University Press.

Quintus Curtius Rufus. *History of Alexander*. Translated by J. C. Rolfe. Loeb edn., 1946.

Radt, W. 1988. *Pergamon: Geschichte und Bauten, Funde und Erforschung einer antiken Metropole*. Cologne: DuMont Buchverlag.

Rassam, H. 1897. *Asshur and the Land of Nimrod*. New York.

Rawson, J. 2010. 'Carnelian beads, animal figures and exotic vessels: traces of contact between the Chinese states and Inner Asia, ca.1000–650 BC', *Archaeology in China*, 1: *Bridging Eurasia*, 1–42.

Reade, J. E. 1978. 'Studies in Assyrian geography I: Sennacherib and the waters of Nineveh', *Revue d'Assyriologie* 73, 47–72.

——1979. 'Assyrian architectural decoration: techniques and subject-matter', *Baghdader Mitteilungen* 10, 17–49.

——1979. 'Ideology and propaganda in Assyrian art', ed. M. T. Larsen, *Power and Propaganda: A Symposium on Ancient Empires*, Mesopotamia 7. Copenhagen: Akademisk Forlag, 329–43.

——1983. *Assyrian Sculpture*. London: British Museum Publications.

——1987. 'Was Sennacherib a feminist?', ed. J.-M. Durand, *La Femme dans le Proche-Orient Antique*, Compte Rendue de la 33e Rencontre Assyriologique Internationale. Paris; Éditions recherche sur les civilisations, 39–146.

——1998. 'Greco-Parthian Nineveh', *Iraq* 60, 65–84.

——1998–2001. *Reallexikon der Assyriologie*, vol. 9, s.v. 'Ninive'.

——1998. 'Assyrian illustrations of Nineveh', *Iranica Antiqua* 33, 81–94.

——2000. 'Restructuring the Assyrian sculptures', eds. R. Dittmann *et al.*, *Variatio delectat: Gedenkschrift für Peter Calmeyer*, Alter Orient und Altes Testament 272. Münster: Ugarit-Verlag, 607–25.

——2000. 'Alexander the Great and the Hanging Gardens of Babylon', *Iraq* 62, 195–217.

——2001. 'More about Adiabene', *Iraq* 63, 187–200.

——2002. 'Shiru Maliktha and the Bandwai canal system', eds. L. Al-Gailani-Werr, J. E. Curtis, A. McMahon and J. E. Reade, *Of Pots and Plans: Studies presented to David Oates*. Cambridge: Macdonald Institute, 309–18.

——2005. 'The Ishtar Temple at Nineveh', *Iraq* 67, 347–90.

——2008. 'Nineteenth-century Nimrud: motivation, orientation, conservation', ed. J. E. Curtis *et al.*, *New Light on Nimrud*. London: British Institute for the Study of Iraq, 1–21.

Renger, J. and Cooper, J. S. 1975. *Reallexikon der Assyriologie*, vol. 4, s.v. 'Heilige Hochzeit', 251–69.

Rivaroli, M. 2004. 'Nineveh from ideology to topography', *Iraq* 66, 199–205.

Roaf, M. 2004. *Reallexikon der Assyriologie*, vol. 10, s.v. 'Persepolis'.

Robertson, D. S. 1969 (reprint). *Greek and Roman Architecture*. Cambridge: Cambridge University Press.

Robson, E. 1997. 'Three Old Babylonian methods for dealing with "Pythagorean" triangles', *Journal of Cuneiform Studies* 49, 51–72.

Rochberg, F. 2000. 'Scribes and scholars: the *tupšar Enūma Anu Enlil*', eds. J. Marzahn and H. Neumann, *Assyriologica et Semitica*, Festschrift for

Joachim Oelsner. Alter Orient und Altes Testament 252. Münster: Ugarit-Verlag, 359–75.

Rollinger, R. 1998. 'Der Stammbaum des achaimenidischen Königshauses oder die Frage der Legitimität der Herrschaft des Dareios', *Archäologische Mitteilungen aus Iran und Turan* 30, 155–209.

——2000. 'Schwimmen und Nichtschwimmen im Alten Orient', ed. Christoph Ulf, *Ideologie—Sport—Aussenseiter Aktuelle Aspekte einer Beschäftigung mit der antiken Gesellschaft.* Innsbruck: Institut für Sprachwissenschaft der Universität Innsbruck, 147–65.

——2006. 'The terms "Assyria" and "Syria" again', *Journal of Near Eastern Studies* 65, 283–7.

Romer, J. and Romer, E. 1995. *The Seven Wonders of the World: A History of the Modern Imagination.* London: Michael O'Mara.

Royle, J. F. 1839. *Illustrations of the Botany and Other Branches of the Natural History of the Himalayan Mountains and of the Flora of Cashmere,* vol. 2.

Russell, J. M. 1991. *Sennacherib's Palace without Rival at Nineveh.* Chicago: Chicago University Press.

——1997. 'Sennacherib's Palace Without Rival revisited: excavations at Nineveh and in the British Museum archives', eds. S. Parpola and R. Whiting, *Assyria 1995.* Helsinki: Helsinki University Press, 295–306.

——1999. *The Writing on the Wall: Studies in the Architectural Context of Late Assyrian Palace Inscriptions.* Winona Lake, Ind.: Eisenbrauns.

Sack, R. 2004. *Images of Nebuchadnezzar: The Emergence of a Legend.* 2nd, revised and expanded edn. Selinsgrove, Pa.: Susquehanna University Press; London and Toronto: Associated University Presses.

Safar, F. 1947. 'Sennacherib's project for supplying Erbil with water', *Sumer* 3, 23–5.

——1957. 'The temple of Sibitti at Khorsabad', *Sumer* 13, 219–21.

Sagona, A. and Zimansky, P. 2009. *Ancient Turkey.* London: Routledge.

Sartre, M. 2005. *The Middle East under Rome.* Cambridge, Mass.: Harvard University Press.

Sauvage, M. 1998. *La Brique et sa mise en œuvre en Mésopotamie des origines à l'époque achéménide.* Paris: Éditions recherche sur les civilisations.

Schaudig, H.-P. 2001. *Die Inschriften Nabonids von Babylon und Kyros' des Grossen.* Alter Orient und Altes Testament 256. Münster: Ugarit-Verlag.

——2010. 'The restoration of temples in the Neo- and Late Babylonian periods', eds. M. Boda and J. Novotny, *From the Foundations to the Crenellations.* Alter Orient und Altes Testament 366. Münster: Ugarit-Verlag, 141–64.

Schwartz, G. and Nichols, J. L., eds. 2006. *After Collapse: The Regeneration of Complex Societies.* Tucson, Ariz.: University of Arizona Press.

Scott, M. L. and Macginnis, J. 1990. 'Notes on Nineveh', *Iraq* 52, 63–74.

Scurlock, J. 1983. 'Berossus and the fall of the Assyrian empire', *Revue d'Assyriologie* 77, 95–6.

——1990. 'The Euphrates flood and the ashes of Nineveh', *Historia* 39, 382–4.

Segala, E. 1999. *Domus Aurea*. Milan: Electa.

Simpson, S. 2005. 'Christians at Nineveh in late antiquity', *Iraq* 67, 285–94.

Smith, G. 1875. *Assyrian Discoveries*. London.

Smith, S. 1925. *Cambridge Ancient History*, 1st edn. 1925, vol. 3, *The Assyrian Empire*, eds. J. B. Bury, S. A. Cook, and F. E. Adcock. Cambridge: Cambridge University Press.

So, J. and Bunker, E. C. 1995. *Traders and Raiders on China's Northern Frontier*. Washington DC: Smithsonian Institute.

Soggin, J. A. 1976. *Introduction to the Old Testament*. London: SCM Press.

Steiner, R. C. 1997. 'The Aramaic text in demotic script', eds. W. Hallo and J. Lawson Younger, *The Context of Scripture*. Leiden: Brill, 309–27.

Stephens, S. A. and Winkler, J. J. 1995. *Ancient Greek Novels: The Fragments*. Princeton: Princeton University Press.

Stevenson, D. W. W. 1992. 'A proposal for the irrigation of the Hanging Gardens of Babylon', *Iraq* 54, 35–55.

Stol, M. 2003–5. *Reallexikon der Assyriologie*, vol. 10, s.v. 'Pflanzenkunde'.

Stone, E. C., Linsley, D. H., Pigott, V., Harbottle, G. and Ford, M. T. 1998. 'From shifting silt to solid stone: the manufacture of synthetic basalt in ancient Mesopotamia', *Science* 280, 2091–3.

Strabo, *Geography*, transl. Horace Leonard Jones, Loeb edn. 1932 revised 1969.

Streck, M. 1916. *Assurbanipal und die letzten assyrischen Könige*. Leipzig: J. C. Hinrichs.

——1998–2001. *Reallexikon der Assyriologie*, vol. 9, s.v. 'Nebukadnezar II'.

——2010. 'Grosses Fach Altorientalistik: Der Umfang des keilschriftlichen Textkorpus', *Mitteilungen der Deutschen Orient-Gesellschaft zu Berlin*, 142, 35–58.

Stronach, D. 1990. 'The garden as a political statement: some case studies from the Near East in the first millennium B.C.', *Bulletin of the Asia Institute* 4, 171–80.

——1997. 'The fall of Nineveh', eds. S. Parpola and R. Whiting, *Assyria 1995*. Helsinki: Helsinki University Press, 315–18.

——1997. 'Anshan and Parsa: early Achaemenid history, art and architecture on the Iranian plateau', ed. J. Curtis, *Mesopotamia and Iran in the Persian Period*. Proceedings of a Seminar in Memory of V. G. Lukonin. London: British Museum Press, 35–53.

Syme, R. 1934. 'Galatia and Pamphylia under Augustus: the governorships of Piso, Quirinus and Silvanus', *Klio* 27, 1–148.

Tacitus. *Annals*.

Tadmor, H. 1994. *The Inscriptions of Tiglath-Pileser III King of Assyria.* Jerusalem: Israel Exploration Society.

Taylor, P. 2006. *Oxford Companion to the Garden.* Oxford: Oxford University Press.

Teixidor, J. 1967. 'The kingdom of Adiabene and Hatra', *Berytus* 17, 1–11.

——1987. 'Parthian officials in Lower Mesopotamia', *Mesopotamia* 22, 187–93.

Thomas, R. 2000. *Herodotus in Context Ethnography, Science and the Art of Persuasion.* Cambridge: Cambridge University Press.

Thureau-Dangin, F. 1924. 'Les Sculptures rupestres de Maltai', *Revue d'Assyriologie* 21, 185–97.

Trigger, B. 1989. *A History of Archaeological Thought.* Cambridge: Cambridge University Press.

Tuplin, C. 1991. 'Modern and ancient travellers in the Achaemenid empire: Byron's Road to Oxiana, and Xenophon's Anabasis', eds. H. Sancisi-Weerdenburg and J. W. Drijvers, *Achaemenid History* 7, 37–57.

Turner, G. 1970. 'The state apartments of late Assyrian palaces', *Iraq* 32, 177–213.

Ur, J. 2005. 'Sennacherib's northern Assyrian canals: New insights from satellite imagery and aerial photography', *Iraq* 67, 317–45.

Ussishkin, D. 1982. *The Conquest of Lachish by Sennacherib.* Tel Aviv: Tel Aviv University Publications of the Institute of Archaeology, 6.

Valentine, L. ed. 1896. *The Poetical Works of John Milton.* London and New York: F. Warne and Co.

Van de Mieroop, M. 2004. 'A tale of two cities: Nineveh and Babylon', *Iraq* 66, 1–5.

Vanden Berghe, L. 1984. *Reliefs rupestres de l'Iran Ancien.* Brussels: Musées Royaux d'Art et d'Histoire.

van der Kooij, A. 2010. 'The story of paradise in the light of Mesopotamian culture and literature', eds. K. J. Dell, G. Davies and Y. Koh, *Genesis, Isaiah and Psalms.* Vetus Testamentum Supplement 135, in Honour of J. Emerton. Leiden and Boston: Brill, 3–22.

Van der Spek, R. 1995. Review of R. Rollinger, *Herodots Babylonischer Logos. Orientalia* New Series 64, 474–7.

——2000. 'The šatammus of Esagila in the Seleucid and Arsacid periods', eds. J. Marzahn and H. Neumann, *Assyriologica et Semitica: Festschrift für Joachim Oelsner.* Alter Orient und Altes Testament 252. Münster: Ugarit-Verlag, 437–46.

——2006. 'The size and significance of the Babylonian temples under the Successors', eds. P. Briant and F. Joannès, *La Transition entre l'empire achéménide et les royaumes hellénistiques.* Persika 9, 261–307.

——2008. 'Berossus as Babylonian chronicler and Greek historian', eds. R. van der Spek *et al., Studies in Ancient Near Eastern World View and Society, presented to Marten Stol,* Bethesda, Md.: CDL Press, 277–318.

Van Leeuwen, R. C. 2007. 'Cosmos, temple, house: building and wisdom in Mesopotamia and Israel', ed. R. J. Clifford, *Wisdom Literature in Mesopotamia and Israel*. SBL seminar series. Leiden and Boston: Brill, 67–90.

Van Nuffelen, P. 2004. 'Le Culte royal de l'empire des Séleucides: une réinterprétation', *Historia* 53, 278–301.

Van Seters, J. 1989. 'The creation of man and the creation of the king', *Zeitschrift für Alttestamentliche Wissenschaft* 101, 333–42.

Verbrugghe, G. and Wickerstam, J. 1996. *Berossos and Manetho, introduced and translated: Native Traditions in Ancient Mesopotamia and Egypt*. Ann Arbor: University of Michigan Press.

Vitruvius. *De Architectura*.

Vogelsang, W. 1992. *The Rise and Organisation of the Achaemenid Empire: The Eastern Iranian Evidence*. Leiden: Brill.

Walker, C. B. F. 1981. *Cuneiform Brick Inscriptions*. London: British Museum.

Wallenfels, R. 2008. 'A new stone inscription of Nebuchadnezzar II', ed. M. Ross, *From the Banks of the Euphrates: Studies in Honour of Alice Louise Slotsky*. Winona Lake, Ind.: Eisenbrauns, 267–94.

Waters, M. 2004. 'Cyrus and the Achaemenids', *Iran* 42, 91–102.

Weissert, E. 1997. 'Royal hunt and royal triumph in a prism fragment of Ashurbanipal', eds. S. Parpola and R. Whiting, *Assyria 1995*. Helsinki: Helsinki University Press, 339–58.

West, M. L. 1995. 'The date of the Iliad', *Museum Helveticum* 52, 204–19.

White, Gilbert. 1876. *Natural History and Antiquities of Selborne*. London: Macmillan.

Wikander, O. 2000. *Handbook of Ancient Water Technology*, Leiden: Brill.

——2008. 'Sources of energy and exploitation of power', ed. J. P. Oleson, *Oxford Handbook of Engineering and Technology in the Classical World*. Oxford: Oxford University Press, 136–57.

——2008. 'Gadgets and scientific instruments', ed. J. P. Oleson, *Oxford Handbook of Engineering and Technology in the Classical World*. Oxford: Oxford University Press, 785–99.

Wilcox, H. 1999. 'Milton and Genesis: interpretation as persuasion', ed. G. P. Luttikhuizen, *Paradise Interpreted: Representations of Biblical Paradise in Judaism and Christianity*. Leiden: Brill, 197–208.

Wilkinson, A. 1998. *The Garden in Ancient Egypt*. London: Rubicon Press.

Wilson, A. 2008. 'Hydraulic engineering and water supply', ed. J. P. Oleson, *Oxford Handbook of Engineering and Technology in the Classical World*. Oxford: Oxford University Press, 285–318.

——2008. 'Machines in Greek and Roman Technology', ed. J. P. Oleson, *Oxford Handbook of Engineering and Technology in the Classical World*. Oxford: Oxford University Press, 337–66.

Wiseman, D. J. 1983. 'Mesopotamian gardens', *Anatolian Studies* 33, 137–44.

Woolley, C. L. 1929. *The Sumerians*. Oxford: Clarendon Press.

——1954. *Excavations at Ur: A Record of Twelve Years' Work*. London: Benn, revised by P. R. S. Moorey, 1982, *Ur 'of the Chaldees'*.

Worthington, M. 2012. *Principles of Akkadian Textual Criticism*. Studies in Ancient Near Eastern Records I. Berlin: de Gruyter.

Yamauchi, E. M. 2003. 'Athletics in the Ancient Near East', eds. R. Averbeck, M. Chavalas and D. Weisberg, *Life and Culture in the Ancient Near East*. Bethesda, Md.: CDL Press, 491–500.

Yardley, J. C. 1997. *Justin: Epitome of the Philippic History of Pompeius Trogus, Books 11–12*. Oxford: Clarendon Press.

Yildirim B. 2004. 'Identities and empire: local mythology and the self-representation of Aphrodisias', ed. B. E. Borg, *Paideia: The World of the Second Sophistic*. Berlin: Walter de Gruyter, 23–52.

Yoffee, N. 1988. 'The collapse of ancient Mesopotamian states and civilization', eds. N. Yoffee and G. Cowgill, *The Collapse of Ancient States and Civilizations*. Tucson, Ariz.: University of Arizona Press, 44–68.

——2006. 'Notes on regeneration', eds. G. Schwartz and J. L. Nichols, *After Collapse: The Regeneration of Complex Societies*. Tucson, Ariz.: University of Arizona Press, 222–7.

Zadok, R. 1984. *Assyrians in Chaldaea and Achaemenid Babylon(ia?)*. Assur 4/3.

Index

Page numbers for illustrations, maps, drawings and photographs are given in italics.

278 *Index*